To the Barlow

Love, Marie

Echoes of NOTRE DAME FOOTBALL

The Greatest Stories Ever Told

Edited by John Heisler

TRIUMPH
BOOKS

CHICAGO

Library of Congress Cataloging-in-Publication Data

Echoes of Notre Dame football : the greatest stories ever told / edited by John Heisler.
    p. cm.
    Includes bibliographical references.
    ISBN-13: 978-1-57243-745-6
    ISBN-10: 1-57243-745-6
    1. Notre Dame Fighting Irish (Football team)—History. 2. University of Notre Dame—Football—History. I. Heisler, John.

GV958.N6E34 2005
796.332'63'0977289—dc22

2005047812

This book is available in quantity at special discounts for your group or organization. For further information, contact:

Triumph Books
542 South Dearborn Street
Suite 750
Chicago, Illinois 60605
(312) 939-3330
Fax (312) 663-3557

Printed in U.S.A.
ISBN-13: 978-1-57243-745-6
ISBN-10: 1-57243-745-6
Design by Patricia Frey
Photos courtesy of AP/Wide World Photos

CONTENTS

FOREWORD

I enrolled at Notre Dame in the fall of 1974, on the heels of Notre Dame's 1973 national championship in football. Ara Parseghian was the coach of that team, Tom Clements was the quarterback, and the 24–23 Irish win over top-ranked Alabama that year in the Sugar Bowl is still considered one of the top bowl matchups of all time.

During my senior year in 1977, Notre Dame won the national championship again. This time Dan Devine was the head coach, Joe Montana was the quarterback, and I have vivid memories of the Cotton Bowl win over No. 1–ranked Texas. I had road-tripped all the way from New Jersey to Dallas with some friends to see the game, and it was well worth it to watch Bob Golic and the Irish defense handle Earl Campbell and the Texas running game. One of Notre Dame's running backs and their captain, Terry Eurick, lived in our suite of rooms in Flanner Hall—and he scored two touchdowns that day and ended up on the cover of *Sports Illustrated* the next week.

In those days I was just a student and a fan, sitting in the stands at Notre Dame Stadium and watching like everyone else. I remember listening to Lindsey Nelson and watching the Notre Dame football replays on Sunday mornings when I was growing up. But it wasn't until I got seriously into coaching that I came to understand the depth of the coverage of Notre Dame's football program.

You don't have to know much about Notre Dame football history to appreciate how it all started with names like Knute Rockne and the Four Horsemen and Grantland Rice. In fact, the Four Horsemen piece by Rice may still qualify as the most well-known piece of journalism in the history of college football. The successes of Irish teams under Rockne, Frank Leahy, Parseghian, Devine, and Lou Holtz only provided more fodder for the sportswriters around the country.

When *Sports Illustrated* celebrated its 50th anniversary in 2004, it published page after page of all its previous cover subjects. No college program had been featured more than Notre Dame football, and it ranked up there at the top of the list along with the Los Angeles Lakers and the New York Yankees. That sort of coverage has been the rule, as opposed to the exception, for Irish football.

This collection of pieces from the print media encompasses nearly a century of coverage of Notre Dame's football program. There are stories from *Sports Illustrated, The Sporting News, SPORT,* and other publications that chronicled Irish fortunes over the years.

I hope you enjoy the pages to come. For an old Irish fan like me, I can only hope there will be many more stories of great moments in Notre Dame football in the years to come.

—Charlie Weis,
head football coach,
University of Notre Dame

INTRODUCTION

Once upon a time, difficult as it may be for some relative youngsters to comprehend, there was no Internet and no World Wide Web. Today, you can of course check out the Web on an everyday basis and find just about anything that's being written about University of Notre Dame football. You can read the sports pages of *The New York Times* and the *Los Angeles Times*, and everything in between—not to mention the various "dot-com" sports sites that have produced a cottage industry by themselves.

When I went off to college in the midseventies, I took out a mail subscription to the *South Bend Tribune*. How else could I regularly follow Fighting Irish football fortunes in those days? There might be outstanding, well-written game stories or features in any one of the daily papers in major cities around the country, but you weren't going to be able to read them unless someone clipped them out and sent them to you.

What all that meant was that national sports magazines, including *Sports Illustrated*, *SPORT*, and *The Sporting News*, probably took on even more national significance over the last half century than they hold in our modern world. Their predecessors, publications such as *Collier's*, bridged that gap in the first half of our century. They also created a media environment in which renowned national writers such as Grantland Rice (of "Four Horsemen" fame), Damon Runyon, Red Smith, and Jimmy Breslin took on near celebrity status, almost becoming cult figures, simply by reputation.

More recently, names like John Underwood and Rick Reilly, from the pages of *Sports Illustrated*, may be familiar—but they also share the stage with dozens of other writers whose words can now be routinely accessed. In effect, everyone qualifies as a national (actually, international) writer these days, thanks to the Web.

This collection of previously published material on Notre Dame football comes from all corners. You'll read pieces from *Sports Illustrated* and *SPORT* and *The Sporting News*, as well as from newspapers in New York, Chicago, and Boston.

You'll read (maybe even reread) tales of some of the greatest games in Irish football history, plus profiles of the players and coaches who participated in them. You'll experience the events through the eyes and words of many of the great names in sports journalism.

We hope Notre Dame fans will enjoy waking up their own echoes of coverage of Irish football from bygone days.

—John Heisler

Dubbed the "Game of the Century" at the time, the 1966 tie with Michigan State in East Lansing featured one of Notre Dame's greatest comebacks of all time.

Section I
THE GAMES

Jim Beach

NOTRE DAME 35, ARMY 13

Maybe no football game put Notre Dame on the map as clearly as its victory over Army in 1913. It proved that the forward pass could be a weapon and that the small Catholic school from the Midwest could be a force even against an established power like Army. College football would never be the same—from then on the Irish would almost always be a factor on the national scene.

A newspaper story datelined West Point, April 18, 1913, announcing the Army football schedule for the following fall, states: "The most interesting home game is likely to be that with Notre Dame."

This refutes a popular notion that the South Benders arrived on the Plains as an unknown, unheralded 11 from "someplace out west." And, to blast another fable, we offer as evidence a quote from the New York *Evening Sun* account of the first "big game": "The cadets admittedly went on the field with the utmost respect for their opponents already lodged in their minds."

The fact of the matter is that many Midwestern coaches hesitated to risk their reputations against Notre Dame. The Irish had ridden roughshod over some outstanding opponents, and even mighty Michigan had fallen before them, 11–3, in 1909. Fielding "Hurry Up" Yost, the Wolverine coach, had tried to shrug off that defeat by saying that it had been in a practice game, but, nevertheless, Notre Dame was named unofficial "Western Champion" that year by the *Chicago Tribune*. In 1912 the *Spalding Record Book* rated them on a par with Wisconsin, the Western Conference (Big Ten) Champions, and this information had wide circulation.

As a consequence, Notre Dame had to go far afield to book five new teams for the 1913 schedule. In addition to the game at West Point, the team played at State College, Pennsylvania; St. Louis, Missouri; and Austin, Texas.

The football prowess of the Blue-and-Gold was well known, but it was baseball that up until then had brought them their greatest fame. This was the opening wedge in the unusual relationship with Army.

The Notre Dame football players and managers were searching for a means to break into the national limelight. In the summer of 1912, Bill Cotter, student manager of athletics, Charlie "Gus" Dorais, captain-elect of that year's team, and Knute Rockne, the left end on the varsity 11, were working at Cedar Point, Ohio, a resort on the shore of Lake Erie. It was then that the idea was hatched: try to arrange a game with Army.

The first correspondence with West Point concerned baseball. Finally in January 1913 a contract was signed—the first written agreement between the two institutions—and on May 24, during an extended swing through the east, Notre Dame's nine met and were defeated by the cadets, 3–0. That was the first Army–Notre Dame sports contest.

The spade work was done and the cadets already knew that the students from the small college that sprawls the meadows of northern Indiana were not plow-jockeys, but rather acceptable and respected opponents in sport.

Meanwhile, Harold Loomis, the cadet football manager, had been in a dilemma that was not of his own making.

It seems that before the Army-Yale game in 1912, Loomis was informed that the gridiron series with the Bulldogs was being discontinued after that year. Ernest "Pot" Graves, the West Point coach at that time, and Lieutenant Dan Sultan, the Army Athletic Association football representative, had decided with the Yale coaches that the annual game between their teams took too much out of the players. Loomis did a little reshuffling under the general supervision of Sultan. He found himself hung up with an open date for November 1. Late in the year he started writing longhand letters after taps to some eastern colleges. Those that answered said that they were filled. Then he wrote to every college he could think of. Into the spring he still had no game until at last he got a bite from Notre Dame, a letter signed by Jesse Harper, who had been hired as the new head coach but was still at Wabash College in Crawfordsville, Indiana. Harper wanted more information—specifically, how much money could be guaranteed for the trip. This was thought to be an out-of-order request because Harvard, Yale, etc., always paid their own way to the Point.

However, the cadet manager was authorized to go as high as $600. Harper replied that Notre Dame had no funds and sent information giving the number of players he would bring and, after figuring expenses, concluded that it would take at least $1,000.

Compared with well-heeled eastern teams, Notre Dame was impoverished. The squad traveled light—each man carrying his equipment under his arm or in a small satchel. Also, the South Benders presented a nondescript appearance; some of them wore shoes that were actually football brogans with the cleats removed.

Football was known in the Midwest as early as 1878, when the University of Michigan and Racine College played a game. The following year Michigan played a rugby match with Toronto, and it was Michigan that introduced football to Notre Dame in 1887, three years before West Point adopted the sport. According to the *Notre Dame Scholastic*, the Wolverines won 8–0, but the boys at South Bend were intrigued and a Rugby Football Association was immediately formed at the school. "What the football 11 needs now is a coacher," remarked the *Scholastic*, but there seems to be no record of a "coacher" until J. L. Morrison in 1894. Frank E. Hering, captain in 1896, however, is usually considered the school's first coach. Notre Dame's first victory was against Harvard School (Chicago) in 1888, by the score of 20–0. Their first undefeated, untied season was 1889 (they had had eight by 1913), but as they played only one game that year, against Northwestern, winning 9–0, the boast loses some of its potency. However, in 1892 and 1893 they again went undefeated and, in 1903, not a point was scored on them in an eight-game season. When they first faced Army in 1913 they already had a record of 115 victories, 13 ties, and 31 defeats.

Semiorganized football had been introduced at West Point in 1890 when cadet Dennis M. Michie gathered a squad of 31 men and coached them for the Military Academy's first intercollegiate game. Like Notre Dame, Army lost in its debut, when Navy defeated it on the Plains, 24–0.

Twenty-three years later a cadet team under the tutelage of Lieutenant Charlie Daly met Notre Dame for the first time.

Before the 1913 football season Daly had returned to the scene of some of his greatest games—in the days when he was an All-American as a cadet—to indoctrinate the soldiers in the style of play taught by Percy Haughton at Harvard. Following his graduation from the Military Academy (class of 1905), Daly had served one year as an officer and then resigned his commission. In the interim he had acted as assistant to Haughton (in 1909) and had been appointed fire commissioner of Boston. The chief of staff recommended that Daly be reappointed to the army—at Daly's own request—and the papers were waiting on the president's desk when Woodrow Wilson assumed office for his first term in March 1913.

Unlike Harper, who was a substitute for Walter Eckersall at the University of Chicago, Daly had been a great star as a player, both at Harvard and later at West Point. He was doing well as a coach, also, and his charges faced Notre Dame with a perfect record.

Army, surprisingly enough to the average fan of today, had earned some fame as a passing team prior to the first game with Notre Dame.

The Vernon Prichard–to–Lou Merrillat and Prichard–to–Jack Jouett passing combinations were rated the best in the east, and records show that the West Pointers defeated Colgate as the result of an aerial attack two weeks before meeting the South Benders.

Dorais, of course, was the Notre Dame passer, tossing the pigskin with what seems to have been unerring accuracy in most instances. The downfield spirals aimed at the ends, Rockne and Fred "Gus" Gushurst, were tremendously successful, but it was the short lobs over the line to halfback Joe Pliska that were the most effective in the westerners' repertoire. These plays had been worked out during the 1912 season, when chalk marks were traced on the gym floor and the exact timing of the pass and the turn by the intended receiver to grab the ball were reduced almost to habit. The passes were thrown on a split-second count, and the Hoosiers never expected a failure.

Notre Dame looked forward to the November 1 date with Army as a red-letter day. It was its first chance to break into the "big time," and it could bring glory to the school and to football beyond the Appalachians—or it could be hurled back into the obscurity of the Midwest.

At Cullum Hall Field, West Point, November 1, 1913, the scene was typical of fall Saturday afternoons on the Plains. Good-sized crowds had been coming since the turn of the century—admission free—to watch the parade of the Corps of Cadets in the morning and a gridiron engagement in the afternoon. For the Notre Dame game the knock-down, circus-seat bleachers were almost completely filled by three thousand spectators, a number that exceeded all expectations for the occasion.

In the growth of the popularity of football, much of what had happened before was merely prologue; the stage was set for the big game.

The team captains—Benny Hoge of Army and Rockne of Notre Dame—shook hands at midfield. The referee's coin was flipped and the visitors would receive the opening kickoff.

The ball was set on a mud tee at the Army 40-yard line and plebe Johnny McEwan, the center, signaled to the officials that he was ready.

Through the intervening years reams have been written about the first big game—and most of the stories are far removed from the truth.

In 1913 Daly, one of the first gridiron mentors to apply systematic methods to coaching, was in charge of the Army men. He had sent captain Tom Hammond, his former teammate, to South Bend to observe Notre Dame in a game with Alma. Alma lost 62–0.

Hammond certainly must have been impressed by the slashing style of play as he sat behind the cow pasture wire fence that kept spectators away from the sidelines at Cartier Field. There was the magnificent ball-handling and quarterbacking of Dorais and the ferocious line smashing of Ray "Iron Eich" Eichenlaub certainly must have been reported to Daly when his scout returned to West Point. And Notre Dame's fast-breaking attack, a startling sight for an easterner to behold, probably alarmed Hammond too.

So Army prepared a defense against power and was primed with an offense based on superior strength blasting a path through opponents with the surging force of the wedge.

The Army Athletic Council had reluctantly agreed to a $1,000 guarantee, and the Hoosier entourage rode railroad coaches from South Bend to Buffalo. There they switched to Pullmans for the last leg of the journey; the varsity men took lower berths while the substitutes crawled into uppers. On their limited budget it was necessary to eat sandwiches made in the campus refectory in order to shave costs on the trip. Notre Dame had brought 18 players . . . and only 14 pairs of cleats.

The Game

First half: Dorais took the kickoff deep in his own territory and was tackled immediately. Dorais was close behind Al Feeney, the Notre Dame center, as he barked the signals. The cadet linemen braced for his impact and Eichenlaub was stopped at the scrimmage. Dorais, probing for an Army weakness, called for two line bucks and on the second—a fumble! Army recovered. It was the first break of the ballgame.

The cadets attacked but Notre Dame piled up the interference in the line and on fourth down Paul Hodgson punted to Dorais. From the safety position, Dorais sprinted 30 yards from his own 5 before he was downed.

Right halfback Pliska grabbed a direct snap from center and drove through the line to the 40-yard stripe. Dorais faded and shot a surprise forward pass toward Rockne in the clear. Army was caught flat-footed but the ball overshot the sprinting left end and tumbled harmlessly along the ground.

Quickly the Hoosiers shifted to punt formation; Dorais was hurried and he booted the ball off the side of his foot out of bounds at the 50. Again Hodgson and Leland Hobbs could make no headway and Hodgson also punted short in return. Dorais was rushed by the cadet flankers and was smeared on the runback. Another fumble!

Two Notre Dame fumbles were evidence that the West Pointers were playing their famous smashing game.

The cadets kicked again and it looked as if a punting duel was in the offing with Army having the edge. It was Army strategy when playing on their home field to take advantage of a prevailing wind that sweeps down the Hudson. The cadets always kicked high, their line checking momentarily and then racing downfield to mob the opposing safety man.

So far, the Hoosiers had shown little in the way of offensive strength, but in a sudden surge Sam Finegan twisted off-tackle and then Eichenlaub plunged up the middle—both for substantial gains on successive plays.

Dorais tossed another forward pass—but again it was too long. Notre Dame reverts to the ground attack and plowed its way to the Army 25 before the soldiers halted the drive.

The grueling Army play was having its effect on the Hoosiers. Rockne was limping badly. On the offense he was side-stepping the cadet tackle instead of throwing a block. Although there was no score in the game, Notre Dame appeared to be taking a beating.

The visitors put the ball in play after a punt and their bantam quarterback cocked his arm to pass. Dorais flipped a long floater over the heads of the soldiers. Suddenly, Rockne was no longer limping; he raced straight away and hauled it in without breaking stride. He was all alone! Touchdown! Dorais made the extra point.

Score: Notre Dame 7—Army 0

Army fought back. Hodgson and Hobbs, with trip-hammer smashes, shattered and penetrated the Notre Dame line.

A pass—Prichard to Jouett—advanced the ball to Notre Dame's 15-yard line. This was the second completed high-angle aerial in a sustained Army drive midway through the first half that threatened the westerner's goal.

The cadets burrowed ahead with plunging power. Army's twin catapults—Hodges and Hobbs—were relentless in their plunges through the forward wall. The Notre Dame line bent and Hodgson bulled his way for a touchdown!

Roscoe "Spike" Woodruff tried a left-footed placement kick—no good. Notre Dame 7, Army 6.

After the kick-off, followed by an exchange of punts and a Hoosier fumble recovered by the cadets, the Army line crashers resumed the pressure on the Notre Dame forwards. Then twice the Prichard-to-Jouett passing combination clicked and again the Hoosiers were fighting with their backs to the wall.

A head-on charge brought Army three yards from the goal. On the next play a holding penalty against the Hoosiers placed the ball on the 6-inch line.

First down and goal to go! Two plunges, including the penalty play, had netted barely a yard, and now Hodgson's signal was called twice for assaults that were stopped cold. Another plunge failed. Fourth down and Prichard took the snap in his close-up position. He faked an underhand lateral and Notre Dame spread to protect the flanks. McEwan at center was low as he drove into the middle, and on a delayed buck Prichard followed in his wake to score!

Hoge kicked the goal after touchdown.

Score: Army 13—Notre Dame 7

The Army kick-off was near the sideline and Rockne barely got back to the 15-yard line before he was dropped. Time was short in the half as Dorais streaked on a quarterback sneak that was run without a shift. Dorais then took Feeney's snap-back and faded. Rockne was covered as he darted downfield, but the pass was to Pliska closer to the scrimmage. Pliska squirmed away from would-be tacklers and covered 30 yards before he was overtaken. Dorais completed another pass to Rockne; then another moved them to the Army 5. Hitting hard and hitting fast, Notre Dame had advanced the ball 80 yards in four plays.

With perfect timing and accuracy, little Dorais got his passes away. Rockne, on the long-lofted aerials and Pliska on the short, bulletlike shots, gathered in the ball while running at full tilt. Army appeared bewildered in the face of this barrage. They deployed in wider formation to protect against the passes, only to lessen their holding power in the line.

Dorais sized up the situation and sent Pliska through the middle for six more points! The score was tied as Dorais waited with outstretched hands on the 12. The pass. The kick. Good!

Score: Notre Dame 14—Army 13

The first half ended as Prichard halted another Notre Dame drive by leaping high to intercept a downfield pass intended for Rockne.

Probably the most common legend about this game is that it introduced the forward pass to football. Actually, the pass had been legalized by the Rules Committee in 1906.

The pass was considered a desperation move by most coaches. Daly at West Point was one who followed this theory. Daly was cautious in his instructions to his quarterbacks; in effect he told them: "You may use it at the last minute or two of the first half when deep in your opponents' territory. The forward pass is a hazardous weapon and must be used sparingly."

Not only was there a difference in theory with regard to the situation in which the pass should be used, but also in the manner of execution in an overhead play. Army passers threw the ball into a zone—a "spot pass"—and it was the responsibility of the receiver to arrive at the point of aim ahead of the ball, or at least simultaneously with it. Contrary to this, Notre Dame (and other "open game" teams) had the passer throw so that the receiver could take it in stride. Both methods required skill, but the latter required more finesse.

The feature of the visitors' style of play that most astounded the cadets was the effectiveness of the pass when used in *conjunction* with a strong ground game, and not just as a last-moment method of *attempting* to gain yardage.

Second half: The cadets started the third period using an improvised floating defense that had the ends moving wide with the Notre Dame flankers—actually playing the first five-man line—and the backfield drifting with the eligible pass receivers when they crossed the line of scrimmage. For a time it stopped the Hoosiers, and at one point Dorais was reduced to attempting a field goal from the 50-yard line.

But this kick went wide, and it was Army's ball on its own 20.

The soldier backs tore into the line for advances but were stopped when they tried the flanks. Ends Rockne and Gushurst were standouts on defense. Not once did they fail to hit the interference on the outside, driving the ball carrier into the line or off tackle directly into the secondary.

The force of the West Point onslaught up the middle was shoving the Hoosiers back. Frank "Shrimp" Milburn was sent in at fullback and there was a resurgence of cadet strength. Army had fought its way past the Notre Dame 15-yard line and, after a plunge for three yards, a holding penalty advanced the ball to the 2.

First down and goal to go! Eichenlaub closed in from his backer-up spot behind the westerners' line and the Hoosiers entrenched.

Army sensed victory. Every West Point rooter from General Leonard Wood, the war department chief of staff, to the lowliest plebe was on his feet, urging the team on.

Hodgson got the first chance to score. He was thrown for a loss by Rockne, who bowled him over from the side. Then Milburn cradled the ball in his arms and lowered his head for the collision. No gain. Prichard dropped back 10 yards to pass. He had excellent protection and he lobbed the ball diagonally to the left. Merillat, the cadet end, was standing in the end zone! Suddenly from nowhere Dorais sprinted, sprang, and intercepted—right at the fingertips of the intended receiver.

Thus was the powerful offense of undefeated Army slowed and then stopped in a magnificent goal-line stand by the men of Notre Dame.

That was the crest of the Army tide, and then to the amazement of the east—and the entire sports world—football tradition was exploded and history was made.

It is impossible to reconstruct a report of the ensuing action. Everything happened so fast that a difference of opinion exists concerning the exact continuity of events. Notre Dame hit its stride after halting the cadets and it seemed that the air was full of footballs.

It was passes—Dorais to Rockne; Dorais to Gushurst; to Pliska; to Finegan. Halfbacks and ends were always at the end of the arc traversed by the ball, and Army was simply unable to fathom this style of play. The cadet defenses were spread-eagled all over the field in vain attempts to break it up.

When Army dropped back to guard against passes, Eichenlaub drove through gaping holes in the line and sometimes skirted the ends. Today the men who manned the Army line that afternoon maintain that it was plunges by Eichenlaub, the biggest man on the Notre Dame team, that did the most damage. In quick succession three more touchdowns were scored.

Although statistics vary, the *New York Evening Telegram* reported that 15 out of 17 Notre Dame passes were completed, and that the Hoosiers gained nearly 300 yards through aerials alone. This may be inaccurate, since the most common figures are 14 completions in 17 attempts, resulting in a net gain of 243 yards through the air.

The feature of the game that most amazed the sports fans in the east was the length of Dorais' passes. Some of the spiral throws traveled 35 to 40 yards to the receiver, an unheard-of distance in those days.

The game did not turn into a complete rout and the tiring cadets battled to the bitter end.

As though in salute to the old-fashioned mass play that became obsolete in a single afternoon, Eichenlaub was given the honor of marking up the last two touchdowns on the scoreboard.

Final Score: Notre Dame 35—Army 13

"NOTRE DAME OPEN PLAY AMAZES ARMY," said the *New York Times* the following day. "The westerners flashed the most sensational football ever seen in the east." "I've always believed such playing possible under the new rules," said Bill Roper, who umpired the game, "but never have I seen the forward pass used to such perfection."

The stunning demonstration by Harper's men converted Daly to the "open" style of play, and Army defeated Navy one month later, 22–9, through constant use of the forward pass—and Notre Dame plays.

One legend that persists is that Harper, Rockne, and Dorais stayed over at the Military Academy to teach the cadets their technique for passing and receiving. This is false information. Both Army and Notre Dame men deny it, and in 1947 Harper told Jim Costin, sports editor of the South Bend *Tribune*, that the team left West Point late that Saturday afternoon, arrived at Buffalo the following morning, and spent Sunday at Niagara Falls. The *Tribune* for November 3, 1913, ran a story that the Notre Dame team returned to campus that day (Monday). Ralph

Lathrop, the Hoosier tackle, told the authors that what is printed here is historically correct.

In this first game, Notre Dame made just one substitution, and that as a result of a freak accident. Finegan broke his shoelace in the waning minutes and Harper ordered "Bunny" Larkin to remove his shoes and give them to Finegan. Larkin refused. After all, he hadn't come 900 miles to sit on a bench. Jesse had no choice; Larkin went in at right halfback.

Damon Runyon, the *New York American*

NOTRE DAME BEATS ARMY, 12 TO 6

It was the shining moment for a Notre Dame player named Johnny O'Brien. It also became known as the "Win One for the Gipper" game, based on the Knute Rockne locker room speech that summoned up the image of a dying George Gipp. Whomever you want to hold responsible for the play of the Irish, it was good enough to knock off a heavily favored Army team at Yankee Stadium in 1928.

A mysterious young man named O'Brien was quietly insinuated into the Notre Dame football lineup by Mr. Knute Rockne at the Yankee Stadium along toward the shank of the evening yesterday. The score then stood 6 for Notre Dame and 6 for the Army.

The advent of this young O'Brien person was almost surreptitious, so quietly did he appear with orders from Mr. Rockne to take the place of [John] Colrick at end.

Few among the eighty thousand slightly incoherent souls packing the stands noticed him, and he didn't look important enough to the Army for any of the Soldiers to request an introduction. There are always so many strangers with names that sound like O'Brien drifting in and out of the Notre Dame lineup that a cadet really hasn't time to get acquainted with them all.

This O'Brien person remained a vague and shadowy presence for the moment. Then it suddenly developed that he is a professional football catcher and had been sneaked into the pastime by Mr. Rockne, maybe with glue on his hands, to catch a 35-yard forward pass from John Niemiec that produced a touchdown and the astounding defeat of the great Army team by a score of 12–6.

The Soldiers went looking for the O'Brien fellow a minute later, but he had quickly retired to the sideline and hid himself under a warm blanket. The Army intelligence department could only develop the information that he comes from the Los Angeles High School and that his first name is John. The last is no clue. Everybody on the Notre

Dame team is named John, including Niemiec, who made the astonishing pass.

It came at a moment when it looked as if the very best the boys could do would be a tie. Even that would have been deemed a moral victory for the South Bend young men over the unbeaten Army outfit. It was the big upset of the season. All our most astute experts figured Army two touchdowns over Notre Dame. But of course they didn't know Mr. Rockne had a guy with glue on his fingers under cover.

Something detained the mighty [Chris] "Onward Christian" Cagle until the game was well into the evening dusk. He had one outburst when he chipped in on Army's only touchdown with a brief gallop and a long pass. Then he subsided to some extent, what with [Fred] Miller and [John] Law and some of those other Notre Dame boys stepping on him even when he was just standing still.

But after the sudden appearance and the equally sudden disappearance of the mysterious kid from Los Angeles, Cagle seemed to get indignant. Perhaps he thought a dirty trick had been perpetrated on the Army. He broke out with a 55-yard whiz. He tore off another blast of speed for about 20 yards. He chucked forward passes around like a man possessed.

He got the old ball down within about 15 yards of the Notre Dame goal, one way and another; then General "Biff" Jones, the Army coach, installed one [Richard] Hutchinson in Cagle's stead to do a little passing. Perhaps he thought Cagle was losing control. Anyway, with Hutch doing the pitching, the Army had the ball within a couple of feet of the South Benders' goal when the game ended.

A handful of serious-looking gentlemen came out on the field after the game and made heavy work of tearing down a pair of goal posts and lugging them around by way of jubilating on behalf of Notre Dame. The Soldiers went away very sad. The crowd was all limp from the hysteria of the last few minutes of the business.

Jake Ruppert has so arranged his ballyard in the Bronx that it holds around seventy-five thousand men, women, and small children. The footballers expanded that capacity to some extent by putting in extra shelves here and there, and I would say that eighty thousand is a very fair estimate of the size of the assemblage, most of the members thereof being New Yorkers.

The noble specs were using crying towels outside the green and gray walls of the colonel's baseball edifice because they couldn't get $50 apiece for the coveted pasteboards, as we speak of them at the club. It is feared that the sucker crop is really decreasing hereabouts.

The West Point cadets marched into the stadium behind their band and paraded the field with an expertness and precision born of long practice this season. The boys are getting plenty of hiking going through the 1928 schedule. The stands were only about half filled at this time. There was a terrific jam on the bridges across the Harlem and even at the subway terminal.

After all these years they are still unable to handle a football crowd in New York as well as they do in New Haven or even Princeton. A milk wagon can tie up the traffic in New York in a hard snarl.

The Cadets took up a position in the left field stand. There didn't seem to be enough Notre Dame rooters on hand to make a representation in any one section. The wandering tribe covers too much territory to carry a cheering section with it.

Mr. Walter Eckersall of Chicago, one of the greatest football players of the prehistoric era and now an able football writer and official, came on the field in short white pants and looked things over. He was the referee.

With him was the *Evening Journal*'s candidate for All-American eating honors, Mr. Tom Thorpe. He also wore a pair of balloon panties. He was the umpire. Mr. Thorpe is growing a bit stout, and, in fact, he can cover more ground sitting down than the Notre Dame team running the ball. F. W. Murphy of Brown and N. E. Kearns of DePaul [in] Chicago were the other officials.

[Mortimer "Bud"] Sprague kicked off for Army at 1:45 [P.M.], and [Jim] Brady ran the ball back 15 yards. Many seats were still empty. The clients were outside fighting bravely.

The folks were eagerly watching Christian Cagle and, after Notre Dame had kicked, following a couple of futile charges, the ball was turned over to the great back of the Army with No. 12 on his jersey. He promptly proceeded to fumble, and then skid on his nose as Miller and [Fred] Collins hit him. It was an inauspicious start. The Army presently had to kick.

Niemiec bucked a neat pass right into Jack Chevigny's paws, but Jack muffed it. He was loose and fell at the time, too. Niemiec tried it again, but picked out [Eddie] Collins this time. The chuck was too long. Niemiec lifted a beaut of a punt to the Cadets' 20-yard line. The field seemed a little soggy. The boys were skidding all over the joint.

Notre Dame got the ball again and Brady flipped a pip of a pass to Chevigny for a gain of 20 yards before [William] Hall nailed the young man from South Bend. That put the ball in midfield, where it started, and Notre Dame proceeded to lose some of the yardage gained by bouncing back off the Army wall. So the South Benders went back to chuck ball. Niemiec put a darb in Fred Collins' arms for a 20-yard gain. Niemiec whistled another through the ambient, but it was muffed. Niemiec had to punt again.

[John] Murrell returned the boot. Brady was dropped by Sprague before he had gone very far and the game developed—or should I say degenerated—into a kicking proposition. Cagle tried to lug the ball a couple of times, but [George] Leppig kept leppiging on him, so to speak, and [Cagle] couldn't get untracked. The boys commenced to get all muddy. The stands were pretty well filled by this time. Never was a crowd more delayed.

Niemiec finally lifted a punt that landed on Army's 2-yard line and rolled out of bounds. Murrell had to kick from behind his own goal, and Brady caught the ball on Army's 30-yard line. On the next play, [Fred] Collins went around Army's left end for the first real run of the game to Army's 16-yard line. Chevigny made five yards through center, and Collins went on by the same route to put the ball within seven yards of Army's goal.

Chevigny went two yards more. With the ball on Army's 4-yard line on the second down, Collins fumbled the pass and Murrell recovered the ball for the Army. So passed an apparently sure touchdown for Notre Dame.

Murrell tore off a 55-yard punt and [Edwin] Messinger, his end, was right on top of Brady as the latter caught the ball deep down in Notre Dame territory. Collins and Chevigny wasted a lot of strength pounding at the Army front before Niemiec had to punt to Nave. Cagle then carried the ball. He made eight yards through center.

Moynihan, the Notre Dame center, halted Murrell. The latter poked through center for five yards before Law nailed him and Cagle squirmed about two yards through center. Murrell couldn't get past that fellow Moynihan, so Army kicked. It was dull stuff.

[Charles] Allan relieved [Richard] O'Keefe in Army's backfield after a long recess during which the Cadets' little tea wagons came out and ministered to the suffering stretched out on the grass. The Soldiers seemed to be getting sniped [a] little.

Starting from their own 40-yard line, Notre Dame took up a march headed by Chevigny, [Fred] Collins, and Hall that carried right through Army's line to Army's 35-yard line before Niemiec punted.

The half ended with the boys tussling in Army territory with the ball belonging to the Army for the moment.

Sprague, the Army tackle who was elected lieutenant of his cadet company only yesterday morning, was laid out in almost the first scrimmage. Sprague had his nose broken in the Harvard game.

It was after a brief delay while the tea wagon was tending Sprague that Cagle cut loose. He first carried the ball from Army's 27-yard line to the 47-yard line. Then he whipped a 40-yard pass to Messinger, putting the ball on Notre Dame's 15-yard line. It was an amazing toss, perfectly hurled and perfectly handled.

With the Army cheering section all abuzz, the Cadet backs began hammering the Notre Dame line. Cagle, O'Keefe, and Murrell smashed away, moving the ball forward by inches, Cagle finally making first down on Notre Dame's 3-yard line. On the next drive, Cagle put the ball on the 1-yard line. He was slightly hurt in that smash, and the tea wagon came for him.

When he got to his feet again the crowd cheered. With only a foot to go, Murrell pushed his noggin through a hole in the center of the line. Sprague failed to kick goal. Score: Army 6, Notre Dame 0.

Sprague had to remove the nose guard that protects his broken beak as he made the kick. Law, the Notre Dame guard, and Collins put up a mighty battle against that last onslaught of the Army.

[Charles] Humber, of the Army, was stretched out early in the third period as Notre Dame was putting on a drive, and [John] Dibb took his place.

Notre Dame shoved the ball by charging to Army's 42-yard line, then Messinger, one of the greatest ends [who] ever wore cleats, nailed Chevigny running with the ball and pushed him back for a loss. Notre Dame had to kick, and Army quickly returned the compliment.

A 15-yard penalty gave Notre Dame the ball on Army's 36-yard line. Collins made four yards through center and then skipped around Army's right end to Army's 24-yard line, where Hall nabbed him.

Chevigny leaped right over the Army center and traveled to Army's 10-yard line before Cagle could bring him down. [William] Parham relieved the wounded Sprague, and Collins went around Army's left end for a brief gain, putting the ball on Army's 9-yard line directly in front of the goal posts. Poor Sprague sat on the sideline all by himself, huddled up under a gray blanket, while Hall took over the job as captain of the Army team.

[Thomas] Lynch relieved the great Messinger. Niemiec crowded the ball to within seven yards of the Army goal where [Louis] Hammack halted him. Chevigny pounded through center and deposited the old melon three yards from the West Point goal.

Hall stopped Collins' plunge. It was first down and about a foot to go. Chevigny was thrown for a slight loss. Collins couldn't gain, Nave stopping him. Collins was halted again. He was hurling himself at center. On the next try Chevigny took the ball and smashed through to a touchdown. Niemiec's kick was blocked, leaving the score tied: Army 6, Notre Dame 6.

Frank Carideo kicked off to Cagle, who rambled back to Army's 20-yard line with the ball. Leppig stopped Cagle's next lunge as the period ended.

They swapped goals and Murrell kicked after one futile charge. The tea wagon moved to the succor of some of the Soldiers during a recess.

Collins suddenly rifled through Army's center for 15 yards before Hall got him. Carl Mark stopped him on his next try. Notre Dame tried a pass which failed, and Army was penalized for offside. That put the ball on Army's 38-yard line.

Carideo carried the ball for a brief gain, and Chevigny failed on a crack at Army's right end. Murrell halted Collins. A pass failed. Carideo dropped back to the 45-yard line and, with Chevigny holding the ball, tried a place kick—a rare attempt these days.

It was a good try, but failed. Cagle made one short gain and Murrell punted, giving Notre Dame the ball on its own 45-yard line. Niemiec tried a pass that failed, then Chevigny hit center for eight yards. Notre Dame kicked to Army's 20-yard line. Cagle tried rushing, but his gains were short. Law was always on top of him. Army kicked. Chevigny got away for a 10-yard gain. Carideo made first down on Army's 45-yard line. Now Chevigny circled Army's right end for 15 yards.

The ball was on the Soldiers' 30-yard line. Collins and Niemiec pounded the Army line for 10 yards. Chevigny joined in, and the ball was on Army's 15-yard line when Chevigny fumbled a pass and the ball rolled back to Army's 30-yard, where Chevigny fell on it for a recovery.

He was so badly hurt as the Army tacklers piled on him that he had to be helped from the field. [Billy] Dew took his place. [Clark] Piper relieved Murrell, of the Army. A Notre Dame forward pass went all askew.

On the next play Niemiec took the ball, ran back to Army's 45-yard line and, pulling back his arm, let fly to a man in a Notre Dame helmet who was drifting down toward the Army goal. It was a coolly calculated pass and covered 35 yards. The ball drifted right into the outstretched arms of O'Brien, who merely had to keep trotting onward a couple of yards to the touchdown.

O'Brien, who had relieved Colrick in the Notre Dame lineup just before this play, was immediately taken out again. Carideo missed goal while the crowd was still roaring.

A moment later it went fairly wild as Cagle began some strange manifestations. He cut loose with a 55-yard run. He chucked a pass to the Notre Dame goal that Carideo just barely managed to break up. He ran 20 yards more a moment later, then was relieved by Hutchinson.

A forward pass from Hutchinson to [Herbert] Gibner and a last-minute charge by Hutchinson put the ball within two yards of the Notre Dame goal as the final whistle sounded.

Wilfrid Smith, the *Chicago Tribune*

LUCK O' THE IRISH

These days it seems that games of the century are a dime a dozen. But this matchup, between Notre Dame and favored Ohio State, was an authentic, original version. This replay takes you back to 1935.

"What though the odds be great or small, old Notre Dame will win over all."

Thousands of Notre Dame men have sung these stirring lines. Millions have known them. This afternoon an inspired Notre Dame team lived those words in a fourth-period attack that beat back the mighty men of Ohio State, 18–13, in a relentless surge, an attack that thrice crossed the Buckeye goal and brought the Irish from the borderland of an impending humiliating defeat to the heights of football fame.

In the annals of gridiron lore are countless tales of famous rallies. Notre Dame men have recorded many in their marches through the years.

But no Notre Dame team has written a more brilliant page in football history than these boys today.

Beaten 13–0 in three periods of play, Notre Dame, almost without warning, rose with tornadic fury to sweep aside Buckeye defenders with as deadly certainty as if an unseen machine-gun sprayed murderous blasts.

Then, when Ohio State's scarlet warriors, in desperation, wedged forward to check the assault along the ground, Notre Dame lifted its attack to the skies. And Ohio State, demoralized by this team it had thought beaten, could not check passes that sailed accurately to sprinting receivers for victory.

Eighty-one thousand saw today's struggle. Every seat was taken and hundreds stood in every available space, filled the entrances, massed in the aisles, and finally rushed over the low restraining walls to line the sides of the gridiron.

Before this throng, alternately cheering the irresistible attack of Notre Dame or praying that time would halt the play while Ohio State still held an advantage, was unfolded a gridiron drama that defies description.

Early in the final period, the thousands saw Notre Dame score its first touchdown. Ohio State's partisans sent a vast cheer to the gray sullen sky when Ken Stilley's place-kick for the extra point struck the crossbar and bounded back. This outburst was only faint applause compared to the Niagara of sound that swept the arena when Wally Fromhart kicked the ball into a surging scarlet mass as he essayed the point after Notre Dame's second touchdown. That play, so thousands believed, had decided the contest. Ohio State still led, 13–12.

Less than two minutes remained to play. But Notre Dame, still believing in its destiny, came back once more. Five plays after the kickoff to Ohio State, Wayne Millner, Notre Dame's left end, grabbed Bill Shakespeare's pass in Ohio's end zone. The unbelievable had become fact, and Notre Dame had given new life to the timeworn copybook adage that a team that *will* not be beaten *cannot* be beaten.

Who led Notre Dame's inspired charge? Believe this, if you can, but it was Notre Dame's second line that battered through the Buckeyes. These were the boys, not those first-team players who had fought to victory over Pittsburgh, that signaled advance. Behind them were Notre Dame's flashing backs, Andy Pilney, Shakespeare, and Steve Miller, who had replaced Fred Carideo after an injury had incapacitated the fullback in the first half.

The line-up changed rapidly with quarterbacks bringing in instructions from the Notre Dame bench. Each man played his role without mistake. But in this list of heroes the name of Pilney stands out in bold capitals. Give credit to all Notre Dame players, but in any division Pilney must receive the major portion.

It was Pilney who touched off the fuse that ignited Notre Dame's dynamite. It was Pilney whose every play in the fourth-period climax was a picture of absolute determination. More than any other man on the field, Pilney refused to accept defeat.

Notre Dame might have lost 13–12 except for an Ohio State misplay, a fumble by Dick Beltz, who unfortunately qualifies as the one man the Buckeyes will blame for defeat. But so great was Irish determination that the thousands in the stands must have felt Notre Dame could not be denied.

Beltz fumbled on Ohio State's first play after the kickoff when the Buckeyes led 13–12, and Notre Dame recovered on its own 49-yard line. Then Pilney, who had led preceding marches, stepped into the breach.

On the first play, he dropped back to pass. Receivers apparently were covered, so Pilney set out on his own. Ohio's left end had retreated to cover for a pass. At that position Pilney started, then cut back down center field, eluding lurching tacklers with a change of pace. Three times he was penned in, had enemy hands clawing at his person, but his churning legs never stopped, and he pulled away. For 32 yards he tore forward, scorning to yield until he was knocked out of bounds on Ohio's 19-yard line by Frank Fisch.

Pilney was knocked out of bounds, badly bruised. There he lay while trainer and doctor worked over him and Shakespeare reported to umpire John Schommer. The sideline throngs parted and Pilney was carried out on a stretcher to the dressing room.

Could Notre Dame now be stopped? Ohio State could no more halt the inevitable than mere man, unarmed, could throttle a raging lion. And Pilney's last contribution, since he was hurled out of bounds, was perfect, for that tackle at the sideline stopped the field judge's watch. Time, against which Notre Dame was fighting, now was checked. The watch could not start until Notre Dame put the ball into play.

Andy Puplis, Pilney's teammate at Harrison Tech in Chicago when that school won a national prep championship, now replaced Fromhart at quarterback. Shakespeare came in for Pilney. Puplis' contribution, as directed by coach Elmer Layden, was to call a forward pass, but the pass failed. In came Jim McKenna for Puplis. Tony Mazziotti took Henry Pojman's pass from center, handed the ball to Shakespeare, and assisted in the blocking, which swept aside Ohio State's desperate linemen.

Shakespeare faded back 15 yards, then threw 35 yards to the western corner of the end zone, where Millner had sprinted. The ball came down in a long arc, spiraling over the head of Beltz, defending halfback, who had failed to see Millner until too late. Millner grabbed the ball for victory.

Notre Dame did not care when Marty Peters missed the kick for the extra point. Points no longer were important.

Seconds remained. Ohio State chose to receive and Notre Dame purposely kicked short to Gus Zarnas at guard, wary of a runback from a longer kick, which might have been received by Joe Williams or other open-field threats.

Ohio had one play. Stan Pincura took the ball for a pass, but as he dropped back, a wave of blue shirts enveloped him and he went down under a flurry of men as the timer's gun sounded the knell of Ohio's hopes.

From the stands a wave of humanity now poured to the field. Hundreds lifted the conquerors to their shoulders and carried them to the dressing room. Disconsolate Ohio State players forced a passage through the mobs. Notre Dame fans swarmed to the goal posts, iron pipes set in concrete bases. They hurled their strength and finally, after 10 minutes, had torn the posts from the ground and formed long lines to escort the trophies outside the stadium. The crowd was loath to disperse. An hour afterward many still huddled in groups, replaying the game.

"It was a great game. Notre Dame made a wonderful finish." This was coach Francis Schmidt's statement from the Ohio State dressing room.

"It was a great game," Layden said in his statement. "What can I say?"

And 81,000 spectators might have chorused with these men: "It was a great game."

Red Smith, the *New York Herald Tribune*

IRISH HOLD ARMY TO SCORELESS TIE

You may not think much of a 0–0 football game. But this one, between Notre Dame and Army in 1946, turned out to be a doozy. The legendary Red Smith makes the prose sing.

Notre Dame's Pyrrhic bid for vengeance over real and fancied grievances of the immediate past died of its own frustration in a bloodless 0–0 tie with the Army today as a carnival crowd of seventy-four thousand rocked and tottered.

Thus came to an inane and bootless anticlimax Notre Dame's great gesture of the first unblemished postwar football championship, which was to wipe out the stigmata of those Army 59–0 and 48–0 scores of the last two years with an Irish victory.

The Irish were stopped once only four yards from the goal late in the second period, but they didn't get close after that. After that, as a matter of fact, nobody got very close, [not] even All-Americans Glenn Davis and [Felix] "Doc" Blanchard, the Army's stellar duo. They wound up trying to comb a lot of Notre Dame digits out of their hair.

That was one pale degree of satisfaction for the stymied Irish. Another was the fact that their tie broke the sequence of Army's 25 straight victories, carried forward from 1943.

Meantime, they pounced upon Blanchard with bellicose relish and flung him boisterously down—sometimes for short gains, sometimes for none at all. They even held the blustering Doctor for downs twice, once on the 14 in the opening period and again on the 34 near the close of the game. He did get away for 20 yards inside Notre Dame's right end, running to the Irish 37 before Johnny Lujack brought him down. But that was the Doctor's only contribution of valid merit.

Davis, too, was string-halted and rendered well-nigh void by the Notre Dame ends, Jim Martin and John Zilly, all the live long day.

Before the game's lamentable end, in fact, the two sockdolager boys from up the river were bogged down so badly they were practically leaving everything to quarterback Arnold Tucker.

The next-to-the-last gesture of note this consummate artist made during an adventurous and singularly theatrical afternoon was to intercept Lujack's pass far down in Army terrain and come rampaging back 25 yards through the serried Irish ranks almost to midfield. His last was to intercept another Lujack cast on West Point's 45, with less than a minute to play.

Tucker then tried to gather the flagging and, by this time, distrait Army forces for a last, desperate gamble for the winning touchdown. But Davis and Blanchard had played the entire 59 half minutes on the clock and didn't have a leg left under them.

Lujack, hampered in his repertoire by the hurtling absence of Floyd Simmons, injured, and Jim Mello, for some reason unavoidably detained on the sideline, wasted no time with meaningless motions. He went into his patter with a 30-yard pass, brilliantly executed, to Bob Skoglund around midfield.

Subsequently, [Lujack] shoveled one back to Gerry Cowhig, who got in the clear around Army's left end and went 18 yards to the Army's 12. Cowhig, reversing to the left at the 15, might have gone all the way to goal, but his own blockers pinched him back long enough for Tucker to make the tackle. Two plays later, Terry Brennan hit the defensive left side to the 4.

It was fourth down and two to go, so Cowhig was reversed out of a shovel pass, this time to the opposite flank. But the Army's [William] West—the only man not taken out of the play—stayed with it all the way into the sideline, forcing Cowhig out for no gain. It was at once Notre Dame's most impressive and disastrous effort of a long and mis-spent afternoon.

At that, Lujack played the entire 60 minutes and was supposed to have only one leg when he started. More than this, he remained to the end the most dangerous of the Irish backs, with his passing, kicking, and occasional runs on a "naked" reverse. [Lujack], in fact, might have kicked the Cadets into defeat in the final, dramatic minutes of the game, for his punt into the coffin-corner had Tucker absolutely licked.

The ball was bounding around inside the 4-yard line with Notre Dame's Jimmy Martin hovering avidly over it. But he hovered too long. He wasn't satisfied with the 4-yard line; he wanted the 2 or the 1. While the young man was trying to make up his mind, the ball suddenly squirted over the goal line for an insipid and meaningless touchback—and Notre Dame's last chance was gone. Not two moments later, the Army's West was quick-kicking 56 yards over Lujack's agitated thatch.

Notre Dame's best chance, however, was its first. It came on the momentum of a 71-yard charge down through the Army defense to the near side of the goal midway through the opening period, the parade starting just after the Irish stopped Blanchard's fourth-down lunge over tackle.

In fact, it might be difficult to say which suffered the more poignantly in the day's uninspired process—unbeaten Notre Dame's repute as an invincible scoring agency, built up around its hitherto awesome total of 198 points in five games this year or the legend that Davis and Blanchard were really something out of this universe.

This bit of amiable nonsense was dusted blithely off like a coat sleeve when the celebrated Army running attack, tied in almost entirely with the maraudings of this distinguished duo, gained 138 net yards from scrimmage, as against 173 for Notre Dame.

The first downs temperately favored the Irish, too, at 10–9, while their five pass completions topped the Army's four in all save acreage. Each side picked up a skimpy 52 yards thereby, though it seemed that Lujack's receivers were mightily intent throughout upon filling in for old doctor fumblefinger, the All-American drawback. Most of the time, they couldn't catch eczema in a county pesthouse.

However, all that ran sensationally up the middle of the street for [Chuck] "E Pluribus" Sweeney. If the Irish had a bare edge in the compiled returns, it unfortunately did not make itself manifest on the scoreboard, and that was the avowed purpose of this reassembled Notre Dame squad—three deep in everything but scoring numerals.

They were going to "get hunk" for those nightmarish trouncings administered by the Messrs. Blanchard and Davis to war-weakened Notre Dame outfits for a scandalous total of 107 points too in 1944 and 1945.

They did contrive to leave more than a trace of emerald tarnish upon the luster of this highly embellished pair.

It was the fourth tie of the series, which now shows Notre Dame far in front by 22 victories to 9.

All told, the day's performance was not a savory dish to set before a notable assemblage, which included General Dwight Eisenhower, Attorney General Tom Clark, Secretary of War [Robert] Patterson, and Navy Secretary [James] Forrestal, among others.

Meanwhile, it was estimated that $15 to $25 million were wagered on the result—which of course was unfortunate.

There wasn't any.

Mike Celizic, the *Chicago Tribune Magazine*

THE BIGGEST GAME

The 1966 Notre Dame–Michigan State battle, a contest between the two top-rated teams in the country, in November in East Lansing proved huge enough that it prompted Notre Dame graduate Mike Celizic to write an entire book about that one football game. The Biggest Game of Them All *was published in 1992 by Simon & Schuster and excerpted that same fall in the* Chicago Tribune Magazine.

Nothing in college football gets the juices flowing in fans like a late-season match between the No. 1 and No. 2 teams in the country. This is because it so rarely happens. In fact, when Notre Dame and Michigan State met on November 19, 1966, it was the latest in the season that such a matchup had ever happened. Even today, when fans expect to see the top teams meet with some regularity in a postseason bowl game, it's rare for both to be undefeated.

To show how serendipitous such games are, when the 1966 schedule was first drawn up in 1960, the Irish weren't even supposed to play Michigan State. Instead they were scheduled to meet Iowa on November 19. Then, after agreeing to the game, Iowa decided it would rather spend the weekend before Thanksgiving in Florida playing the University of Miami Hurricanes, a team that hadn't yet gotten football religion. Needing a 10th game to fill the schedule, Notre Dame's athletic director, Edward W. "Moose" Krause, called his old friend Clarence L. "Biggie" Munn, who was Michigan State's athletic director.

So it was that two grown men called Moose and Biggie, strictly as a matter of courtesy and convenience, scheduled a game that would outlive them both. Neither man had any clue that the game would amount to anything special. At the time they came to their agreement, the Spartans and the Irish were both in a bit of a decline. No one knew that Ara Parseghian would bring his "Era of Ara" to Notre Dame, that by 1966 Notre Dame would be back on top of the heap, and that Michigan State would be there to meet them.

As big as the game was, the world didn't stop spinning on its axis as of Sunday, November 13, 1966, no matter what the sportswriters thought. An unmanned spacecraft was busy snapping pictures of the moon, where America intended to plant a flag and swat a golf ball by the end of the decade. A manned *Gemini* craft was orbiting the Earth. Ralph Nader was filing a $26 million lawsuit against General Motors. Joe Namath was finishing his sophomore season with the New York Jets. Ronald Reagan, a retired actor, was basking in the glory of having been elected governor of California. "The Poor Side of Town" by Johnny Rivers, last week's hit song, was giving way to "You Keep Me Hanging On" by The Supremes.

Somewhere, people were concerned with all of these things. But not at Notre Dame or Michigan State. The moment Notre Dame dismembered Duke 64–0 and the Spartans thrashed Indiana 37–7, the world may as well have stopped spinning. A week of classes remained, a week that at Notre Dame included midterm exams. Few cared. All that mattered was Saturday and the Game of the Year, the Game of the Decade, or the Game of the Century, depending on who was writing about it.

The Wall Street Journal ran a front-page story about the pregame madness. *The Journal* usually didn't cover sports, and if it was writing about the game and had reporters at both campuses, it meant only one thing—big money was at stake.

Those who just wanted to watch the game on TV had another problem. Notre Dame had used up its allotment of national television. The game could only be broadcast regionally, as part of the first college football double-header. The second game, between USC and UCLA, would determine the Pac 8 champion.

Until that Saturday, the nation had one game and one game only each week. But ABC thought showing two big games back to back was an idea whose time had come. Because the Notre Dame–Michigan State game could not be shown nationally, ABC announced that the South and Pacific Northwest would get a different game, while the rest of the country got the Game of the Millennium, which would be beamed for the first time via the Lani Bird satellite to Hawaii, Vietnam, and the U.S. armed forces in Europe.

Several weeks before the game, Beano Cook, the publicity chief of ABC Sports, began to sense what he had to look forward to when a petition arrived asking that the game be shown nationally. It was signed by twenty thousand people. In all, fifty thousand pieces of mail buried the ABC offices. Faced with this unprecedented demand, ABC finally hit on a compromise that the NCAA could live with. It decided to broadcast the game on a tape delay to those parts of the country that were blacked out.

The bookies had made Notre Dame a 3½-point favorite, and the line rose during the week to 5 points.

Parseghian was asked whether he liked going into the game as the top-rated team. "Sure I do," he said. "Absolutely. I have no qualms about it, but . . . there's not enough difference between No. 1 and No. 2 to say that whoever wins, it could be an upset."

Notre Dame's All-America halfback, Nick Eddy, was sidelined with an injured shoulder, and early in the game Irish quarterback Terry Hanratty was put out of action after a bruising hit by MSU's Bubba Smith. Irish center George Goeddeke was injured during the same series and had to leave the game too.

And that's the way it went, with the two teams testing each other in what most of the players would recall, even years later, as being one of the hardest-hitting games any of them had ever played.

After a scoreless first quarter, Michigan State scored on a four-yard run by fullback Regis Cavender. The Spartans' barefooted kicker, Dick Kenney, converted. Michigan State 7, Notre Dame 0. Later in the same quarter, Kenney hit a 47-yard field goal, and the Spartans led 10–0.

With 4½ minutes left in the first half, Notre Dame halfback Bob Gladieux, playing for the injured Eddy, scored the only Irish touchdown on a 34-yard pass from quarterback Coley O'Brien, playing for the injured Hanratty. Kicker Joe Azzaro converted. Michigan State 10, Notre Dame 7.

The third quarter, like the first, was scoreless. Gladieux was knocked out of the game with a quadricep injury after a tackle by MSU safety Jess Phillips.

On the first play of the fourth quarter, Azzaro tied the score with a 28-yard field goal. Azzaro had a chance to put the Irish ahead with 4:39 left on the clock, but his field-goal attempt from 24 yards out was wide.

The Spartans took over but after seven plays had moved the ball only to their own 36-yard line. Now it was fourth-and-four, and the clock was down to the last two minutes of the game. If Michigan State punted, Notre Dame could finish the game on offense by getting a first down or two and the Spartans wouldn't get another chance. But if [they] didn't punt, the odds weren't good on making a first down on fourth-and-four. A turnover in [their] own territory might hand Notre Dame the game.

Michigan State head coach Duffy Daugherty weighed all that and decided to punt. His thinking was that he could get lucky and get a fumble on the punt return. Or, failing that, Parseghian would have to put the ball in the air from deep in his own territory, and [Daugherty's] defense might get a shot at picking one off. Then, with the wind at his back, Kenney could try a field goal, which would be dangerous anywhere from midfield on in.

[Daugherty] considered the possibilities and sent Kenney in to punt. [Parseghian] sent his men in after Kenney, but the Spartan line did its job, and despite a low snap, Kenney got the ball away. It was a high kick, and [Daugherty] almost got his wish immediately. Safety

Tom Schoen moved under it at the 30, signaled for a fair catch, and dropped it with six Spartans almost on top of him.

Footballs bounce funny ways—everyone knows that—and this one bounced the funniest way of all, which is to say it didn't bounce a bit. Schoen was able to drop to the ground, reach out his left arm, and sweep the ball to safety just before the green wave landed on top of him.

All across the country the Notre Dame faithful spent a couple of seconds trying to recover from its collective heart attack. But the Irish had the ball with 1:24 on the clock and timeouts left. There was still time.

While the fans were pleading with their televisions during Michigan State's last drive, [Parseghian] was weighing his options. For all his fire on the sideline, Parseghian didn't operate on impulse, as Daugherty sometimes did. If the risk of failure greatly outweighed the chance of success, he didn't do it. [Parseghian] explained his thinking immediately after the game and hasn't changed a word of it in more than a quarter century. He had brought in a team that started without Eddy. On the second series, it had lost its starting quarterback and center. Later, it lost another halfback. Still it had rallied from a 10–0 deficit against some of the greatest defensive players in the country and had forged a 10–10 deadlock. He had had a chance to win it, but the field goal had trickled wide at the last moment. It was, he said, "one of the greatest comebacks in Notre Dame history."

His choices were obvious only to him. To everyone else, he had only one choice: put the ball up and hope the guy who catches it is wearing a white jersey. But he knew he didn't have to win to reach his goal—he just couldn't lose. At the same time, Daugherty did have to win. That was because this was [his] last game. He had no bowl to go to, no chance for redemption, no overtime. Notre Dame did have overtime—its final game the following week against nationally ranked Southern Cal. Tie this one and beat Southern Cal, and the national championship might still be attainable. Lose this one on a stupid play in the closing minute and there was no chance of winning the championship.

So [Parseghian] sent O'Brien in, and on first down, with the Spartans rushing five men hard, the Notre Dame coach sent O'Brien around right end on a power sweep that picked up four yards. On second down O'Brien dropped back as if to pass, the Spartans dropped back to cover, and then he handed it to halfback Rocky Bleier on a draw, good for three yards.

On third-and-three, Notre Dame packed it in tight, and O'Brien handed off to fullback Larry Conjar for two yards. Now it was fourth-and-one on their own 39 with less than a minute to go. Duffy had kicked on fourth-and-four and was looking for Parseghian to do the same, but again [Parseghian] refused to go along with the plan. It was a gamble to go for the first down, but it was a gamble [he] could control. The alternative was to punt, and the chances of a bad snap, a blocked kick, or a big return were better than the chances that his huge offensive line would fail to get a yard in front of O'Brien on a quarterback sneak.

[Parseghian] figured it right. The line fired out into the Spartan defense and pushed the whole pile forward two yards for the first down at the 41. [Parseghian] had figured that if he got to the 45, he could risk one pass to get close enough for a field goal. Complete the pass, and he still had timeouts. But he wasn't going to stop the clock until he thought it would help.

After O'Brien sneaked for the first down, the Spartans saw what was going on and called a timeout. Less than half a minute remained. In the huddle, Smith and Charlie Thornhill were screaming at their teammates, saying that Notre Dame was trying to run out the clock.

On first down from the 41, [Parseghian] finally called a pass. With the clock at 10 seconds and the crowd booing, O'Brien dropped back on a sprintout. But [Smith] timed the snap perfectly, blew past the center, and dragged O'Brien down seven yards behind the line of scrimmage before Coley could get out of the way. As [Smith] hit the ground, he signaled frantically for another timeout. He got it, but the game was over. O'Brien ran a sneak for five yards, and that was that.

The players hauled themselves off the tattered grass and looked around as if to say, "Is that all there is?"

The players distinctly remember that the stadium, which had been so incredibly noisy, went dead silent at the final gun. No one left. Like the players, the fans just stood around, thinking it couldn't be over, it couldn't be a tie. Somebody had to win.

The photographers were rushing onto the field, snapping pictures, but the players were unaware of them. [Parseghian] and [Daugherty] found each other, patted each other on the back, and went their separate ways. Neither one of them looked happy. Neither one was.

Ara Parseghian never thought, "Let's get a tie," as he managed the last minutes of the game. He didn't hum the fight song to himself and substitute the words that appeared in *Sports Illustrated* and provoked a magazine-burning on the Notre Dame campus: "Tie, tie for old Notre Dame." First, he wanted to win. Second, he wanted not to lose. There was no third. "I knew there was going to be a winner and a loser, and I thought we were going to win," he says. "I never thought about a tie. The last thing Duffy Daugherty or I wanted was a tie."

What he thought about as he left the field was what he was going to tell his players. He had heard a drunk who had run on the field and shouted that they were going for the tie, and that angered him. His players had spilled their guts on that field, just as the Michigan State players had. It may not have been the prettiest game in history, but it was, [Notre Dame] linebacker Jim Lynch said, the hardest-hitting college football game he had ever been in. It was also the biggest he ever would be in. "The Super Bowl was not as big as the Michigan State–Notre Dame game," he said after having played in both. "If we had won that game, we would have gone down in history as the greatest football team ever," Thornhill said. "There's not a month that passes that somebody doesn't mention it."

Thornhill may exaggerate, but he may also be right. Certainly, few defenses have ever put together four athletes like Jess Phillips, George Webster, Bubba Smith, and Charlie Thornhill, and then filled in with the likes of Phil Hoag and Jeff Richardson, and still [had] a George Chatlos in reserve. Notre Dame sent more men to the pros, but Michigan State's best were better than Notre Dame's best.

That's not an insult to Notre Dame. It's impossible to insult the abilities of players like Jim Lynch, Pete Duranko, Alan Page, and Kevin Hardy. No one would believe you. But people who play against Webster swear there was no better defensive player in college football. Notre Dame had a collection of offensive linemen who would go on to play more than a half century of professional ball. Every interior lineman on the team had a pro career. And not one of them could hold a block on Webster. These were players who simply blew away everyone else they faced, who were the engine of an offense that averaged 400 yards a game when that was an enormous figure. They got just over half that against the Spartans—219 yards: 91 on the ground and 128 in the air.

The Spartans, like the Irish, played clean. Only five yards in penalties were assessed against Notre Dame, and 32 against the Spartans. The officials didn't call a single holding penalty, personal foul, or pass interference penalty. That says a lot about the play of the game. It was hard and it was clean, as football is supposed to be and so seldom is.

It was left to a few, led by Dan Jenkins of *Sports Illustrated* and Jim Murray of the *Los Angeles Times*, to set the agenda for the ages. They saw the game as a case of [Parseghian] purposely playing for a tie. Jenkins began his lead story in the nation's sports magazine, "Old Notre Dame will tie over all. Sing it out, guys. . . . No one really expected a verdict in that last desperate moment," he wrote. "But they wanted someone to try."

That's the legacy of the game, and Parseghian saw it coming as soon as he talked to the first wave of newspaper reporters. The first thing he did when he got off the field and had his few minutes with his team in the closed locker room was explain to his own players what had happened. They had come off the field thinking that their dreams of a national championship were finished. They thought they had lost, and when they got behind closed doors, they sat at their lockers and wept.

[Parseghian] asked for their attention and explained that they hadn't lost, and that was the main thing. He told them how magnificently they had played to come back and tie the Spartans with five key players hurt. He told them that college football did not have overtime in a game, but that they had overtime in their season. Michigan State was through, their record carved in stone at 9–0–1. But Notre Dame had USC yet to play. Beat them, and they could still save the season, still win their championship.

The players listened, and the players believed because Parseghian had never misled them. They still felt empty, but no longer as empty as the Spartans, who were raging in their own locker room at the cruel trick fate had played on them. When the writers came in, [Smith] led the charge by telling everyone how Notre Dame had played for a tie and how it was Parseghian's fault.

The writers ran over to the Notre Dame locker room and asked [Parseghian], "What about it?" They've been asking the question ever since. [His] answer never changes. The more the writers questioned his strategy, the more frustrated [he] became. What, he said, could he have done in the last minute that he hadn't done in the first 59? He had tried everything. There was nothing left to do but get out and win the title the next week.

Most coaches understand that. The goal is not to win any one game but the big prize at the end of the season. If a pro coach tied the score on purpose and got into the postseason because of it and went on to win the Super Bowl, he'd be a genius. "That's what you're playing for," says George Young of the Giants. "It's not how you win things. It's whether or not you do."

"I made the judgments for all the games I coached, and I wasn't going to let some writer in the press box make a decision about what I should have done at the end of the game. Who knows better my team and the capabilities of the team?" [Parseghian] argues, his eyes flashing. "One of the writers said, 'Well, why didn't you throw the bomb out of bounds to make it look good?' What? I'm not trying to impress anybody. Doing that would be truly phony to me."

Over the years, since he retired from coaching because he was afraid the job would kill him, the question that comes up most is, "Why did you go for the tie?" It has become an obsession with him, his Moby Dick that he keeps sticking harpoons into but can't kill. And having always relied on the power of reason, he has never been able to say, "Screw it. I did what I did and that's that. End of discussion." He seems to feel that if he can only get people to see the game the way he did, if they could only look at the big picture instead of the little picture, they'd understand.

In fact, most of the people who count *do* understand. Bleier, one of the few among the Irish who openly questioned [Parseghian's] strategy, said, "It makes sense now. If I were coaching today, I'd probably do the same thing. It's just at the time, the mentality of the player was to throw the ball, throw the ball, throw the ball. But we were running the ball, and you don't even get the satisfaction of saying, 'Hell, we tried.' If you lose, it takes away from the success of the whole season. I would tie it for the guys because if you lose it, nobody remembers you. If you lose, you can say all you want, 'We could have won. We went for it.' But that's bull. Who cares? To win the championship, which was our goal, you have to win every game or, in this case, not lose that game. That's the point. We didn't lose the game."

On the other side of the field, Smith, who was most vocal in criticizing Parseghian, has come to appreciate the fact that nobody won the game: "I told George Webster that the best thing that ever happened was that the game ended in a tie. The only person it has really driven crazy is Ara, and the older he has gotten, the more it has preyed on him, because the game comes up every year. But he did exactly what he should have done. I knew during the game that Ara's strategy was right. I was calling them names because that's all we had left to do—play head games. I told our guys in the huddle, 'If this game ends in a tie, Notre Dame is going to win. All the sportswriters are Catholic.' I said, 'Do you think we're going to win the national championship even if they run the clock out? We got too many niggers on this team to win the national championship. We have to find a way.'

"I was saying that to try to motivate the guys, but it's true. I don't think any other school would have won the championship if they had done that. But he did the right thing. They couldn't have thrown the ball against the defenses we were running. I'm just being honest."

[Daugherty] himself, before he died, never criticized [Parseghian] for his strategy. He and Ara were friends. [Daugherty] told [Parseghian] that he had done the right thing.

But again, the problem was that the writers needed a winner. They had to vote for one in the polls, and how could they vote if the game was tied? [Daugherty] got it right when he said Notre Dame and Michigan State should be co–national champions. The awarders of the MacArthur Bowl, one of the national championship awards, did just that. They split the award between the two teams. Notre Dame kept the trophy for six months, and Michigan State kept it for the next six.

The two polls came out on Monday, with Notre Dame leading the AP version and Michigan State first in the UPI coaches' poll.

Epilogue
The AP poll soon became the most coveted of all the championships, but over the years at least 15 organizations have awarded such honors.

Some of those championship races created more national interest than others, and the biggest of them mark pivotal points in the continuum. Notre Dame–Michigan State was one of those pivotal points because it demonstrated the power of television and showed how far beyond the stadium a game could reach. It ushered in the modern TV-football era.

Everyone wanted a piece of the frenzy that Notre Dame–Michigan State had inspired; everybody wanted to be No. 1. To do that, they would have to follow the rules that the voters—sportswriters and broadcasters—were making up as they went along.

The University of Alabama went undefeated and untied in 1966 but could do no better than third in the polls. The pollsters decided the Crimson Tide had not proved itself because it hadn't played any intersectional schedule. That year Bear Bryant started talking about the need for his team to play three national games every year, along with seven conference games. To win those games, Bryant knew he'd need to have some of the black players who were being recruited away in ever-increasing numbers by midwestern and western schools.

All in all, 1966 was an important year for black college athletes. First, Texas Western became the first major college to put five blacks on a basketball floor, on its way to beating all-white Kentucky to win the national championship. Then Michigan State went undefeated with a majority of blacks on its football team. The old prejudices that said blacks weren't leaders or didn't have the alleged "necessities" pretty much died right there.

It's doubtful that Duffy Daugherty was consciously trying to drag the rest of college football into the modern world. More likely he was just trying to win a championship, and he realized that color wasn't important. Talent was. He probably would have preferred that his rivals continued to wallow in their ignorance and bigotry. That way he could have kept the best talent for himself. But, consciously or not, he helped change recruiting.

To be No. 1, boosters were willing to do anything, and university presidents went along with their desires. The following years saw the construction of special dorms for athletes at many schools. The abuses that had always existed—altering transcripts, spreading money around, getting cars for the star players—reached new levels as well; recruiters started going after kids who would never have been able to get into most schools before the frenzy began.

The huge rewards of success made trainers, coaches, and players more willing to turn to the medicine cabinet to gain an edge, and more players started going to the weight room. The discovery that a class of drugs called steroids could add enormous bulk in a short time accelerated the process, which continued until men the size of Smith and Hardy were no longer the exception on the line, they were the rule. At the same time, coaches demanded more and more that athletes stick to one sport.

It all followed the new importance of what would become college football's cash cow—television. Notre Dame–Michigan State was the first megagame of the modern television era: the first monster game seen in color with instant slow-motion replay. ABC had even flown in a special zoom lens from England for the game, a lens that allowed viewers to see not only Kenney's bare kicking foot, but whether he had dirt under his toenails. It was the first time a lens of such power had been used to cover a sporting event.

The players, too, would discover the all-seeing eye. In Notre Dame's first game that year, against Purdue, Hanratty and split end Jim Seymour had to be coaxed by an ABC employee to turn away from the game and smile into the sideline camera. Waving an index finger and mouthing, "Hi, Mom" was out of the question. You watch a tape of any game from that year, and you'll see the same attitude. In the Michigan State–Notre Dame game, not one player from either side can be seen gloating over a fallen opponent. The contest was filled with monster defensive hits, with great efforts, with tackles for losses, tackles for no gains, passes broken up along with the receivers who were trying to catch them. And after every great play, the athletes picked themselves up and got back into the huddle. That was it. No pointing. No gloating. No woofing. Not even a little leap of triumph. Just business.

But a new generation would soon be watching Joe Namath take the New York Jets to the Super Bowl while wearing white football shoes and sporting hair that hung out of the back of his helmet. Cool. Then Billy "White Shoes" Johnson would join the Houston Oilers in 1974 and introduce the sport to the end-zone boogie. After Johnson, Mark Gastineau did the same thing for defensive linemen with his sack dance. And every time someone did something unusual on the field, the cameras picked it up and the replay machines showed it again and again on the sports shows. It got to the point where the first thing players did when they made a play was jump up and down and dance and gesture for the cameras. Then they'd look for a teammate to celebrate with.

Television did all that, and the Game of the Century gave television its stage. The enormous ratings the game attracted—33 million viewers for a game that was shown on tape delay in the South and Northwest—attracted the most attention of all. It was the largest audience ever to see a college football game. The 22.5 Nielsen rating for the game was also the greatest ever and remains the second highest in history for a regular-season game, surpassed only by the 22.9 rating for the 1968 Notre Dame–Southern Cal game in O. J. Simpson's senior year. No one knows what the rating would have been if the two sections of the country hadn't had to wait to see the game until after it was broadcast on the radio.

One game was not the whole cause of all these changes. Just as someone would have discovered the forward pass without Knute Rockne and Gus Dorais, the combination of television and football would have grown into the monster it is without The Biggest Game of Them All. The point is that the game defined a turning point and pointed out the possibilities that lay down the road. It accelerated the process. Part of that had to do with the times. Much more than football was changing.

A big part of the new generation was the quest for social justice, for fundamental fairness. That, too, was mirrored in college football in rule changes that governed how national champions were chosen and who went to bowl games. Michigan State might have won the national title that year if it could have gone to a bowl game—and if the final polls were taken after the bowl games. But Big Ten rules prohibited the Spartans from going to the Rose Bowl because they had been there the year before. The Rose Bowl was considered a treat to be spread out among the conference members, not an end in itself.

The Pac 8's rule was different but equally inequitable. That conference voted on a representative, a policy that prevented UCLA from representing the conference after the 1966 season. Because of the uproar that arose when both UCLA and Michigan State were shut out of the bowl, both conferences changed their rules. From then on, the conference champion would go.

Once bowl games became an important part of the race for the national championship, Notre Dame, which for decades had contended that postseason play would detract from the academic mission of the university, changed its mind too. Predictions that the school's no-bowl rule would be dropped appeared immediately.

But people don't still talk about Notre Dame–Michigan State for any of those reasons. They still talk about it because it ended in a tie—an immortal tie. They talk about it and argue about which was the better team.

In the fall of 1991, Ara Parseghian sat in his downtown South Bend office, surrounded by the relics of a great career, defending himself again for his strategy. I listened to him that day, and finally I said, "Ara, you did the right thing. If someone had won or lost, it would have been a great game, but we wouldn't be sitting here talking about it 25 years later."

We may never talk about a game for as long again.

(Notre Dame won its final game, beating USC 51–0. In the end-of-season polls, the two wire services, AP and UPI, voted Notre Dame No. 1 and Michigan State No. 2.)

Rick Telander, *Sports Illustrated*

PLUCK OF THE IRISH

Notre Dame's 1988 victory over top-rated Miami was as memorable and satisfying for Notre Dame fans as any in Irish history. And it proved the Irish were back for good. It also marked the first of three Sports Illustrated *cover appearances for Irish quarterback Tony Rice in a span of 10 weeks.*

Do you want to call this good triumphing over evil? Did Notre Dame's 31–30 defeat on Saturday of previously unbeaten and No. 1–ranked Miami remind you of Milton's archangels whupping up on Beelzebub and the crew from Chaos?

Well, OK, winning by one point while getting outgained 481 yards to 331 isn't exactly the way Michael handled the devil. But you catch the drift. Did you fall for those signs and T-shirts that sprouted in South Bend during game week comparing Notre Dame to the Sistine Chapel and the University of Miami to the river Styx house of detention? If you did, then you probably feel now that all is right with the world and that God is in his place.

But if you happen to be a Hurricane fan, you might argue that Miami was jobbed out of a fourth-quarter touchdown—or, at least, possession of the ball at the Notre Dame 1-foot line—when the officials ruled that Miami fullback Cleveland Gary wasn't down before he fumbled the ball as he tried to extend it across the goal line. Or you could contend that Hurricane coach Jimmy Johnson didn't have to go for a two-point conversion after wide receiver Andre Brown made a brilliant catch of an 11-yard touchdown pass with 45 seconds left in the game to make the score 31–30. Miami could have just accepted a tie, the way Notre Dame did against Michigan State in their famous battle of undefeateds in 1966.

And, you could insist, the Irish upset would not have occurred if Notre Dame defensive tackle Jeff Alm wasn't 6'7" and hadn't batted down one of Hurricane quarterback Steve Walsh's passes and intercepted another just by extending his damn arms. And who knows how bad the Hurricanes might have thrashed Notre Dame if they hadn't had seven turnovers—three interceptions, one of which was returned 60 yards for a touchdown by free safety Pat Terrell, and four fumbles, two of which were recovered by Irish nose tackle Chris Zorich, the human groundhog.

Yeah, you could argue about a lot of things, particularly the good versus bad stuff, but you couldn't change the fact that the university library overlooking Notre Dame Stadium seemed to be raising its arms a little higher in blessing over coach Lou Holtz's boys.

"The afternoon was absolutely perfect," said Notre Dame defensive end Frank Stams (one tackle for a loss, two fumbles caused, and one fumble recovery), celebrating in the locker room after the game. "This is what college football is all about."

The Irish scored first on junior quarterback Tony Rice's first-quarter seven-yard option keeper, on which he waltzed into the end zone unscathed. Rice, who's listed at 6'1" and 198 pounds but who looks much smaller, took a pounding on most of his other carries (21 rushes for a net of 20 yards), but he remained upbeat throughout the game. "The glass isn't half empty for Tony," said flanker Ricky Watters afterward. "It's always half full."

In between the beatings, the occasionally scatter-armed Rice even completed 8 of 16 passes for a career-high 195 yards. Included in that number was a rainmaking 57-yard, second-quarter bomb to wide receiver Raghib ("Call me Rocket if you can't say Raghib") Ismail, which traveled almost 70 yards in the air. Said the smiling Rice in the locker room, "Never say bad things about a little guy, because the little guy will fool you." Meaning himself.

Miami scored seven minutes after Rice's touchdown on an eight-yard pass from Walsh to Brown. The Irish then went ahead 21–7 on a short scoring pass from Rice to fullback Braxston Banks and Terrell's return of that tipped Walsh pass. Not the swiftest or gainliest of athletes, Walsh nevertheless chased Terrell to the bitter end, diving and cutting his chin in a futile attempt at a tackle near the goal line.

A normal team might have folded at that point. The crowd was wacky, the enemy was fired up, and Miami's quarterback was bleeding: you could almost hear Rockne and the Gipper cackling from on high. But the Hurricanes, who had whipped Notre Dame in the schools' last four meetings by a combined score of 133–20 and who were unbeaten in 36 straight regular-season games, are not a normal team. They are a testy street gang that has transformed itself into the high-wire act of college football—the Miami Pound Machine, a club that can score from anywhere at any time, a traveling bomb squad that four weeks earlier had trailed 30–14 at Michigan with less than six minutes left in the game and won 31–30 using just one timeout. And Walsh, the gunner, is a man who is ultracool under pressure.

In the final minutes of the second quarter Walsh threw a 23-yard touchdown pass to halfback Leonard Conley. Then he mounted a 54-yard drive in just 48 seconds, capping it with a 15-yard touchdown strike to Gary, whose 11 catches for 130 yards set a Miami single-game reception record for running backs. The teams ran off at halftime tied 21–21, and the general feeling of the stunned Golden Dome fans was Heaven help us, Miami is possessed by the devil.

Earlier in the week Walsh, who would complete 31 of 50 passes for a career-high 424 yards and four touchdowns against the Irish, suggested that the Miami air attack is so sophisticated that nobody can stop it. "If I get the time, there's always somebody open," he said, adding that this is why he has not allowed himself to be sacked this year. "I'd rather throw the ball away than get sacked. An incompletion? Big deal. If it's third-and-eight, third-and-ten, we'll get that. We have entire third-and-long scrimmages. We're so used to it, it's nothing."

His three interceptions and two fumbles were his undoing, however, and almost undid any chance that the Hurricanes would win their second consecutive national title. The long-armed Alm quashed one third-quarter Miami drive, and the hard-working Stams twice looped in from Walsh's blind side to jar the ball from his clutches. "He seemed real comfortable back there," said Stams with a shrug, knotting his tie and listening to the wild Irish fans outside the locker room. "He seemed to think he had more time than he did. Yes, I think I'll party tonight."

Long before the game Miami coach Johnson knew that his time for dominating the Irish was coming to a close. People kept harking back to the 1985 game in which Miami wiped out Notre Dame 58–7, a contest Irish fans said branded Johnson with the mortal sin of running up the score. Whatever the truth of that charge, the rout was an arm shove out the door for departing Irish coach Gerry Faust, a man who, at the time, was almost certainly the worst tactical coach in the country. In his five years at Notre Dame, Faust was so overmatched that he made the faithful tremble in fear over the prospect of facing the likes of Air Force. The fidgety, driven, inspirational Holtz followed Faust and after 2½ years has the Irish back where they belong—in the ozone.

"They say we're fast, but look at these times," said Johnson after Thursday's practice, holding up a Notre Dame football guide to a page listing the players with the fastest times in the 40-yard dash. "They've got four guys under 4.4. The only guy we have under that is Randal Hill."

Johnson flipped through the pages and then said, "Sixteen of their starters were high school All-Americas. Four were honorable mention. They have quarterbacks backing up Rice who were All-World. And we've got guys like Russell Maryland starting, guys who weren't even offered scholarships. Poor old Notre Dame."

Needless to say, the poor, old, ever-feisty Johnson isn't well-liked in South Bend. One T-shirt popular on the Notre Dame campus was emblazoned "TOP TEN REASONS TO HATE MIAMI." It listed reason

No. 10 as "THEY THINK 'LEAVE IT TO THE BEAVER' IS A METHOD FOR GETTING HOMEWORK DONE," and No. 1 as simply "JIMMY JOHNSON."

Bear in mind that Notre Dame students, a generally restless, brainy, and athletic group of wise guys (and not a few wise gals), rise like fish to meal when it comes to slogan painting and hero bashing. They jumped all over the Hurricanes and their lingering reputation as a band of outlaws. "CAN YOU READ THIS? MIAMI CAN'T" said a banner high up on Flanner Tower. Another hot-selling T-shirt read "YOU CAN'T SPELL SCUM WITHOUT U.M." Another: "CATHOLICS VS. CONVICTS." There were others as well that crossed the line into bad taste—for instance, one with a drawing of Johnson as the devil above the words "JIMMY JOHNSON PORK FACE SATAN."

The hate-Miami atmosphere had become so volatile that Notre Dame administrators designated the pregame days as Spirit Week, a sort of rah-rah alternative to overt meanness. Holtz wrote an open letter to the student body, published on October 6 in *The Observer*, the campus newspaper, asking students to behave themselves during game week. The Irish tri-captains, Mark Green, Ned Bolcar, and Andy Heck, also wrote a letter to the paper, asking students to support the team "in a *positive* manner."

But what the heck, it wasn't like the Notre Dame kids were going to steal Miami's gold jewelry or something. They were just getting excited about the fact that Notre Dame, which was ranked No. 5, was going to play a top-rated team in South Bend for the first time in 20 years. "As far as hatred goes: "Hey, God hates things, too," summed up *Observer* news editor Mark McLaughlin in his column.

In the second half, what Johnson hated was the sight of Irish freshman tight end Derek Brown catching two passes for 46 yards, which helped Notre Dame sustain time-eating drives. A 6'7", 235-pound bruiser who can run like a deer, Brown is from Merritt Island, Florida— 'Cane country—and Johnson had recruited him like crazy, knowing what Brown would be able to do in Miami's offensive system. But Brown visited Notre Dame in the dead of winter and, miracle of miracles, fell under the Irish spell.

"I came here on a gut feeling," he said after the game. "I couldn't believe it, either." And what could he tell the disappointed fans in south Florida? "I'd just like to say, 'Well, I made the right choice.'"

With speedsters like Brown, Rice, Watters, Ismail, and running back Tony Brooks, Notre Dame is no longer a lead-footed team. Miami found that out in the third quarter as the Irish pulled ahead 31–21 on a touchdown and a field goal set up by a couple of big passes from Rice and crafty running by Brooks.

But then it was Miami prime time. Everybody had the same thought: could this team possibly roar back in the fourth quarter the way it had earlier this year in that game against Michigan in Ann Arbor, or the way it had last year against Florida State, when it had scored three times in just 4:57 to win 26–25? It would take faith. And as Walsh said before the game, "Notre Dame hasn't cornered the market on Catholic football players." Walsh is Catholic, as are the "big three" who preceded him at quarterback: Jim Kelly, Bernie Kosar, and Vinny Testaverde. All Miami's starting offensive linemen, including tight end Rob Chudzinski, are Catholics too.

The Southern Catholics came back against the Midwestern Catholics. Miami scored on a field goal and then on a Walsh-to-Brown touchdown pass with 45 seconds left. Everything—or, at least, an Orange Bowl berth and the national championship—may have been hanging on the two-point conversion attempt. Johnson never considered playing for a tie. "We always play to win," he declared solemnly afterward.

But Walsh's floating pass, intended for Conley, was batted down in the end zone by Terrell, and Notre Dame won its sixth game in row. In the locker room where Bertelli, Lujack, and Huarte used to dress, Rice smiled with pure satisfaction. Critics have questioned whether an option-type quarterback—a black kid from the Deep South, for goodness' sake—is suited to lead this hallowed institution on the gridiron. Well, after the Miami game, Rice's suitability is no longer in doubt.

Before the game, in the tunnel under the stadium, a fair-sized dust-up had broken out between Notre Dame and Miami players, and somebody had grabbed Rice's face mask and tried to punch him. "It was No. 18," said Rice after the game. That would be Miami backup wide receiver Pee Wee Smith. Gee, has anybody ever been hurt by a guy named Pee Wee?

Rice laughed. It was no big deal. One time during the game he had come to the sideline and wiped off "a big gob of spit on my forehead." That was no big deal, either.

What is a big deal is that Rice now fits in at Notre Dame, both on the field and in the classroom. A former Proposition 48 casualty, Rice is pleased to announce that he got an A- and a B on two recent psychology midterms. How has he turned things around?

"They have so many people helping you here—how can you fail?" he replies. "Unless you don't want it. I want it."

Well then, welcome back, Notre Dame.

Dan Shaughnessy, the *Boston Globe*

HOLTZ WINS HOME GAME

Maybe the most memorable, if not shocking, story of game week for the 1993 Notre Dame–Florida State contest came when Irish coach Lou Holtz invited all the visiting media to his home for barbeque on the Thursday night prior to the big game. This is the report by one of those visiting journalists.

Today is "the game of the century." Florida State vs. Notre Dame. We've got all the trappings. Florida State is No. 1; Notre Dame is No. 2. Both teams are 9–0, winners of 16 straight. The game is being played at Notre Dame, where they have real grass, weather-beaten brown bricks, Touchdown Jesus, and the Golden Dome. Tickets are said to be going for more than $1,000.

With the game of the century just hours away, I'm still thinking about my dinner with Lou.

It was an unlikely happening. I'd never met the Notre Dame coach until Thursday. After his daily press briefing, he invited everybody to his house for dinner. A blue sheet of paper—directions to the home of Lou and Beth Holtz in Woodland Hills—was handed out to members of the national media.

This was extraordinary. Trust me when I tell you that the ink-stained wretches were not invited to the home of John and Ellen McNamara the night before the first game of the 1986 World Series. Bill Fitch did not—*did not*—invite us for beer and pretzels at his downtown apartment before the 1981 playoffs. Bobby Knight didn't have us over for dinner two nights before the NCAA championship final in 1987.

It was a tad bizarre. Was Lou trying to court favor? Was this a damage-control measure, a counterstrike against *Under the Tarnished Dome*, the tell-all book that portrayed Holtz as mean, petty, and something less than holy?

We made the decision to go to dinner. Who could pass on an opportunity like this? It was a chance to see Notre Dame's main man in his own home less than two days before the game of the century. It was a chance to probe the mind of the man who'll call the shots today. It was a chance to maybe learn more about today's game plan. And let's not forget, it was a free meal.

Holtz' house is about a 10-minute drive from the Notre Dame campus. The coach and his wife greeted us behind the bar of their huge downstairs rec room. They could not have been more gracious. Lou was glad-handing all the sportswriters. He kept saying, "What can I get you?"

We asked for a beer. Bud Light, to be precise. Lou handed over a Bud Light and, laughing, told his wife, "Bud Light is running ahead of Miller Lite."

The downstairs den is Lou's shrine. "I'm not allowed to have anything on the walls anywhere else in the house," he said. "Except for here."

It is museumlike. Trophies, plaques, murals, pictures. Lou with Ronald Reagan. Lou with George Bush. Lou with Bill Clinton (when Clinton was a young Arkansas attorney and Lou was coach of the Razorbacks). Lou with Johnny Carson, sitting in on the *Tonight* show. Over the fireplace, there was a painting of Lou with the other coaches of Notre Dame lore—Lou with Dan Devine, Ara Parseghian, Frank Leahy, and Knute Rockne (FSU wide receiver Kez McCorvey this week referred to the last as "Rock Knutne").

Lou's telephone is a golden Notre Dame helmet. The books on the shelves are sports classics. I looked long and hard for *Under the Tarnished Dome*. Couldn't find it. Lou says he never read the book. Maybe it's true. I didn't check to see if it was hidden under his pillow. Investigative reporting has its limits.

Lou told us that his only requirement for any house is a pool table. He loves his pool table. He said he always wanted a home with a big rec room, a place where his kids could bring their friends. He said he wanted his kids to bring their friends over, rather than have his kids going to other kids' homes. He sounded like a lot of parents I know.

On the downstairs bathroom wall was a touching poem about a father leaving his son with a good name. I asked Lou about it and he took me into the bathroom to explain where it came from and how he felt about it. I couldn't help but think, "The game of the century is 40 hours away and Lou Holtz is standing in his downstairs bathroom going to great lengths to reveal himself to someone he's never met."

We sat side by side at dinner, and Lou said he'd called former Holy Cross coach Mark Duffner to see how things were going at Maryland. Lou recruited Duffner at William & Mary. He said he likes to call people when they're down. He said he hadn't yet spoken with Holy Cross coach Peter Vaas. Vaas was a Holtz assistant before taking over at H.C. "I told him it was a mistake," said Lou. "They were losing the scholarships. It was a no-win situation."

He drank A&W root beer. He ate chicken and ribs. He kept asking, "Can I get you anything?"

"I did a radio show this week," he laughed. "And they asked me, 'What do you do all week?' It's true. I only work one day a week."

Sure. One day a week. That's why he's sleeping only four hours a night. That's why he looks like he weighs about 135 pounds. And that's why his secretary says he's booked through 1994.

Back in the rec room, Lou sat on the couch with his daughter and watched ESPN. It was halftime of the Brigham Young–San Diego State game, and much of the halftime show was devoted to today's game of the century. Lou watched himself say his team will not be intimidated. He watched FSU coach Bobby Bowden say Lou will be going crazy today on the sideline eating grass, and stuff like that. ESPN ran some footage of Lou's famous headlock on an official during last year's Brigham Young game.

Lou had his arm around his daughter as he watched. When the ESPN analyst said Notre Dame must keep FSU pinned in its own end, Holtz laughed and said, "He ought to see our punter."

At one point, during the heavy TV analysis of the game of the century, he said, "It's just a game."

Beth Holtz gave us cookies in a napkin as we left. What a feed. I felt like the Golden Dome was hovering over my belt buckle. My new friend Lou gave us a small box of golf balls. Payola party favors.

That settled it. It doesn't matter if Florida State wins today by four touchdowns; I will write only good things about Notre Dame. I have broken bread with Lou. After today's game of the century, I will have only one question.

What time is dinner before the BC game?

* * *

Editor's note: Two days after Irish coach Lou Holtz played host to the visiting media at his home, Holtz and his second-ranked and unbeaten Notre Dame football team defeated unbeaten and top-ranked Florida State 31–24 in Notre Dame Stadium, vaulting the Irish into the top spot in the polls.

Johnny Lujack was a Heisman Trophy winner at Notre Dame and went on to quarterback and captain the Chicago Bears.

Section II
THE PLAYERS

Jim Beach, *Saga*

GIPP OF NOTRE DAME

George Gipp may well have been as talented a football player as has ever worn a Notre Dame uniform. His exploits on and off the field remain legendary at Notre Dame—and they certainly were not hurt by the fact that his part in a renowned sports movie was played by one soon-to-be President Ronald Reagan. This piece appeared in Saga *in the fall of 1958.*

At 7:00 on the bone-chilling winter evening of December 14, 1920, a young man lay close to death in St. Joseph's Hospital, South Bend, Indiana, suffering from a streptococcus infection that had now reached its critical phase.

At that hour the entire student body of the University of Notre Dame was joined in prayer. Some of the boys were kneeling in chapels on campus; others knelt in the snow, reciting the rosary on the hospital grounds.

At the Oliver Hotel on North Main Street, there was a spirit of gloom in the rooms where the smart money guys, card sharks, and traveling salesmen had gathered for the nightly dice, poker, and rummy sessions which the sick man had regularly attended.

A few minutes past 7:00, the hotel lights dimmed and flickered, and although there had been no prearranged signal, this message from the desk clerk was correctly interpreted to mean that George Gipp was dead.

George Gipp—the first Notre Dame man to be chosen All-American by Walter Camp—was a football star who, in his brief 25 years on Earth, had been raised to the stature of a demigod. His astounding feats inspired Ring Lardner to write that the Notre Dame team seemed to have only one formation and one signal: "Line up, pass the ball to Gipp, and let him use his own judgment."

The innocent years immediately preceding, during, and following World War I are commonly thought of as the "Old Siwash" era. It was an era typified by a moleskin-clad lad named Gipp, who could run with the speed and power of a stallion, pass a football through a needle's eye at 40 yards, punt soaring spirals, and drop-kick field goals with the precision and poise of an automaton. George Gipp was a national celebrity, regarded with the same awe as Woodrow Wilson, "Black Jack" Pershing, and Douglas Fairbanks.

As a youngster living at Laurium, Michigan—a small mining and industrial community located near the shores of Lake Superior—Gipp first revealed his athletic ability. In those days, baseball and basketball were his sports. He did play some football at Calumet High School, but he was slight of build and got banged up too often. On the basketball court [Gipp] made up for his fragile frame with speed and accuracy, and he starred on a team that won 24 out of 25 games and brought Calumet its first regional championship.

It was baseball, however, that brought him hometown fame. Old codgers around Laurium still recall him as a dark-haired, gangling schoolboy who could belt the ball for extra bases against grown-men pitchers. In one four-game series with Iron Mountain, [Gipp] made seven hits in 12 times at bat: three triples and four doubles. Newspaper records show that he batted .494 one season and belted the longest wallop ever seen in the Laurium ballpark.

While he excelled in sports, his scholarship was a different story. He managed to get passing grades, but after he and some of his buddies were accused of vandalism, [Gipp] was suspended from school. The result was that he didn't get a diploma and took a job driving a taxi.

Hacking soon put Gipp wise to the shadier aspects of life in the tough copper country. He matured far beyond his years in many respects, but he had no plans for the future.

"George," his older brother Alex finally told him, "the best thing for you is to get out of town."

[Gipp] spoke in short, clipped sentences. "I like it here," he replied. "Besides, who are you to give me advice? You came back home after college, didn't you?"

"But you've got the brains in this family, kid," Alex argued.

But the most Alex could accomplish was getting [Gipp] to go to work on a line gang for the Michigan Bell telephone company—rough and dangerous work. The lanky 20-year-old had the strength and stamina required, and he was agile and quick, climbing telephone poles to string and repair wire. Away from the job, though, [he] was restless and unable to settle down.

His stern, bearded father, a hard-working carpenter and laborer who had sired a family of eight children, and his gentle, Scotch-Irish mother didn't approve of their youngest son's shiftlessness. They were alarmed, too, at the time he spent hanging out in saloons and pool parlors.

"Matthew," his mother would chide her husband when he criticized [Gipp's] shiftlessness, "he'll find out what he wants to do soon enough."

[Gipp] resented the strict Baptist discipline maintained in [his] home. He escaped from the constant prodding and carping by following a well-worn path away from the frame house on Hecla Street toward the bright lights of Calumet. He would prowl the honky-tonks, shooting pool and playing cards with pals from his Calumet High days, and he indulged in the conventional vices.

A girl named Hazel—the town beauty—was one of the reasons [Gipp] remained in Laurium. But because he considered her to be on a higher social level, [he] admired her from afar.

The mounting friction in the Gipp household reached a climax in the summer of 1916, when Bill Gray, a baseball catcher who had been signed by the Chicago White Sox after playing college ball at Notre Dame, returned home to Calumet for a few days. [Gray] told [Gipp] he would be a cinch for a scholarship at Notre Dame—then a minor university—and that he thought he could arrange it for him. Although [Gipp] expressed little interest, Gray got him an offer of free tuition if he would play baseball. He could earn his bed and board working as a waiter in a student dining hall.

At the age of 21, George Gipp packed his pool cue and some clothes and set out for Notre Dame.

When Gipp came down the pike it wasn't difficult to pass muster at the registrar's office. He indicated a willingness to study and was assigned a bed in the Brownson Hall dormitory. To his dismay, he had to pay for books, classroom supplies, registration fees, and other routine expenses, and he was charged for his laundry and other incidental items. It wasn't long before he had only 15 cents left.

Notre Dame was primarily a poor man's school, where virtually all students dressed in the same manner and ate the same meals regardless of bloodlines, bank accounts, or religious background. The average fellow thought he was flush if he had a dime and a nickel to rub together. It was a Spartan existence, characterized by a strong spiritual undercurrent from which [Gipp] felt apart. Men like the fathers and brothers of the Congregation of the Holy Cross, who taught and administered at the Catholic university, were strange to him.

Although it took him a while to become accustomed to the strict ways of life in a Catholic college, George grew to respect and admire the priests for their devotion, sacrifice, and faith. But, as in the case of Hazel, he admired from afar and followed the path that led him to the bright lights of South Bend.

One afternoon, Knute Rockne, then a Notre Dame chemistry instructor who doubled as assistant to football coach Jesse Harper and as team trainer to supplement his meager income, was strolling across the recreation field alongside Brownson Hall. Suddenly, he stopped in his tracks and watched a 60-yard punt sail in a lazy spiral over his head. He looked around to see who had kicked it, and there stood George

Gipp—wearing street shoes. By now, [Gipp] was a 175-pound six-footer with lean muscles, long legs, and broad shoulders.

"Why aren't you out for the freshman squad?" the burly man with the knuckle-dented nose asked.

"Football isn't my game," Gipp replied.

"Afraid?" Rockne said, laughing.

"Like hell I am!"

"Oh, you're tough?"

"As tough as I need to be."

"Think it over. I'll be handing out equipment over at the Field-house in an hour or so. I've got just the pair of cleats for you."

"A special pair?" [Gipp] asked.

"Yeah," Rock said, "they belonged to Ray Eichenlaub."

"Who is he?"

"Around these parts he was known as a *real* Notre Dame man."

Rockne had gauged the kid correctly. The barb stung Gipp's pride, and he reported for practice.

The name George Gipp first appeared in sports page headlines a few weeks later. He made the freshman team and was a starter at left halfback against Western State Normal School at Kalamazoo, Michigan, where his brother Matt was living. In the fourth quarter the score was tied, 7–7. Notre Dame had yardage to go for a first down. On fourth down, quarterback Frank Thomas barked the signals for a shift from the "T" to punt formation, with Gipp back in kicking position.

As the ball was snapped from center, Notre Dame end Dave Hayes took off at full speed to get down under the punt. He sprinted straight for the Western State safety man, but slowed down when he saw the player turn around to face his own goal. Then [Hayes] became conscious of the cheering crowd.

"What happened?" Hayes asked.

"That sonofabitch kicked a field goal," the State safety man told him.

Gipp, not wanting to settle for a tie, had drop-kicked—62 yards between the uprights and over the crossbar. The record still stands in the books.

Gipp wasn't at all ruffled by the applause he received for his remarkable feat at Kalamazoo, and he accepted prestige as a matter of course. Once his status as athlete was established, he moved from Brownson Hall to Sorin Hall, where he bunked with athletic scholarship men. Yet he still had to don a waiter's white jacket and sling hash.

[Gipp] played freshman basketball that winter and ran anchor in the intramural track relays. The evening hours usually were spent in the recreation room with his roommate and friend Elwyn "Dope" Moore.

"Make you a proposition, Dope," Gipp said one night. "You teach me three-cushion billiards, and I'll stop taking your money at pool."

"Since I lose to you all the time, old buddy," Moore said, "I guess that's a pretty good deal for me. You've got yourself a teacher, and I'm the best."

"The best for now, but not for long," [Gipp] said.

For a number of weeks afterward [Gipp] concentrated on perfecting his smooth cue stroke at billiards, a game he found both challenging and stimulating. Meanwhile, he shot Kelly pool and snooker for small change. Since the financial returns were limited around the campus, [Gipp] soon set out in search of bigger action. This meant taking the Hill Street trolley to the billiard halls of South Bend.

Playing pool, [he] was, as always, the picture of nonchalance. He would saunter into the room, remove his jacket, and hang it on a wall peg. Then he would take his stick down from the rack and chalk up, all the while sizing up the skills of the men at the tables. Having selected his victim, he would begin the customary pregame con.

"How many will you spot me?" he would ask an unwary stranger.

The poolroom loafers who had seen [Gipp] play, or who knew him by reputation, would cluster around the table as Gipp flubbed a few practice shots.

"It would be foolish, you playin' me," the mark would say.

"Put some money where your mouth is."

"OK, laddie buck. I'll spot you 10 balls. For 10 bucks."

At this point, Gipp would dangle a cigarette from the corner of his mouth and say, "Why not make it more interesting?"

"Are you good for $25?"

"If he ain't, I am," the proprietor would say.

"It's like a license to steal," the patsy would remark. "Anytime you're ready, buster."

Gipp would always lose the first game. Then he'd ask, "How about a chance to get even?"

"Be my guest," the stranger would say.

"For a hundred bucks?"

"You got yourself a bet."

[Gipp's] opponent would then scatter the balls and Gipp would settle down to work. It wasn't at all unusual for him to make 50 consecutive shots when it was worthwhile. It was how he made his living.

Gipp's behavior was not unusual in a period when the tramp athlete was a fixture at most colleges. Notre Dame had adopted strict standards of eligibility for athletes—insisting on a 76 percent grade, instead of the 70 percent commonly accepted by most of the big colleges. But [Gipp] took advantage of his growing fame, and his individuality was regarded with leniency by certain members of the faculty.

Knute Rockne, himself a nonconformist, made it his business to be Gipp's protector and apologist. He had a deep-rooted fondness for [Gipp], based on respect for his native intelligence and athletic ability.

In football, [Gipp] applied himself solely to theory. It bewildered his coaches that he improved as a player without going through the intermediate steps of instruction and practice. "He doesn't have to be told anything twice," Rock said to Harper. "And more often than not, he does the correct thing the first time without being taught. For him, football is strictly a game of brains. . . ."

[Gipp] absorbed most of his knowledge of football at the noon chalk-talks conducted in the off-season by Harper and Rockne. He was counted on for regular varsity duty in his sophomore year, 1917, when America entered the war and 10 Notre Dame lettermen enlisted.

Gipp spent the summer vacation playing professional baseball. When the squad assembled for fall practice, [he] was among the missing. Rockne finally learned that he was playing for the Simmons Baseball Club in Kenosha, Wisconsin. Rock chased up north to investigate and found [Gipp] sitting on the bench.

"Hiya," the coach said. "Been playing much?"

"Some."

"The manager tells me not at all. Guess he was afraid it would cost you your amateur standing."

"Maybe."

Rockne told Gipp he had no future knocking around the country, picking up a few dollars here and there. And when [Gipp] argued that there was no percentage in it for him to go back to college, Rock had the answers to prove [him] wrong. They talked well into the night, but Rockne knew he needed Gipp, and when he took the train back to South Bend, his star backfield man went with him.

The subject of Gipp's borderline professionalism was kept secret. It never came up again, even though [he] would often pick up a few dollars playing "town ball" under assumed names on Sundays. But Rockne couldn't kick—he had done the same thing in his undergraduate days at Notre Dame.

In 1917, Gipp showed signs of fulfilling his promise of gridiron greatness. He was hampered by a muddy field in the Nebraska game. But under the same weather conditions at West Point, he stole the show from cadet Elmer Q. Oliphant by playing the full 60 minutes and sparking Notre Dame to a 7–2 victory.

When the team arrived at the South Bend railroad station after the Army game, [Gipp] flashed a wry smile as the students mobbed him. Then he left the party to join some of his downtown cronies. He had bet some money for them and was bringing home the winnings, part of which was his commission for handling the transactions.

Gipp's first varsity season was cut short the following Saturday. In a game with Morningside at Sioux City, Iowa, he was tackled and thrown against an iron post near the sideline. His leg was broken. After spending a short time in the infirmary, he went home to Laurium on crutches.

The following spring [he] still walked with a limp, and the draft board deferred action on his case. But when word reached the board the next fall that Gipp was playing football, an induction notice was drawn up and mailed special delivery, ordering him to report for military duty at South Bend on October 19, 1918. But the Armistice was signed on November 11, and Gipp's only uniforms were baseball flannels and a blue football jersey with a big 66 on the back.

In the 1918 season—Rockne's first as head coach—Gipp became a full-fledged star. Yet, he never had the spirit and attitude expected of a football hero. Football ordinarily requires a basic urge for tooth-rattling, rock-'em sock-'em body contact. The average player gets fun out of the sport by putting his strength, skill, and courage to the bloody test without hesitation. Gipp was an exception. It wasn't that he disliked the game; he just took no particular delight in it. Moreover, his physical condition was seldom up to taking the punishment. A priest at Notre Dame once asked him why he didn't do more blocking and make more tackles. "I let the strong boys do that," [Gipp] answered.

In Sorin Hall bull sessions, Gipp was often the number one topic. Right halfback Grover Malone, whom [Gipp] preferred to have blocking for him, spoke with authority on the subject. "The thing that makes him a slick customer is that he avoids trouble. When he is hit with a solid tackle, he relaxes and goes down. He's always saving himself for next time."

"How come you knock yourself out for him so much, Grover?" someone asked.

"I dunno," Malone said. "I want to run the ball as much as anybody, but Gipp has me doing the heavy work—and liking it."

Rockne, a stickler for physical conditioning, tried to take George to task for his indifference to training rules. "Aw, cut it, Coach," Gipp told him. "You know I don't need to mess with that muscle stuff."

Rock reluctantly agreed. "Yeah, maybe you're right, George. As long as you're in shape on Saturdays, I guess I can't complain."

[Gipp] made his own hours on the practice field, and he wouldn't work out more than three times a week. The other players were usually taped, suited up, and gone before Gipp wandered into the locker room. They had been catching punts and running wind sprints for half an hour when he finally joined the practice. [Gipp] would kick a few and say, "Let's go. I'm ready."

During the play, Gipp disguised whatever excitement he may have felt with a quiet calm. He used razzle-dazzle to good advantage, and speed was his strongest point. He had the habit of talking to his blockers as he advanced downfield: "*Take him to the outside . . . let this one go . . . go after the safety man.*" Then he would slither off tackle, change pace to outrace the secondary, and, using the cross-over dodge, fake other defenders with a hip, an eye, and a burst of power that left them grabbing at a shadow.

One of the compensations for the grind, the bruises, and the postgame exhaustion was the hero-worship of thousands of cheering sports fans. But more important, football gave him a chance to make money—by betting on himself.

Notre Dame went through its schedule undefeated in 1919, and much of the credit was given to Gipp. And all the while [he] was paying less and less attention to his classroom studies, barely skimming through as a prelaw major.

"The faculty is getting on my neck," Rockne told him one day.

"What are they kicking about?"

"They say you never crack a book."

"That's for the grinds," [Gipp] sneered.

Eventually there came a showdown with one of his law professors. "Tell me, Mister Gipp, how were you able to answer the examination questions when your notebook contains nothing but blank pages?"

"A friend loaned me his notes," [Gipp] said. "College isn't hard when you know the shortcuts."

"That's an arrogant remark, Mister Gipp. You have a flair for evasive tactics—"

"Have I been evasive with you?"

"No, you've been forthright. And in being forthright you have revealed your weakness. God blessed you with a remarkable intellect, but you are letting it lie fallow."

[Gipp] always weathered his scrapes with the faculty with an air of toughness and self-assurance. He was popular and he was witty, but he was distant and aloof, except with his few old-time buddies.

Gipp began spending more and more time in downtown South Bend and made Hullie and Mike's poolroom on Michigan Avenue his headquarters. After beating the best pool sharks in northern Indiana and surrounding territories, he branched out. He supported himself for a while at three-cushion billiards, then he turned to the poker tables. Eventually he and a man named Peaches Donnelly rented a suite of rooms and conducted their own card games.

From the time Gipp first arrived in South Bend, he was a big man with the ladies. Hazel had married soon after he left Laurium, but his soft-spoken charm registered strongly with the Indiana girls. "George was always a gentleman," said one lovely blonde, whom he numbered among his intimate friends, "and he always treated me like a lady." This particular gal was always good for a touch when Gipp suffered a streak of bad luck gambling, but he never failed to pay her back.

Another girl he favored was the manicurist in a downtown hotel. Also there was a pretty little French girl, who was sometimes seen with him in side street cafés. And then there was Irene.

Irene was the girl [Gipp] loved. Other girls were good for laughs, but she was the girl he wanted to marry. Irene adored [him]—despite her family's disapproval of him—and reached him in a way no one else ever had. She was sensitive, cultured, tender, comforting, and encouraging. [Gipp] loved her, but he couldn't marry her. She was already married, though separated from her husband. They finally broke off their romance, and [he] resumed his carousing.

Finally his hell-raising came to the attention of the priests at Notre Dame when he was caught in an off-limits South Bend hangout. He was immediately expelled from the university. [Gipp] packed up and went to Indianapolis to get a job with that city's American Association professional baseball club. By now, however, he was famous as a football star, and Indianapolis knew nothing of his baseball ability. They advised him to peddle himself to the independent team at Lafayette, Indiana. When [he] failed to sell his baseball services in Lafayette, he reasoned that he had but one alternative open to him.

For months Gipp and several other Notre Dame players had been receiving offers to play football for the University of Michigan. There was a big drive on by the Michigan alumni to recruit all state residents playing for other colleges. Two men who were prime targets in the campaign were Bernie Kirk, the Notre Dame left end, and George Gipp.

Kirk accepted the profitable deal, and [Gipp] went with him. Gipp actually went to the Michigan campus and remained for two weeks before deciding just as suddenly that he couldn't play for Fielding H. Yost, a longtime antagonist of Rockne and Notre Dame.

Another offer that had come to him was from the University of Detroit. Leonard "Pete" Bahan, a Notre Dame halfback, had already accepted the bid to switch to that college, and [Gipp] decided he would join him. Part of the arrangement with Detroit called for a summer job in Flint, Michigan, playing baseball with the Buick-Chevrolet team.

West Point was also after Gipp. General Douglas MacArthur, superintendent of the Military Academy, had instituted a new system for recruiting sports stars into the ranks of the Corps of Cadets. On July 27, 1920, a telegram arrived in Laurium from West Point:

You have been recommended for appointment to United States Military Academy . . . please wire me collect whether or not you will consider acceptance.

> Capt. Philip Hayes
> Charge of A.A.A.

[Gipp] never received that telegram. His family had no idea where to forward it.

Gipp was floundering badly at this stage of his young but full life. He was running away from the only security he had known since growing into manhood—his football fame at Notre Dame.

That summer in Flint, George became interested in the Catholic religion for the first time. He borrowed prayer books and pamphlets from Pete Bahan. Notre Dame, and what it stood for, became more important to him. And when Rockne traced him and offered him an assistant coaching job for the following year so he could complete his law courses, Gipp reversed his plans and took a train for South Bend.

In the meantime, Rockne, confident that he could get [Gipp] to return, had sold the priests on giving Gipp an examination to make up the previous year's class work. But the panel of professors was instructed to throw the book at [Gipp, whom] they felt was a bad influence on the other students and a detriment to the reputation of Notre Dame.

Rockne chewed a cigar butt to shreds waiting in his office while [Gipp] was undergoing the ordeal calculated to flunk him out of college.

"How'd it go, George?" Rock asked when it was over.

"I passed," Gipp said.

And he had—with flying colors. Gipp's brilliant mind had saved him. It was the general impression that he was finally ready to knuckle down.

However, it wasn't long before Gipp began to crack under the restrictions of school life. Because he preferred to be alone, he registered at South Bend's Oliver Hotel. And within a few days he fell back into his old pattern of behavior.

Prohibition had been in effect in Indiana long before the Volstead Act was passed, but it didn't bother the South Bend citizens. Speakeasies were open for business all over town, and Gipp was a good customer.

The long hours spent in dissipation began to show on him. His complexion, always pale, faded to a pasty white. He was losing weight, and in the shower his teammates noticed his ribs sticking out. But on the field, he continued to be the attraction that drew the crowds.

In the opening game that year—only four days after [Gipp] had been readmitted to school—he was stricken with a sudden attack of nausea. The attacks recurred every game.

In one game Joe Brandy called for Johnny Mohardt to run. "Check!" Gipp shouted. Brandy repeated the signal, but Gipp checked again. When this happened a third time, Rockne knew that something was wrong. He waved Brandy over to the sideline and, upon learning the trouble, yanked Gipp. Star or not, George was told in no uncertain terms that he was to obey the quarterback. George took the reprimand and used different tactics to gain his point from then on. When signal-caller Chet Grant, a crafty war veteran who was even older than Gipp, entered the Nebraska game with instructions to play it safe, George told him that some of this South Bend friends had bet that Notre Dame would win by a greater margin than 16–7—the score at that moment, late in the fourth quarter.

Gipp said, "Let me throw one. We need another touchdown."

Grant made Gipp promise that he would pass long to avoid an interception, and he let [him] toss twice to end Eddie Anderson. Both were incomplete.

Grant said, "That's all, George."

Gipp shrugged his shoulders. "All right," he said.

The players who didn't know that Gipp was gambling heavily on the games mistakenly thought he had developed a star complex. But the few guys who knew the truth worked all the harder for him, trying to get him even. They knew he was betting $500 and $600 each week, big money in those days.

The week before the Army game, [Gipp] placed a bet that he alone would score more points than the entire cadet team.

On October 20, 1920, when the teams were going through warm-ups and signal drills at West Point, Gipp gave the fifteen thousand fans a fabulous demonstration of drop-kicking skill. Russell "Red" Reeder, the Army point-after-touchdown specialist, was matched against him in an impromptu competition, but he dropped out when Gipp backed up to the 40-yard line. Then [Gipp] walked to the midfield stripe and called for four footballs. From there he kicked two balls aimed at one goal, then, turning around, sent two more toward the opposite goal. All four balls sailed between the goal posts.

The game that day was the dramatic crest of Gipp's football career. He gained 124 yards from scrimmage, threw passes for 96 yards, and ran back kick-offs and punts for 112 yards—a grand total of 332 yards accounted for by one out-of-condition young man.

But he blew his big bet. For in that game, if in none other, he was a team player. On defense he was far from great, as he sat on his rump and watched cadet Walter French scamper for two long runs, one of them a touchdown. But on offense, he recovered a fumble, punted beautifully to keep Army in its own territory much of the time, and time after time acted as a decoy while other players cashed in on the opportunities he had set up. Mohardt scored twice, as plays were run to the left to outsmart an Army team that was prepared to stop Gipp on the other flank. [Chet] Wynne plunged over for a third touchdown while the cadets chased [Gipp] as he ran wide. Gipp threw a pass to end [Roger] Kiley for one more touchdown in the Notre Dame 27–17 victory. [Gipp] himself marked up three points on conversions. He did win some money, however. The entire team did, with the exception of Wynne, who hadn't had any money to bet. When [Gipp] heard about this, he hit his teammates for a percentage of their winnings, put $10 in the pot himself, and handed it over to [Wynne] with the comment, "Here, you earned it."

After that wonderful Army game, [Gipp] suffered a decline. He injured his left arm in the first half against Indiana, when Notre Dame was trailing 10–0. Rockne taped him from shoulder to wrist, however, and he went back on the field. Although he had a relatively poor day as a ground gainer, he contributed to a close Notre Dame victory by setting up one touchdown and pulling off an amazing fake while Brandy sneaked across for the score that won the game.

[Gipp] didn't get off the return train at South Bend that night. Instead he continued on to Chicago to help out Grover Malone, a Notre Dame graduate who was coaching a high school team. But [they] never got around to teaching the finer points of football to schoolboys. They went on a rip-roaring three-day drunk, stopping at every joint they could smell out. When Malone poured Gipp aboard a South Shore railway car headed for South Bend, he noticed that [Gipp] was coughing.

"Better take care of that, kid," Malone said.

"I've already swallowed the best medicine for what ails me," Gipp told him.

On Saturday Rockne didn't put Gipp in the starting lineup. It wasn't until the second quarter that [Gipp] trotted to the center of the stage in front of the first homecoming crowd at Notre Dame. Two plays later he sprinted 70 yards and over the goal line. But the play was called back, and Notre Dame was penalized 15 yards. Again Gipp carried—and this time went 85 yards to plant the ball in the Purdue end zone. [He] was untouched but completely bushed.

Rockne, with his keen sense of showmanship, coupled with worry about [Gipp's] health, substituted for his first-string left halfback. "Always leave 'em wanting more," he told Gipp.

By the middle of the week [Gipp] had developed a sore throat that complicated his sick condition. He didn't mention this to Rockne, but it was evident to the coach that the infection had sapped Gipp's strength and energy.

"You're sitting out the Northwestern game," Rock told [Gipp].

"That's jake with me," [he] said.

"Feel well enough to come with us?" Rock asked.

"Oh, sure."

"Good. At least we'll give the people who pay the money a look at you, huh?"

But the fans in Evanston, Illinois, wanted more than a look. "We want Gipp!" they yelled without letup.

"What do you say, George?" Rock asked between halves.

"Why not?" Gipp answered.

In that game he threw two incomplete passes and was smeared catching a punt. That was all Rockne could bear to watch. Rock couldn't know then that Gipp's playing days had ended forever.

The night of the annual South Bend community banquet for the Notre Dame team, Gipp excused himself early, whispering to Rockne on his way out that he was sorry to disappoint the loyal rooters. The day of the game against the Michigan Aggies in East Lansing, his name was on the critical list at St. Joseph's Hospital.

Father Cornelius Haggerty was assigned by Notre Dame to look after [Gipp's] spiritual needs. "Anything I can do to help?" the priest asked.

"No thanks. I'll pull through this," [he] said. "Everything's jake."

Telegrams arrived by the batch to wish him a speedy recovery. Among them was a wire from Bill Veeck Sr., of the Chicago Cubs, confirming details of a contract agreement already worked out that was to pay [Gipp] the high salary of $3,500 for his rookie year in major league baseball, plus a bonus of $1,500 if he should make the regular batting order.

But George's mind was occupied with other affairs, and he had long conversations about himself with a nun who nursed him. It was that good sister who called in Father Haggerty the day Dr. McMeel gave up all hope of saving Gipp's life.

In the privacy of the hospital room, [Gipp] examined his life and his cynical outlook, and by the time the priest arrived he had come to a conclusion. "I want to be a Catholic," he said.

"Have you been baptized?" Father Haggerty asked.

"As a Methodist, in my mother's church," [Gipp] said.

"Then I'll have to give you conditional baptism in the Catholic faith," the priest said.

"No, better not. Not now, anyway. My mother would be furious."

For a number of days [Gipp] stalled the priest. Intermittently he had lapsed into delirium, but once his mind was clear he said, "Father, be sure and don't let me go out without being fixed up."

Rockne telegraphed Laurium when [Gipp] began to sink fast. [His] father couldn't get time off from his job, but his mother made the fearful trip. Matt Jr. met her at the train, and George's sister Dolly came, too.

At 4:00 on the afternoon of December 14, George was given conditional baptism, conditional absolution, and the sacrament of extreme unction, the last rites of the Catholic church. Then he went into a coma and died three hours later.

It is uncertain whether or not Gipp really made the famous deathbed speech so often attributed to him: "Sometime, Rock, when the team is up against it, when things are wrong and the breaks are beating the boys, ask them to win one for the Gipper. I don't know where I'll be then, Rock, but I'll know about it and I'll be happy."

But that is the version Rockne is supposed to have related to his players before the 1928 Army–Notre Dame game to inspire his underdog team to victory.

Shortly after Gipp died, Rockne told a few intimate friends a different story:

"It must be tough to go, George," Rockne said.

"What's tough about it?" Gipp rasped through a lopsided grin.

Possibly, Notre Dame had had some influence on George Gipp after all.

Bob Curran, *SPORT* Magazine

"OUTLINED AGAINST A BLUE-GRAY OCTOBER SKY ..."

Thanks to the Four Horsemen, Notre Dame played in and won its first bowl game in 1924, then won its first consensus national title that same season. They took the Irish football name national. A columnist for the Buffalo Evening News, *Bob Curran provided this look at the fabled quartet for* SPORT *magazine in 1962, 38 years after their last magic moments in Irish uniforms.*

The 1924 Notre Dame team was the most colorful football team ever assembled. It contributed more to football than any other team.

Making such a statement won't win a man a fat lip as fast as the Irishman's boast that "I can lick any man in the house," but it will get some action if spoken in such spots as Ann Arbor and Columbus, Palo Alto and New Haven, Massillon and Canton, and Green Bay. In each of these towns people remember great local football teams—powerful college teams, destructive high school teams, machine-tough pro teams. Still, was there ever a team like the Fighting Irish of 1924—the team of Knute Rockne, the Seven Mules, and the Four Horsemen in their prime?

The Four Horsemen of Notre Dame. Has any name in American football been known to so many for so long? Can anyone name the Four Furies? The Dream Backfield? Seven Blocks of Granite? Why, a fellow could win enough beers to float Notre Dame by betting no one in the crowd can name one member of that famous Fordham line. How about the Iron Men of Brown, or the Vow Boys? Or a Team Named Desire? Good—yes. Immortal—no. All knew only contemporary fame.

But the Four Horsemen name endures, and so do the names of the men who formed this famous backfield—Layden, Stuhldreher, Crowley, and Miller. Ironically, the Four Horsemen of Notre Dame, as recorded by Grantland Rice, are better known than the Four Horse-men from the Book of Apocalypse, as recorded by St. John. Such was the magic that flowed from coach Knute Rockne's 1924 Notre Dame team.

Any discussion of the 1924 Notre Dame team must start with a hard look at Rockne. And a hard look means that one must accept Rockne not so much as an inventor as an improver. Certain legends insist that Rockne invented the forward pass and the backfield shift. Not so. Rockne *developed* and *improved* both, to the point where both reached a zenith with the Four Horsemen.

Many writers have tried to describe Rockne's elusive skill. Edwin Pope of the *Miami Herald* called Rockne's greatest talent "inspira-tional salesmanship." Harry Mehre, a Rockne player, went into that deeper when he said, "He was the greatest salesman sports ever had. Not just football but all sports. Rock sold football to the man on the trolley, the elevated subway, the baker, the butcher, the pipe fitter who never went to college. He made it an American mania. He took it out of the thousand-dollar class and made it a million-dollar business. Rock sold football to the Notre Dame players. He changed the 'die gamely' routine to 'fight to live.' Rockne captured the imagination of the nation."

But in 1924 this was yet to come. The supersalesman had previ-ously won some big games and produced some big stars, but he had never taken a national title. His 1924 team would prove to be the best sales tool he would ever have, but no one, including Rockne, could have dreamt that in 1921. That's when the future Four Horsemen were freshmen, and Rockne, writing about them in 1930, said, "The football epic of the Four Horsemen is the story of an accident. The four did not play as a backfield in their freshman year—remember, I had seen them in practice and survived the experience. . . . Stuhldreher of the lot had the most promise. He sounded like a leader on the field. He was a good and fearless blocker, and as he gained in football knowledge he showed signs of smartness in emergencies. Layden had speed—he could run a 100-yard dash in under 10 seconds at a track meet. But speed and some kicking ability seemed to be all his football wares. Jimmy Crowley was only less humorous in play than in appearance. He looked dull and always resembled a lad about to get in or out of bed. He showed very little as a freshman—certainly none of the nimble wit that made him as celebrated for repartee as for broken-field running. Don Miller traveled that first year on the reputation and recommen-dation of his brother, Red Miller, the great Notre Dame halfback who made such havoc when his team beat Michigan in 1909. Don, an also-ran in his freshman year, surprised me when he came out for spring practice and with his fleetness and daring, sized up as a halfback to cheer the heart of any coach."

One of Rockne's main jobs each fall was deflating the heads of big-time high school stars, and it is easy to see how he could remember the boys as he wanted to think of them then. The people who sent the Horsemen to Notre Dame thought otherwise.

Crowley had been a high school sensation in Green Bay, Wisconsin, having been steered to South Bend by Green Bay's Curly Lambeau. Layden was a star at Davenport (Iowa) High School, which had been coached by Rockne's top scout, Walter Halas. Stuhldreher came from Massillon, Ohio, which was then the American football capital. Actually, both Stuhldreher and Crowley were prominent from the first day they put on a Notre Dame uniform.

If Miller and his brother Jerry, who started at Notre Dame with him, hadn't been football stars, it would have been one of the most surprising upsets in Notre Dame history. Three of the older Miller boys from Defiance, Ohio—Red, Ray, and Walter—had been Notre Dame stars. Jerry was in the freshman backfield with Stuhldreher and Crowley, but from the middle of the following year on, Don took care of the Miller tradition.

There is evidence Rockne suspected which brother would be the star and gave him some of the famed Rockne psychological treatment. When the freshmen first reported, all the suits had been handed out by the time Don Miller reached the equipment counter. When Don finally got a uniform, it looked like something out of the original Rutgers-Princeton game.

Rockne's policy prevented sophomores from being regulars because they hadn't had the time to absorb his system. He broke that policy for Don Miller, who became a regular as a sophomore and All-America as a junior. Crowley, Layden, and Stuhldreher made All-America as seniors.

As freshmen the Horsemen did not play as a unit. As sophomores they didn't start the season as a unit, but even early in the year they contributed to the team's success.

Moving to the varsity as sophomores in 1922 helped all the Horsemen. As part of the traveling squad they had a chance to get in on the lighter side and spirit of Notre Dame football. And because they did travel a lot—Notre Dame backs get "shifty from getting in and out of upper berths," Stuhldreher once told an opponent—Rockne encouraged them to enjoy the trips.

One such player on the 1922 squad was Mickey Kane, the Notre Dame baseball captain. Although a halfback who seldom saw action, Kane made all the road trips. The minute Kane caught the comical Crowley's act, a new combination was made. Prohibition was the issue that year, and wherever the Notre Dame train stopped, Crowley made a temperance speech from the rear platform while his campaign manager Kane kept the crowd agitated.

In the Georgia Tech game, the sophomore Horsemen had a big part in the 13–3 win, even though Stuhldreher made what Rockne called "the biggest mistake of his career." With the ball on the Tech 5-yard line, Harry passed over the goal line—incomplete. In those days that meant a touchback, with Tech getting the ball on the 20. It was a lesson that was remembered. "Never again did Stuhldreher make a tactical error," Rockne said.

Then came the Butler game and an injury that meant the birth of the Horsemen's unit. [Paul] Castner, the fullback, was knocked out for the season. Rockne made an unusual and keen decision. He called in Layden and told him he was the new fullback.

"I can't play fullback," Layden answered. "I'm not heavy enough."

"That's where we're going to fool them, Elmer," Rock said. "Everyone is accustomed to the big lumbering line plunger who packs a lot of power. But in you we're bringing a new type to the game. You are very fast, and we're going to make you into a slicing and quick-opening fullback."

This was the salesman talking. It's clear that he didn't expect the results he got, because after the Carnegie Tech game, Layden's first at fullback, Rockne said, "Layden amazed me by his terrific speed at fullback. He adopted a straight-line drive that made him one of the most unusual fullbacks in football. He pierced the line through sheer speed, cutting it like a knife."

While the 162-pound Layden was amazing Rockne, the Horsemen, playing as a unit for the first time, were amazing everyone watching the Carnegie game. Their timing was perfect as they won, 19–0.

It was a good year, with only a 0–0 tie with Army and a 14–6 loss to Nebraska spoiling things.

As they prepared for the 1923 season, Rockne knew he had something special in the Four Horsemen. He went to work on making the unit even better. Stuhldreher and Crowley were just a bit slower than Layden and Miller. Rock gave them lighter shoes, stockings, and thigh pads. It worked for Crowley but not Stuhldreher. So Harry dropped thigh pads entirely. It worked, and eventually the backfield became so fast, Rock had to move their lining-up positions farther back from the line.

The Horsemen lined up in the traditional T formation. When the shift signal was given, they'd go into the Notre Dame shift. On a shift to the right, Crowley would be left half or tailback, while Miller was right half or wingback. On a shift to the left, Miller would be the tailback (they didn't use that term), while Crowley would be the wingback.

Stuhldreher would line up between guard and tackle on whichever side they'd shifted to, while Layden would be behind the tackle on that side.

Stuhldreher did most of the passing, and his chief targets were the other backs. This was a case of Rockne improving on an old weapon—until [he] came along, passes were thrown exclusively to ends.

The 1923 season opened with a 74–0 win over Kalamazoo. Lombard College was the second win. Then Army in New York. This game was best remembered for the Crowley antics that were helping spread Notre Dame color around the country. At one tight point in the game, Notre Dame had third down and 10 yards to go in its own territory. As Army waited for the big play, Crowley called time. He paced off the yardage to the first-down marker, turned, and yelled to his huddle, "It's only 10 yards. A truck horse could run that far." He made the 10 yards, and Notre Dame made the final score 13–0.

The Horsemen and Mules bowled over Princeton, 25–2, Georgia Tech, 35–7, and Purdue, 34–7, on the next three Saturdays. Then came Nebraska, which had only a fair record but a big weight advantage over the Irish. The weight difference told in the second half as Notre Dame ran out of stamina. Nebraska won, 14–7, again ruining the Irish unbeaten record.

In this game Rockne made the wisecrack that coaches have been throwing at unlucky football players ever since. In the last period Rock told Max Houser, one of the team's prime comedians, to relax. "I'm saving you for the junior prom, Max." The crack joined the growing Irish legend.

Promises of revenge—spoken and unspoken—were made after the Nebraska loss. Rockne was to make sure there would be no more late-in-the-game letdowns.

His line was set. The soon-to-be-named Mules had never played as a unit, but they were seasoned and well led by captain Adam Walsh. But the Horsemen would be a problem. They had honed their talents to the keenest points. Miller was the most dangerous broken-field runner, a good blocker, and defensive back. Besides being a fine runner and punter, Layden was a top pass defender. The nervy, 164-pound Crowley was making a name as the best blocker for his weight that Notre Dame had ever seen and as the back to look to on the big third-down play.

But there was still the weight problem in the face of the murderous schedule. Nobody in the entire starting lineup weighed [more than] 190 pounds. The Seven Mules were Ed Hunsinger (185) and Chuck Collins (162) at the ends, Rip Miller (190) and Joe Bach (190) at the tackles, Noble Kizer (160) and Johnny Weibel (160) at the guards, and Walsh (190) at center.

Rockne's answer was the "shock troops"—a team of substitutes who would play the first four or five minutes of the first and third quarters.

Rock was about 20 years ahead of his time; his shock troops idea led to the two-platoon system.

The opener was Lombard, and the shock troops and third team did most of the work as the Irish won, 40–0. Against Wabash the regulars saw more action as Notre Dame won, 34–0.

Then it was off for New York City, where one of the best Army teams ever was awaiting them. At this time Army could use players who had already graduated from college, and it was quite ordinary to find ex–All-Americas in the Army lineup. This year was no exception. And arriving in New York, the Irish had problems. Walsh had a broken hand and Stuhldreher was having trouble with his throwing arm. But a new liniment developed, according to Rockne, by a New York doctor must have helped him.

The best report on how that game went is part of journalistic and football history. It was written by the king of American sportswriters, and it began like this:

By Grantland Rice
Polo Grounds, New York, October 18, 1924. Outlined against a blue-gray October sky the Four Horsemen rode again.

In dramatic lore they are known as famine, pestilence, destruction, and death. These are only aliases. Their real names are: Stuhldreher, Miller, Crowley, and Layden. They formed the crest of the South Bend cyclone before which another fighting Army team was swept over the precipice at the Polo Grounds this afternoon as fifty-five thousand spectators peered down upon the bewildering panorama spread out upon the green plain below.

A cyclone can't be snared. It may be surrounded, but somewhere it breaks through to keep on going. When the cyclone starts from South Bend where the candle lights still gleam through the Indiana sycamores, those in the way must take to the storm cellars at top speed. The cyclone struck again as Notre Dame beat the Army 13–7 with a set of backfield stars that ripped and rushed through a strong Army defense with more speed and power than the warring Cadets could meet.

The line did its usual great job. Walsh broke his good hand and (two-for-two) kept opening big holes for the Horsemen.

After the game Rockne confessed to Stuhldreher that the "magic liniment" was the liniment they always used.

The Four Horsemen name and Rice's description instantly caught the imagination of a country always alert for new heroes to worship. Nobody let the idea die. Bill Fox, sports editor of the *Indianapolis News*, asked George Strickler, then Notre Dame student sports publicity director (another Rockne first was creating the job of college athletic information director), to set up a picture of the Four Horsemen atop horses. The picture was spread all over the country.

It was only natural that someone should think up a name for the seven linemen. Well, the Seven Mules were glamorized, too, but the man who gave them the name is unknown.

The week after the Army game the Irish came east again, beating Princeton in a game more lopsided than the 12–0 score indicated. Crowley gained 250 yards and two touchdowns, and he had another called back. Princeton never played the Irish again.

Next came Georgia Tech, and the subs saw a lot of action as Notre Dame won, 34–3. Then Wisconsin was buried 38–3. Miller scored two touchdowns and a Stuhldreher-to-Crowley pass broke the Badgers' last stand before halftime. Next came Nebraska, again.

Some of the Nebraska players had been at the Wisconsin game, and Rock had made sure they had a chance to mingle with the Notre Dame players afterward. They fell into the trap and kidded the Irish about what they would do to them the next week. But Rock didn't need any tricks to get his team "up" for the game. They had good memories. And they were aware that they now had a chance at the mythical national championship.

On the day of the game, played at Notre Dame, Rock started right off with some typical philosophy. He sent six full teams out to warm up. When the awed Nebraska coach, Fred Dawson, said, "Which one is your first team, Rock?" Knute shot back, "All of them."

The shock troops started the game poorly. They fumbled on the 3-yard line, and Nebraska scored a touchdown, then missed the extra point. At the start of the second quarter, Stuhldreher started throwing and the Irish quickly scored a touchdown. Crowley kicked the point after. From then on there was never any doubt about who'd win. Crowley ran 80 yards with a Stuhldreher pass for a score. Two more of [Stuhldreher's] passes connected with Miller's hands for touchdowns. Layden, slicing the line as predicted, plunged for another touchdown. Final: Notre Dame 34, Nebraska 6.

As so often happens in college ball when a team gets "up" for a game—a letdown came the next week against Northwestern. The Irish were also bogged down physically: the field at Grant Park was all mud. And to make the day complete, Moon Baker, Northwestern's star half-back, had one of his best days. He kicked, passed, and ran, and when the Mules kept him from scoring, he booted two field goals.

Unable to move in the mud, Stuhldreher gambled on throwing the soggy ball. He kept passing until the Irish scored. Crowley kicked. It was 7–6.

In the second half Northwestern also started throwing the ball, with less success. Layden ran one back 45 yards. Notre Dame won, 13–6.

The next day Knute Rockne was baptized a Catholic. The news surprised many people, who assumed this man who had graduated from Notre Dame and done so much for the college was, like most of his players and colleagues, a Catholic. (No, there is no record that shows that any of the Notre Dame wits considered this the season's most important conversion.)

There was only one game left—with Carnegie Tech at Forbes Field in Pittsburgh. The date was November 29, and the field was muddy. No day for passing. But someone forgot to tell the Irish. After the Scotchmen had scored, Crowley hit Miller with a 25-yard touchdown pass. Both teams scored again in the second quarter, and it was 13–13 at the half.

In the second half Stuhldreher completed 19 passes in what many old hands call the greatest throwing exhibition ever put on by a Notre Dame back. That's a mouthful of praise when you recollect that almost every Irish team has had a top thrower. Notre Dame won, 40–19.

Now the Irish could claim the national championship—their first ever—and most of the country was ready to give it to them. Most, but not all. Out at Palo Alto the Indians of Stanford had a great team going to the Rose Bowl. An invitation to meet them was sent to the Irish. For the first time in its history, Notre Dame decided to play a postseason game.

The famed Pop Warner was coaching Stanford that year, and his big star, the biggest individual star in the country, was Ernie Nevers. He had been out most of the season with ankle trouble, but his teammates had still managed to tie for the conference championship and win the Rose Bowl bid. With Nevers back, they were sure that they could handle the Irish.

They couldn't. Nevers, playing with two tightly taped ankles, made all his boosters—most of the crowd of eighty thousand—look good as he ripped apart the Notre Dame line. But every time he closed on the goal line, the Mules held him back. Twice, Layden set the Indians back with 80-yard punts.

Rockne had told the boys they couldn't match the Stanford power and shouldn't try. So they played the kicking game until Stanford spent most of its steam. When the Indians tried doing it the easy way—by air—Layden took over. Twice he intercepted passes and ran for touchdowns of 60 and 55 yards. It was typical of the Horsemen that one of them would always come through with the big day. This was Layden's. Besides scoring three times, he averaged 50 yards from scrimmage on punts. The final score was Notre Dame 27, Stanford 10, and there was no longer any question about who was national champion.

But Rockne and the 1924 team did more than win a national championship. They pioneered modern football. Southern California, impressed by the drawing power of the Irish in the Rose Bowl game, invited them back to the coast and started what is now a great traditional rivalry.

When it became clear that Notre Dame drew crowds all over the country, the larger backyard neighbors who'd been ducking the Irish came calling on them. The attitude now was, "We have everything to gain—especially money—and little to lose." There were no cries of "break up Notre Dame." Instead, the other schools fought to reach the Notre Dame level. This led to better competition and improved the quality of football.

Until this time football had been a game followed by college men. It had also been a fairly dull game, featuring "four-yards-and-a-cloud-of-dust" type offenses. The appearance of Rockne's national champions with their great speed and daring passing game brought a new excitement to football.

There's no better way of showing how firmly the Irish gripped the country's imagination than by looking at that once-in-a-lifetime wonder—the "subway alumni of Notre Dame." The name comes from the thousands of New Yorkers who adopted the Irish as their team. Paul Gallico described this extraordinary occurrence:

> The annual visit of the football team of the great University of Notre Dame to New York for the football game with West Point brings about a phenomenon, one of the strangest and most curious in all this country and therefore in the world, since it could happen no place but in this mad grand land. This is the annual gathering of that amazing clan of self-appointed Notre Dame alumni which will whoop and rage and rant and roar through our town from sunup until long after sundown tomorrow in honor of a school to which they never went. The West Point supporters at the Yankee Stadium tomorrow will be numerous and vociferous, but of the seventy-eight thousand spectators, three-quarters will be bawling at the top of their lungs for Notre Dame du Lac. . . . And this business is a phenomenon purely for this one game. There are no self-appointed Colgate or St. Mary's or Tulane or Purdue alumni when those teams come to visit our town.

But membership in the subway alumni wasn't restricted to New York; all over this country Notre Dame was picking up followers who had never seen a subway. Eventually many of these people turned their loyalties to a nearby school.

From then on football did nothing but grow. From the seeds of interest planted by college ball grew more high school football below, more pro football above. And as the game grew, the Mules and the Horsemen kept contributing to it. Layden coached at Notre Dame and was a commissioner of the National Football League; Crowley made Fordham a pre–World War II national power; Stuhldreher was head man at Wisconsin; Kizer at Purdue; Walsh at Santa Clara, Bowdoin, and with the Cleveland (now the Los Angeles) Rams; Rip Miller has been assistant athletic director at Navy for years. Chuck Collins and Don Miller both coached before [Collins] went into business and [Miller] became a federal attorney and then a judge.

All who went into football spread the gospel according to Rockne—*fight to live.* And if football ever replaces baseball as our national pastime—indeed, if it hasn't already—it will finish the story that began in 1924, when a bald-headed supersalesman began making his biggest sale.

Paul Zimmerman, *Sports Illustrated*

THE GOLDEN BOYS

The post–World War II years produced some interesting personnel combinations in the college football world. And perhaps no team boasted more outstanding players than did Notre Dame. Some 50 years after their salad days, Paul Zimmerman authored this look at the late forties Irish teams for Sports Illustrated.

I met John O'Connor in the bar of San Francisco's Olympic Club in the summer of 1967, and when he shook my hand, he almost crushed it. Big guy, size-18 neck, 46-inch chest, still an active AAU [Amateur Athletic Union] wrestler at 40. On the bridge of his nose was a telltale helmet scar.

"Where'd you play football?" I asked.

"Notre Dame, 1946 and 1947," he said.

"Greatest collection of college football talent in history," I said. "How much did you play?"

"Not at all—for the varsity," he said. "B team. Scrimmaged against the big boys every day." He paused. "The greatness of those teams will never be realized. You ever hear of Art Statuto?"

Sure I had. He was the classic example of the postwar talent amassed by Irish coach Frank Leahy. Statuto never earned a monogram at Notre Dame, but he played three years of pro football afterward.

"We had lots of Art Statutos," O'Connor said. "There were guys who'd been starters and then gone off to war and couldn't win a monogram when they came back. There were people who weren't even issued jerseys, but in high school their uniforms had been retired. There were guys no one ever heard of and were never heard of again. You ever hear of Chick Iannuccillo?"

No, never had. So he told me the story of Iannuccillo. He was one of those prospects a coach glimpses once in a lifetime, if he's lucky. He was a fullback, 5'11", 225 pounds—a monster in those days. He had speed and a real killer instinct. "He used to go, '*Vavoom! Vavoom!*' when he was running," O'Connor said, "and he'd bring up a forearm and flatten guys. Leahy used to have this drill for backs to see how tough they were: all the linemen would line up single file, and the back

70

would run at them, one at a time. The back got tackled by every one. The veterans lined up near the end so they could get the runner when he was tired. When Iannuccillo ran it, all of a sudden guys would start dropping out of line. One guy needed a new chin strap, another one would have something wrong with his shoelaces."

Late in the summer of 1946, two men from the Department of Veterans Affairs paid a call to Iannuccillo. "He'd been in an infantry unit in Italy, and he'd caught a flesh wound in the leg," O'Connor said. "He was getting a full disability pension from the government. They let him know that playing football at Notre Dame would seriously compromise his disability benefits." The result: Chick Iannuccillo, ex-fullback.

"Notre Dame had given him a job raking leaves in front of the athletic office," O'Connor said. "Every day on the way to his office Leahy would have to pass by Chick, raking leaves in his army fatigues, getting fatter and fatter. Leahy would just shake his head, and Chick would keep raking and whistling."

The players fought for positions, playing time, a monogram, a smile from the coach. "There have been great college teams through the years," says Leon Hart, an All-America end at Notre Dame and the last lineman to win the Heisman Trophy, in 1949. "But for a sheer collection of talent, nothing could match our teams of 1946 and 1947."

Which team was better? Hard to say. Both were national champs, both were unbeaten—although the 1946 team was held to a scoreless tie by the Doc Blanchard–Glenn Davis Army outfit. The statistics of the 1946 Irish were eye-popping: No. 1 nationally in total offense and defense, first in rushing offense, fifth in rushing defense, third in pass defense, only 24 points (four touchdowns, no extra points) allowed during the nine-game season. The stats of the 1947 squad were slightly less impressive, as the Irish finished second to the Michigan single-wing machine in total offense but ranked in the top 10 in seven categories, including, for the first time, passing offense. Notre Dame gave up eight touchdowns and 52 points for the season.

Most veterans of both teams give a slight nod to the 1947 squad. "We were better, we'd played two years together," says Bill "Moose" Fischer, the All-America guard and winner of the 1948 Outland Trophy as the nation's best lineman.

"Our sequence of plays was slightly smoother in 1947," fullback John Panelli says, "probably because we'd gone away from Leahy's two-unit system of 1946. But that system kept you fresher."

Leahy's biggest problem was sorting out all the talent that came back from the war, so in 1946 he played his first unit, on both offense and defense, in the first and third quarters, the second group in the second and fourth. "It was a tremendous advantage to play on that second unit," says George Ratterman, who split quarterback duty with All-American Johnny Lujack in 1946. "The first unit would beat the hell out of them. We'd come in against guys who were worn out. Look it up. We scored twice as much as the firsts did."

Sure enough, the Irish had 6 touchdowns in the first quarter, 14 in the second, 6 in the third, and 14 in the fourth. If Ratterman had come back in 1947, Leahy might have used the two-unit system again, but Ratterman was a gifted four-sport athlete and had had his fill of playing behind Lujack. At age 20 he signed a contract with the Buffalo Bills of the All-America Football Conference, a deal worth $11,000, including a $2,200 bonus if he finished among the league's top five in passing. He collected the bonus in a breeze, making second-team all-league. In South Bend he would have been second-team Notre Dame.

"Just look at the guys from those teams who never did much at Notre Dame but played pro football," Ratterman says. "I'd say the pros are pretty good judges of talent, wouldn't you? There's no question in my mind that Notre Dame would have beaten any team in professional football except the Cleveland Browns."

Forty-three Notre Dame players from either 1946 or 1947 (or both) played in the NFL or the rival AAFC. Yes, there were two leagues, but the total number of teams was only 18, or 60 percent of today's total. And squads were about 30 percent smaller.

The Notre Dame count is not easy to establish. What do you do about Bob Hanlon, for instance? In 1943 he was a monogram-winning fullback and linebacker on Leahy's first national championship team. He came back from the war in 1946 and was moved to guard. "A tough nut," says Jack Connor, a reserve guard who is the brother of Notre Dame All-America tackle George Connor and the author of *Leahy's Lads*, the definitive book on that era in Irish football. "In early fall practice Bob broke George's hand in a scrimmage and suffered a deep thigh bruise. He could barely walk. Leahy told him to run it off. He said the hell with it and transferred to Loras College in Dubuque, Iowa." Where he made Little All-America. Then the squad of the 1948 NFL Western Division champion Chicago Cardinals. Then the Pittsburgh Steelers. If you count Hanlon, it's 44 Domers from 1946 and 1947 in the pros, but we won't count him.

How about Luke Higgins? He'd been a monogram-winning tackle on Leahy's 1942 team, ranked No. 6 nationally. "A shot put champion, one of the strongest guys in the school," Connor says. The NFL's Cleveland Rams drafted Higgins in 1945 while he was serving in the infantry in Italy, but when he returned home with a Purple Heart, he chose to stay at Notre Dame. Before going off to war, however, he had made an unforgivable mistake: one day he had told Leahy he was tired. In 1946 Higgins found himself on the B team. On the afternoon that Notre Dame beat Purdue, he had a career day in the B team's rout of

Great Lakes Naval Training Station, which had walloped the Irish varsity the year before. In 1947 Higgins was wearing the uniform of the Baltimore Colts. Yes, we'll count him.

In his book Connor wrote about being selected to run in the infamous murderers' row drill, at which Iannuccillo had excelled, on his first day of practice in 1946. Connor faced 14 guards. "Eleven had lettered on previous teams," he wrote, "and six of them had each earned two monograms." Three—John Mastrangelo, Bill Fischer, and Marty Wendell—would go on to make All-America.

"I was one of the few players who hadn't been in the service," says Hart, who arrived at Notre Dame as a 17-year-old freshman in 1946 and would become one of the school's greatest stars ever. "I was one of 21 ends, 11 of them monogram winners."

One of Leahy's favorite routines was to have his assistants take on the linemen in drills. "It was brutal but very effective," says Fischer. "Player blocks coach. Techniques can be corrected immediately. Much better than hitting a sled. It kept the assistants in shape, too. Now Moose Krause, the tackle coach, was the kind of guy who didn't want to embarrass you in front of Leahy, so when I went against him, he kind of retreated, inch by inch, and Leahy said, 'Oh, Bill Fischer, that's the way we want you to block.' He always used that formal form of address, first and last names. When Leahy left, Moose said, 'One more trip,' and he slammed me with an elbow to the throat and walked me back to the green fence and said, 'Don't you ever forget who's boss here.'"

Fischer was one of six members of the 1946 and 1947 squads who would make All-NFL. Nine players on the 1947 Irish team were All-America at some point in their careers; two of them, Lujack and Hart, won the Heisman; two more, Fischer and George Connor, earned the Outland Trophy. Seven would be chosen for the College Football Hall of Fame. Who were the superstars? Hart, of course, a 6'4", 252-pound end who made All-Pro with the Detroit Lions on offense and defense, just as Connor did for the Chicago Bears. And Lujack, the Bears' All-Pro quarterback who was equally gifted at defensive back. In his first NFL game, in 1948, Lujack picked off three passes, tying a Bears single-game record that still stands. He finished his rookie season with eight interceptions, equaling a club record that would stand until 1963.

"When I was at Notre Dame, everyone went both ways," Lujack says. "I loved defense. My first game as a Bear, we were playing the Packers, and the guy I was covering kept yelling at me, 'You All-American SOB, you're gonna have a long day today!' I was shocked. No one had ever said anything to me on the field before. So I picked off three, and next time we played them, they didn't throw to him."

George Connor, a member of the NFL Hall of Fame, was the finest interior lineman in Notre Dame history, a demon blocker with enough speed to make All-Pro as a linebacker. His brother tells the story about the week before the Purdue game in 1947, when George was worrying about an ankle he'd sprained in a scrimmage and Leahy had him test it against half a line—guard, tackle, center—all by himself as the backfield ran plays at him.

"They ran off-tackle plays, traps, up-the-middle plays, quick openers," Jack Connor wrote in his book. "They did this for a half hour, and the offensive team never gained more than a yard or two. At the end of the drill, George was convinced that his ankle was fine. Years later Frank Leahy told his nephew, 'Jack, in all my years of playing and coaching football, it was the greatest exhibition of defensive tackle play I have ever seen.'"

The other big stars were Wendell, a short, blocky guard and linebacker with a devastating initial pop, and Jim Martin, an end with an interior lineman's body. (In 1949, his senior year, Martin switched to tackle and made All-America at the new position. He followed that with a 14-year NFL career as a linebacker.) And, of course, there was Leahy.

Almost everyone on the team could do a passable Leahy imitation—his habit of calling each player by his full name, his formal, almost prissy way of speaking. His practices were no joke, though: mean, grueling affairs, heavy on full scrimmages, born out of Leahy's years as a 185-pound tackle under Knute Rockne at Notre Dame, from 1928 to 1930, and reflecting Leahy's boyhood in Winner, South Dakota, as the son of a freight handler who taught his four boys boxing and wrestling almost as soon as they could walk.

"What I remember is that we fought every day—fought to win a job and then to hold it," says Martin, who went to Notre Dame after serving as a marine in the Pacific, where he was decorated for swimming ashore and doing reconnaissance work before the invasion of Tinian. "I was a mature 22-year-old freshman. I remember when I was visiting Notre Dame before I enrolled. George Tobin, a guard, was showing me around and said, 'How about a movie?' I said, 'How about a bar?' You had guys like me, and then you had the older service vets, and practice was tough on them. They'd had enough of war, of guys beating the hell out of each other, but that's what practice was every day, a war."

Notre Dame corralled many of the best high school recruits, of course. But World War II scrambled the process, as many blue-chip recruits joined the service. And Leahy, a navy officer in the Pacific with the assignment of organizing and supervising athletic and recreational activities for submarine crews returning from the Far East, did some serious recruiting among servicemen.

"I was stationed at Pearl Harbor," says George Connor, who had been All-America at Holy Cross in 1943, "and one day a command car pulled up and a guy said, 'Ensign Connor, Commander Leahy would like to see you at the Royal Hawaiian.' He talked me into coming to Notre Dame. He said we'd win the national championship, and I'd make All-America. It all came true."

The 1946 season was Leahy's first one back, after two years in the service. The Irish had been nationally ranked in 1944 and 1945, but two lopsided losses to Army, and another to Great Lakes in 1945, had marred those seasons. The word got out early that a mighty collection of talent was gathering at Notre Dame in 1946. Phil Colella, the second-leading Irish ball carrier in 1945 and a navy vet who had been on two ships sunk by Japanese torpedoes, came out to preseason practice, took one look at the backs Leahy had stockpiled, and transferred to St. Bonaventure.

"Our paper strength still has to transform into playing strength; we could lose three or four games," said Leahy, whose legendary pessimism was part con, part paranoia. Notre Dame's first opponent was Illinois, which had opened its season with a 33–7 win over Pitt, a game that Leahy had scouted. "It's an awful assignment," he said, "the toughest any Notre Dame team has ever tackled in its first game. Their line is the biggest I've ever seen in college. Their backfield is two and three deep, and with Buddy Young, it has tremendous speed."

Notre Dame won 26–6. Young, who would become one of pro football's most scintillating runners, gained 40 yards. Until the last 30 seconds of the game, Illinois had been in Irish territory only once.

Pitt, coming off a 33–7 win over West Virginia, was the next to fall to Notre Dame. The Panthers threw up a 5-4-2 defense, forcing the Irish to pass. Lujack and Ratterman obliged with 211 yards in the air, and Notre Dame added 257 on the ground in the 33–0 rout. Pitt made three first downs, 42 total yards. Leahy was furious at what he saw in the films, or at least that's what he told the *South Bend Tribune*'s beat writer, Jim Costin. It was a technique Vince Lombardi would later use at Green Bay: rip 'em when they're riding high, leave 'em alone when they're down. Leahy blasted player after player by name until Costin finally asked him, "Didn't anyone play well?"

"Bob McBride," Leahy said. McBride was a third-string guard.

The following Saturday the Irish beat Purdue 49–6. In practice the next week Leahy was annoyed with his punt-return unit. He hollered to Bill Earley, the B team coach, "Send me a punt returner!" and along came Coy McGee. He ran one back all the way against the varsity. Then he did it again. "My goodness," Leahy said. "Who is that lad?"

Are you old enough to remember Fox's Movietone newsreels of 1946 and 1947? Seems like every week there was another thrilling punt return by McGee and the familiar narration: "There he goes again, folks. Another one for little Coy McGee." He was a jackrabbit runner from Longview, Texas, whose weight fluctuated between 146 and 158 pounds. "His legs would go every which way," says Terry Brennan, the Irish starting halfback in 1946. "In the open field he was almost impossible to tackle."

McGee made the 36-man traveling squad for the next game, at Iowa—a team of which Leahy was "scared to death." Someone showed him a pool card. The Irish were favored by 19. "It's a typographical error," Leahy said.

McGee turned in a few nifty runs in the 41–6 slaughter, but he didn't even make the traveling squad for the next game, a 28–0 victory over Navy. It was simply too crowded. "Guys killed themselves to make the traveling squad," Fischer says. "One day years later I asked Bill Earley, 'Why did we always have that two-hour scrimmage on Thursday in full pads, with only the first team exempt?' He said, 'The coaching staff would spend hours and hours trying to select the traveling squad. The idea of the Thursday scrimmage was to see who got hurt. That would help us select the squad.'"

Unbeaten Army was coming up, at Yankee Stadium. On the Saturday morning of the game a motorist drove around the stadium with a sign offering a $3.30 end-zone ticket for $200. He sold it. "My girlfriend in Cleveland called and said she needed two tickets, probably for her and some other guy," Martin says. "So I sold her two for 50 bucks apiece. I made her pay. I never saw her again. Can't be lucky all the time."

It was buttoned-up football, close to the vest—too close, some Notre Dame players would say years later. The Irish had been a two-unit team all season, but now Leahy went with his firsts. "Let's face it. He just chickened out," Martin says. "They had a great first unit, but we could have worn them down with our squad. Leahy could have put Ratterman in and opened things up."

Lujack had been iffy until game time with a sprained ankle. Although the Irish outgained Army by 35 yards, his passing was way off. He made the defensive play of the game, though, bringing down Blanchard in the third quarter with an ankle-high tackle in the open field. Notre Dame mounted the most serious threat of the game, getting a first down on the Army 12 in the second quarter. But Billy Gompers was stopped on fourth-and-one at the 3. "I told Lujack, 'Hell, you should have given me the ball,'" Panelli says. "That was the end zone where my parents were sitting. I'd have scored."

The amazing thing about the newspaper accounts of the scoreless tie was that no one suggested that Notre Dame should have kicked a field goal. "Uh-uh, not Leahy's style," Lujack says. "It would have been an admission of defeat." Field goals were still in their infancy at South Bend. The Irish kicked none in 1946, two in '47. In 1945 they were still drop-kicking their extra points, and Stan Krivak missed 13 of them.

"Look, the game ended 0–0, and people are still talking about it," Lujack says. "If it had ended 7–0, would they still talk about it?"

The rest of the season was anticlimactic. The only unknown each week was which Notre Dame player would break loose. Emil Sitko romped for 107 yards on 15 carries in a 27–0 victory over Northwestern. Gompers (10 carries for 103 yards) and former South Bend high school star Ernie Zalejski (7 for 101) ran wild in the 41–0 annihilation of Tulane in New Orleans. After that game still other players went wild, notably All-America right tackle Zygmont Peter (Ziggy) Czarobski.

"A few of us had celebrated at the Old Absinthe House," Fischer says, "and we finally got to the train and took over the club car. Ziggy was leading the party. Ziggy led all the parties." To this day, when the old players get together, the night is called a Ziggy. Everybody has a Ziggy story. At the Notre Dame sports publicity office they still have the questionnaire he filled out as an incoming student. *Church preference?* "Red brick." *Hobbies?* "Plant collecting, bee hunting, surf-riding [Ziggy came from the South Side of Chicago], dancing."

One time Leahy found Ziggy taking a shower before practice. "Zygmont Czarobski, what in the world are you doing?" he asked.

"Coach, it just gets too crowded afterward," Ziggy said.

When Ziggy, who tended to put on weight, got married, Terry Brennan wired the father of the bride: "You are not losing a daughter, you are gaining a ton."

As Ziggy led the revelry in the club car after the 1946 Tulane game, in walked Leahy. "Ziggy hollered, 'Hey, Coach, I want you to meet a friend of mine,'" Fischer says, "and he turned to the girl on his lap and said, 'What the hell's your name again?' Leahy turned and started walking out the door, and some of the guys booed him. Oh, boy, now this was a dilemma. He couldn't ignore it. He couldn't beat up the whole first team in practice that week, not with Southern Cal coming up and a shot at the national title. And that's when he got a gastroin-testinal attack and checked into the hospital. Thank God he put Moose Krause in charge. We had a great week of practice."

The Irish rushed for 517 yards in a 26–0 victory over the Trojans, and McGee, who'd always been a favorite of Krause's, broke two daz-zling runs and wound up with 146 yards on six carries. Southern Cal had one consolation. It scored the only touchdown against Notre Dame's first unit all season. WHAT?

The Irish were national champions. They had terrorized the college football world—well, all of it except second-ranked Army, whose unbeaten streak now stretched through three seasons. But Notre Dame would have one more shot at the Cadets, in South Bend the following year. That game would be the last in a 34-year Notre Dame–Army series, whose cancellation by West Point would become a sore point with the Irish.

Only three Notre Dame starters would graduate in the spring of 1947, and Leahy sounded a rare note of optimism when he told the *Chicago Sun-Times* in March, "We should be in very good shape next season." By September he was back in form: "Army will come out here undefeated on November 8," he said. "As for us, who knows? No telling how many games we'll have lost."

The preseason forecasters, unfazed by the pessimism, were saying that this Irish squad might be the greatest collegiate team ever assembled. "Intercollegiate football will be divided into two groups in 1947, Notre Dame and The Rest," Tom Siler wrote in *Pic* magazine. "The best games will be the intrasquad scrimmages at South Bend."

When the Eastern sportswriters visited South Bend in the preseason, the first thing Leahy complained about was a lack of size and speed in his backfield. "Instead of halfbacks, we have nine small fullbacks," he said. How about Brennan, a gifted, versatile back who would often line up as a flanker and had led the Irish in scoring and receiving in 1946?

"Heart alone," Leahy said. "He hasn't the speed or physique of a great halfback."

Then what about Sitko? Now there was a guy who could fly. "For 50 yards," Leahy replied. "After that his legs tighten up, and tacklers get him from behind."

Coy McGee?

"He ran well in one game."

And so on, right down to Leahy's announcement that Zalejski would be lost because of a knee injury. "A terrible blow," the coach said. Terrible. Only 15 backs left.

The start of the season revealed a new wrinkle in the offense. The Irish were opening things up. They were throwing the ball: 204 yards in a 40–6 win over Pitt, 184 in a 22–7 victory over Purdue, two teams that had loaded up to stop Notre Dame's fearsome array of runners. The Boilermakers' seven-man line held the Irish backs to 89 yards. That simply had to be addressed. The defense was not a problem. It never was.

What Leahy didn't see was that his team was wearing down. The two months of spring practice ("Goofy," says Brennan. "You started with snow on the ground, and you ended in June.") and the brutal fall practices, with their two-hour scrimmages, had sapped the players' strength. "After the Purdue game there was almost a mutiny," says Brennan, who would succeed Leahy in 1954 and would coach the Irish for five years. "Our captain, George Connor, went to Leahy on behalf of the team and said, 'Look you've got to start backing off on the practices.' Then Warren Brown, the sports editor of the Chicago *Herald-American*, told him the same thing. It had gotten to the point that all you wanted to do in practice was survive. It didn't prove anything. This was a veteran team. Leahy knew who his best football players were, he knew who was going to play hard for him. He didn't have to kill them off on the practice field."

"The games were Cub Scout meetings compared with the practices," says Panelli, the fullback. "Boy, I'll tell you, we lost a lot of good people in those scrimmages."

"The amazing thing was that Leahy listened to Warren Brown," Brennan says. "This guy was not a friend, so he listened. Leahy wound up cutting back on the practices, and it saved our season."

The team responded with three straight shutouts: 31–0 over Nebraska, 21–0 against Iowa, and 27–0 over Navy. The only sour note was the news that came over the wire and was announced on the public-address system during the Iowa game. At Baker Field in New York, Columbia had upset Army 21–20. Notre Dame players, who had wanted to be the ones to halt West Point's four-year streak, kicked the ground in disgust.

The Notre Dame–Army game still produced a record crowd in South Bend. There was a bitter undertone on the Irish side, a resentment of the Cadets for abandoning the series. It was a nasty, windy day. Army's kickoff was a shank out of bounds. The next one was a line drive that Brennan had to take a step backward to catch. "The kick got there ahead of the coverage," Brennan says. "I took few steps up the middle and froze the first four guys. I saw a crack, made my break, and I was gone." Ninety-seven yards, touchdown.

The rout was on. The cold and wind limited the Irish to 28 yards passing, but Leahy unleashed a merciless set of backs: Brennan, the darting Sitko, and the bruising, slashing 190-pounder, Mike Swistowicz. The new wrinkle was Martin on end-arounds, picking up 47 yards on five carries. "I've never seen such a bunch of speedy, hard-driving backs," Army coach Earl Blaik said after his team's 27–7 defeat. So much for Leahy's preseason moaning about having nine small fullbacks.

The following week Northwestern gave the Irish their closest battle of the year, scoring a late touchdown before losing 26–19. "I never felt that we were in trouble," Lujack says. "We never trailed in the game." Or in any game during 1946 and 1947.

Next Tulane come to South Bend with its great fullback, Eddie Price, and fell 59–6. The Irish scored 32 points in the first quarter.

Before Notre Dame's season finale, against Rose Bowl–bound USC in Los Angeles, the city was hit by a rainstorm. "I think the Trojans have a good chance of upsetting Notre Dame," said UCLA coach Bert LaBrucherie, whose Bruins had lost to USC 6–0. "They've beaten favored Notre Dame teams in the past."

"Everything points to a Southern Cal victory tomorrow," Leahy said. "I'll be the happiest Irishman in Los Angeles if we can win by a single point."

How about 31? Sitko, whose legs supposedly tighten up after 50 yards, broke the game open with a 76-yard touchdown run on the opening play of the second half, and the Irish went on to win 38–7. "I was watching a telecast of the game," says Mike Hudson, who was then a Palo Alto High student and would go on to be a UPI [United Press International] desk editor. "They had this very pro-USC announcer doing the game, and on Sitko's run there was only one guy left between him and the goal line—Gordon Gray, the safety. The announcer kept saying, 'Can Gordon Gray make the stop? Can Gray make the stop?' It was hilarious. Notre Dame had an absolute mob of blockers downfield, and Connor just left the pack, knocked off Gary, and returned to the group, and when Sitko crossed the goal line, everyone was still looking for people to block."

"One thing Leahy always liked," Connor says, "was linemen who could run."

The Irish beat out undefeated Michigan in the polls for the national title. There was newspaper talk about matching the teams in some kind of charity game, but it was just talk. "It would have been interesting," Brennan says. "Two distinct systems, our T formation versus their single wing, one unit against Michigan's offensive and defensive platoons. I often wondered how we'd have done under that system. Maybe we'd have been even better."

There was speculation about how Notre Dame would have done against a pro team. "It's too bad football can't have a world series, with the winner of the two major professional teams meeting for the right to tackle Notre Dame for the championship," the Newspaper Enterprise Association's lead sportswriter, Harry Grayson, wrote. "Notre Dame, in this observer's opinion, would beat the best of the pro teams."

The next summer 14 Irish players made the trip to Chicago for the College All-Star Game against the NFL champion Cardinals. The collegians were coached by Leahy. Art Statuto, the fifth-team Notre Dame center, with 10 minutes of playing time in 1947, made the squad. So did five Irish backs and four tackles. What the hell, the Notre Dame reserves were better than other people's first teams. Someone asked Czarobski what was the toughest team he had faced. "The Notre Dame second unit," he said, for once being serious. The All-Stars lost to the Cardinals 28–0.

Many of the 1947 Irish players drifted off to pro football. Lujack, the Heisman winner, signed what was then a hefty contract as the Bears' number one draft choice: four years at $17,000, $18,000, $20,000, and $20,000, plus a $5,000 bonus and an endorsement deal with Wilson Sporting Goods. "I found out later," he says, "that [Bears owner and coach] George Halas had paid only $2,000 of that bonus. The rest was an advance on my Wilson royalties. Halas had tricked me. Fifteen years ago, I was approached to contribute to the Halas Hall Foundation. I said, 'I already contributed $3,000.'"

After Hart finished his eight-year career with the Lions, he became active in the NFL Alumni Association. He has maintained a strong interest in football at all levels. "Notre Dame would have beaten any pro team," he says. "The talent at that time was all in college.

"What is football now? It's push-pull on the line and an aerial show. An athletic contest consists of three things: effort, stamina, and ability. The substitution rules have canceled the element of stamina. Effort? Well, everyone knows he's playing for big bucks, and he's only one play away from oblivion, so that erodes the element of effort. All that's left is ability, and what you see along with it are gloves and towels and low-cut shoes, everybody trying to look good.

"Blocking techniques have almost vanished," Hart continues. "I produced a film for the Notre Dame National Monogram Club, *The Golden Age of Notre Dame Football*, and it's wonderful to see the way the game was played. The precise timing of the blocking, the way the holes opened up. It isn't just running to daylight, running for some seam, behind a whole lot of pushing and shoving. It was beautiful football. The kind of football Frank Leahy taught."

Leahy died in 1973 at the age of 64. In 11 seasons at Notre Dame he produced six unbeaten teams and four national champions. His 1946 and 1947 teams were the best, though, and who can argue that they weren't the best of all time?

Ed Fitzgerald, *SPORT* Magazine

GLAMOUR? SPELL IT L-U-J-A-C-K

Johnny Lujack, quarterback at Notre Dame, ranked as the poster child for Irish football when he starred in South Bend in the late forties. He then went on to a career with the Chicago Bears. SPORT *magazine editor-in-chief Ed Fitzgerald put together this look at Lujack in 1951, when Lujack was in his fourth and last season with the Bears.*

The luncheon-bound businessmen and their expensively dressed ladies turned and stared as the glass doors swung open and admitted the crowd of football players into the quiet, thickly carpeted hotel lobby. Trooping across the elegant room toting suitcases, cardboard boxes, and GI duffel bags crammed with personal belongings, the king-sized athletes looked as out of place as a band of cowboys at a society girl's coming-out party.

These were the Chicago Bears, disheveled from an overnight train ride, and you recognized a number of them: black-haired George Connor, the Big Moose from Notre Dame; Ed Sprinkle, the roughest end in the National Football League; [Clyde] "Bulldog" Turner, the indestructible center; and there, in the middle of the parade, seemingly smaller than the rest but walking with the special assurance that is the hallmark of the born captain, Johnny Lujack, the quarterback. If the group in which he was walking had been twice as large, you still wouldn't have had any trouble spotting [him].

It's hard to say exactly what it is that makes Lujack so conspicuous. Although he stands an even 6', he looks like a boy among men when he's with the rest of the Bears gang. Quiet and restrained in his speech and his manner, he does nothing to attract attention to himself. Nor is it just that he's handsome enough to pass for a movie star; it goes deeper than that. Lujack radiates confidence and class. He's a natural-born Big Man on Campus, and it doesn't make any difference that his current campus is the professional gridiron. When you get to know Johnny, you can't help wondering if it would make any difference what career he chose to follow—he'd be sure to reach the top.

"He can make a million dollars if he wants to," Frank Leahy says of his former pupil. "He has everything it takes for success—brains, character, and personality."

There is no question about Lujack's unusually heavy endowment of personal gifts. You may have seen hundreds of pictures of [him] in newspapers and magazines through the years since his Notre Dame days, but you are unprepared for the impact of your first face-to-face meeting. If you didn't know him and somebody introduced him to you as Lana Turner's new leading man, you wouldn't bat an eye. Freed of the heavy trappings he must wear on the field, he has remarkably even features bearing in their strong cast a trace of his Polish ancestry, friendly brown eyes, and perfectly straight brown hair that always looks a little mussed and probably makes every bobby-soxer who sees it want to muss it up a little more.

The Lujack voice, easy and pleasant in conversation, staccato and unmistakably commanding on the playing field, is good enough to have helped him star in his own radio program a couple of years ago. *The Adventures of Johnny Lujack*, it was called, in the best soap opera tradition, and it served as a summer replacement for the Jack Armstrong network show. "Unfortunately," [Lujack] says, "it was just a sustaining show. We weren't able to get a sponsor, and I guess in that business that's the only thing that matters."

Since then, [he] has had more than one opportunity to plunge into other radio or television ventures, but he wants to make sure he picks the right one next time. "I don't want one of those routine question-and-answer programs," he says. "They're no good. I want something that's going to stand up."

Now playing his fourth season of professional football, [Lujack] himself is standing up very well. Like most hardworking National League backs, he has been hurt a number of times, but he has always come back for more—and soon. "Let's see," he said, counting off on his fingers when I asked him about his injuries. "There was that torn back muscle the first year, the bad cartilage in my knee, the two shoulder separations . . ." He was trying to remember something. "Oh, yeah, that chipped ankle bone that they had to put in a cast."

"You've been hurt a lot."

"More than I ever imagined I would be," he said seriously. "This is a hard game." Then he grinned. "But the pay is good," he said. "I'd never be able to make this kind of money doing something else. Not for a long time, anyway."

"Is the pay still as good as it was before the other league folded?"

"I don't know," [he] said. "I've only signed one contract with Halas. That was when I first got out of Notre Dame. It was for four years and this is the last year."

Informed guesses place [Lujack's] paycheck under the four-year agreement at approximately $20,000 per annum, a nice sum for a 26-year-old youth to take home to his young wife and child. Even at that, the Bears would be the first to admit they're getting a bargain. In an era which has seen football virtually taken over by the specialist, [Lujack] is a throwback to a bygone day. He runs, he passes, he kicks—thereby qualifying as a full-fledged triple threat. In addition, he doesn't bow out cavalierly when the other team gets the ball. As a linebacker, pass-defense expert, and unflinching safety man, Lujack gives the Bears 100 cents of football for every dollar they pay him.

When [Lujack] first signed on with the Monsters of the Midway, the great Sid Luckman, who retired last year, was still pitching touchdown passes and calling signals with most of his old-time finesse. Halas had intended to break the new recruit in gently, but he took one look at his ferocious play on defense and decided to let the collegiate glamour boy play his way into the league.

Lujack's first league start was on September 26, 1948, against the Green Bay Packers. In the first half alone, he intercepted three Green Bay passes and his knifing, diving tackles made boss Halas relax his customarily grim face into an expression of smug satisfaction. Just by way of giving a hint of what might be expected from him in the years ahead, [Lujack] scored a touchdown on a quarterback sneak and kicked a pair of extra points as the Bears rolled to a 45–7 victory. By any standard, it was a passable debut.

The cold type of the National Football League record book shows plainly how valuable Lujack has become to the proud Chicago team. He held the record for the most yards gained on passes in a single game, 468, until Norm Van Brocklin netted 554 yards in an LA Rams–New York Yanks game this year. In all the league's long history, he ranks third in most passes completed in one game—29 against the defense-minded New York Giants on October 23, 1949. He holds fifth place in the all-time ranking for most points scored in a single season, having accounted for 109 in 1950. He stands third in the matter of most yards gained on passes in one season, pushing up right behind Sammy Baugh and Luckman, by pitching for 2,658 yards in 1949. As the current season began, his major-league lifetime percentage of pass completions was a glowing 50.4.

[Lujack] isn't satisfied, though. It is typical of him that he brushes aside his accomplishments and tells you sadly that he has never played on a championship Bears team. Obviously, this rankles him because the Bears are used to being on top and Lujack doesn't want to be the quarterback to lead them into a different tradition.

Ever since his kid days in Pennsylvania, [he] has been accustomed to winning. He grew up in the small town of Connellsville, population seventeen thousand. The fourth child in a family of six and the youngest of four boys, he was exposed to all kinds of ballgames from babyhood. All his brothers—Val, Allie, and Stan—were good high school athletes, and Allie made a reputation for himself as an end at Georgetown University. Johnny, who was named after his father, a boilermaker on the Pittsburgh and Lake Erie Railroad, had to follow a tough act when he became the fourth Lujack to play for the local high school. But the older boys saw to it that he knew a little about the game before he reported to the coach. When he was just 10 [or] 11, they'd go off to play semipro games on Sunday afternoon, and they never blew the whistle on him when he hid in the trunk of their crowded car. "They knew I was there," [Lujack] grins. "But they pretended they didn't see me because Mom would've bawled them out for taking me so far from home."

The boys wouldn't let [him] play tackle, but when they fooled around in touch football games around home, they encouraged him to get on their team, and it wasn't long before they began to respect his throwing arm. How seriously they regarded his ability even then is illustrated by an incident the family remembers from one of those touch games. Johnny had thrown a bad pass to Allie, and his brother bawled him out when he returned from his long run. "What's the matter?" he growled. "You're getting careless."

One of the other fellows in the game thought Allie was being a little hard on the kid. "Take it easy on him," he said.

"I can't," Allie said. "I have to talk to him that way. It'll make him a better passer."

[Lujack] was only 13 years old and weighed a skimpy 120 pounds when he got his first taste of organized football competition, at Cameron Junior High. He made the varsity at Connellsville High as soon as he was eligible, as a sophomore in 1939. They haven't forgotten him yet, and it's doubtful if they ever will. He was a ball of fire on the gridiron for three years and had enough energy left over to win his letters in basketball and track, too. He didn't play baseball in high school, but he was so sensational as an infielder in a local amateur league that he got a feeler from the Pittsburgh Pirates, which he turned down without a second thought.

There was never any question about [Lujack] going to college. "I was lucky," he will tell you. "Dad was doing better after all those years working for the railroad, and I didn't have to feel it was necessary for me to get a job right away." The scholarship offers poured in, eagerly extended by scouts, coaches, and alumni attracted by [Lujack's] dazzling football record. As the word got around of feats, like his intercepting two passes against Mount Pleasant High and running each one back 70 yards for a touchdown, the pile of coaxing letters mounted. In the end, 35 colleges had beckoned to him, and he had been offered an appointment to West Point if he wanted it.

He didn't want it. He didn't want any of the other propositions either. All he wanted was to go to Notre Dame. It was the dream of his life. To the young Catholic boy who had avidly followed the exploits of the Fighting Irish since he had been old enough to read the newspapers and listen to the radio, the dignity and prestige of Notre Dame were greater than all the offers of the other colleges put together. He went where his heart told him to go, and he has never regretted it.

[Lujack] had to suffer through one acutely embarrassing moment before he settled the business of which college he would attend. At his high school graduation exercises, [Lujack], the president of the senior class as well as the school's premier athlete, was eulogized by Congressman J. Buell Snyder. This well-meaning gentleman climaxed his verbal outpouring with the breathless announcement that he was appointing [Lujack] to the United States Military Academy at West Point. Applause and cheers echoed through the auditorium. In a place like Connellsville, it's a big thing for one of the town boys to get such a break. It singles him out, stamps him indelibly as one destined to make his mark in the world. So the people clapped hard and exchanged happy grins, craning their necks, as people do, to see how Mom and Pop Lujack were taking the news. It was in the middle of that storm of applause that [Lujack] walked to the center of the small stage and said, with nervous humility but complete conviction, "I'm very thankful for the honor you have bestowed upon me. But my heart is at Notre Dame. I want to complete my education there and, if I can, play football on that team."

How [he] fulfilled that ambition is one of the brightest chapters in the American football story. He became one of the superstars, a giant to take his place alongside the fabulous ones of the past: Red Grange, Jim Thorpe, Chris Cagle, Ernie Nevers, Sammy Baugh, Sid Luckman, Tommy Harmon. They'll remember the kid from Connellsville as long as they talk about football under the shimmering Golden Dome. They'll remember the way he stepped into Angelo Bertelli's shoes when the "Springfield Rifle" was called for active duty with the marines five days before the 1943 game with Army. All the sophomore replacement did before the seventy-eight thousand wild-eyed partisans in Yankee Stadium was throw two touchdown passes, score another himself on a quarterback sneak, and call plays with all the skill and daring of Frank Leahy himself. Furthermore, he kept right on doing things like that until he graduated in June 1948.

Just as impressive was his reaction to the staggering amount of nationwide publicity which suddenly engulfed him. Bill Heinz, the reporter, tells an illuminating story. According to Heinz, Lujack was being interviewed before practice during his senior year. As he sat on the locker-room bench getting into his uniform, answering the questions of the newspaperman, he kept reaching out when other members of the squad walked by. Playfully, he would tug at their clothing or kid them in the obscure, private way that men gruffly use in exchanges with close friends. Afterward, the interviewer discussed the incident with another reporter. "The way I interpret it," he said, "Johnny was trying to show the other guys that this interview wasn't of his doing, that he hadn't asked for it, and didn't especially want it. I think that as he reached out and grabbed at the others, he was simply trying to maintain his identity with the rest of the squad."

Like all great athletes, Lujack has an enormous amount of self-confidence. But the training that had been begun by his older brothers and refined by the master psychologist, Leahy, had taught him the absolute necessity of team play. A pleasant, gregarious youth by nature, fond of his friends and eager to give them credit, [Lujack] has never even come close to succumbing to the "Great I Am" disease.

"Luje," as the other Bears call him, unconsciously reveals a good deal about his character when he admits that few of his exciting experiences as a college football player pleased him as much as the game-saving tackle he made of Doc Blanchard in the most ferocious Army–Notre Dame game of them all, the classic encounter of 1946. That was the game [that] saw Leahy and most of his prewar stars troop back from the service, hoping to avenge the 59–0 and 48–0 losses handed the Irish in 1944 and 1945 by the colossal Black Knights of Glenn Davis and Felix "Doc" Blanchard—"Mr. Outside" and "Mr. Inside." The newspapers termed it "The Battle of the Century," and, fittingly enough, it ended in a scoreless tie. But it might not have if Johnny Lujack hadn't nailed Blanchard when it seemed that the spectacular Army fullback would surely race over for a touchdown in the third quarter.

Arnold Tucker, the Army quarterback, had intercepted one of Lujack's passes on the West Pointers' 10-yard line. Speeding back up the field, hugging the sideline, Tucker reeled off 32 yards before he was downed. The Irish went into a five-man line. Junior Davis was the flanker as Army set up a counter off to the right, with Blanchard running in the opposite direction. Doc poured it on, burst through the surprised Notre Dame line, and was away. Picking up speed, he shot past the Irish secondary and had nobody between him and the goal line but Lujack. The gifted "Mr. Inside" roared toward the sideline in search of running room, measuring the distance to the point where he would probably meet the Notre Dame safety man. At the last possible second, Blanchard deliberately slowed up, then shoved down the throttle again, and broke for the end zone. But Lujack wouldn't be shaken off. Taking dead aim, he smashed Blanchard head-on in a violent collision. Doc went down on the Notre Dame 36, and the roaring thousands in the jam-packed stadium knew what had made Lujack an All-America.

Leahy loves to tell of the little exchange he had with [Lujack] in the dressing room afterward. Lujack had had a bad day throwing the ball. Of 17 passes attempted, he had completed only 5. Army had intercepted four of them, Tucker grabbing three by himself.

"Tell me, John," the coach inquired amiably, "how did you happen to throw so many passes to Tucker?"

"Well, it was this way, Coach," Johnny grinned. "He was the only man I could find open."

The old college try that characterized Lujack's do-or-die crash into Doc Blanchard and the good humor that lay behind his response to Leahy's teasing have remained with him in professional football. While it's plain that nothing ever could supplant Notre Dame in his affections, it is equally clear that the Bears have a place of their own in his heart. He has a fierce pride in the team's background; he wants badly to be remembered as a valuable Bear player.

It was almost inevitable that [Lujack] would sign with the Bears when he made up his mind to take a fling at pro football. Leahy and Halas have been friends for a long time. Luckman made more than one trip to South Bend to help polish [Lujack's] ball-handling on the T. Although the great civil war was going on in the sport at the time, and he had been drafted by both the Bears and the Chicago Rockets of the All-American Conference AAC, [he] never seriously considered playing for the newer team. He regarded the Bears as the biggest of the big-leaguers.

He wasn't, however, so hungry to sign a contract for Halas that he neglected to bargain. He insisted upon a measure of security in the shape of a long-term agreement—and he got it, a bonus of $5,000 for signing. There were other opportunities to cash in, too. Testimonials by the score, personal appearances, all the emoluments of fame. The Wilson Sporting Goods Company signed Lujack for its advisory board and made a deal with him to manufacture a football bearing his name. That football, still a steady seller in its fourth year, has earned him a lot of money.

Things looked so bright that [Lujack] and his steady girl, Patricia Schierbrock of Davenport, Iowa, decided to get married. They had met at Notre Dame, where Pat had gone to visit Genevieve Pollard, Leahy's secretary. They had fallen in love almost immediately. Father Tom Brennan of the Notre Dame faculty married them at the Sacred Heart Cathedral in Davenport on June 26, 1948. They have their own home now in Park Ridge, Illinois, a suburb of Chicago. A two-year-old baby girl, Mary Jane Lujack, occupies the nursery.

To show how completely [Lujack] has fitted into the pattern of the lawn-mowing, house-painting, odd-job-burdened suburbanite, he even plays softball in a Park Ridge league—and gets a big kick out of it, too. But Halas might not be so happy about it if he saw his prize quarterback racing around the ballfield in the red-hot neighborhood competition. [Halas] is inclined to take a dim view of any activity that might conceivably injure or even tire his key man.

"The first two years I played for the Bears, I bought tickets for all the Notre Dame games on weekends we were playing in Chicago, and then Halas wouldn't let me go," [Lujack] recalls. "He said it was too tiring a trip for me to take, from Chicago to South Bend and back, the day before a ballgame. So I don't even bother to get tickets any more. I just watch the games on television when I get a chance. I saw a lot of them last year."

Johnny's principal recreation is golf. "I love the game," he says with feeling. "I'm a terrible golfer, though. Anything in the low nineties is good for me. I've had a really terrific day if I do that good. But I love to play, and I never go on the course without feeling that this is the time I'll shoot in the seventies."

Being one of the most widely known sports personalities in the country, Lujack is constantly being asked to go to this or that banquet, to this luncheon, to that testimonial. He tries to rule out all such appearances during the playing season because, as he says, "Halas is forever calling meetings without notice, especially for the quarterbacks and the coaches, and I hate to promise somebody I'll show up at an affair and then have to disappoint them. They never believe it when you tell them you have to go to a meeting, anyway, and it just makes for bad feelings." After the season, he goes to more of them, but he still does his best to keep the total down. "I feel," he said seriously, "that after being away so much during the late summer and fall, I owe all the time I can spare to my family."

When you consider that he scored 109 points for the Bears last year, you can scarcely say that Johnny had a bad year in 1950. But the truth is that this season he will be gunning for a return to the passing form he showed in 1949. That was, all things considered, his best year as a pro. There were at least two games that season in which he was so ruthlessly efficient, so imaginative and so fearless, that you couldn't help but rank him with the very best quarterbacks who ever played the game.

Against the New York Giants at the Polo Grounds on October 23, 1949, Lujack completed 29 forward passes. The Giants won the game, 35–28, but if there had been a few more minutes in the game, [Lujack] might well have come away with no worse than a draw. With the embattled Giants ahead by seven points, he completed six straight passes in the last minute and had the ball on the Giants' 16-yard line when the clock ran out.

Then there was the astonishing exhibition of passing skill he staged at the expense of the Bears' crosstown enemies, the Cardinals, on December 11, 1949, at Wrigley Field. In a steady drizzle, on a field sloppy with mud, the water freezing cold on his reddened hands as he gripped the ball to pass, Lujack threw six touchdown passes and set a National League record (since broken by [Norm] Van Brocklin) by gaining 468 yards through the air. He beat Sammy Baugh's old yardage record by 22, completing 24 passes in 40 attempts. Spearheading the Bears to a one-sided 52–21 triumph, Lujack hit his receivers for four touchdowns in the first half alone, giving his team a 31–7 lead by halftime.

In the first five minutes of the game, he spiraled a 52-yard pass into George McAfee's arms for the first score and threw 17 yards to end Ken Kavanaugh for the second. Later in the half, he hit Kavanaugh again for 37 yards and a third touchdown, then hurled an 18-yard touchdown pass to J. R. "Jackrabbit" Boone. Then, after George Gulyanics carried the ball for the Bears' only touchdown overland, [Lujack] threw twice to fullback John Hoffman, the first for 6 yards into the end zone, the second a 65-yard beauty.

Lujack was so hot that day he might easily have racked up three more touchdowns. In the first quarter, he pitched 12 yards to Julie Rykovich only to have the former Illinois back fumble on the 1-yard line. Kavanaugh was brought down from behind on the 2 after taking a 10-yard pass in the third quarter, and Kavanaugh again was nailed on the 12 after [Lujack] hit him with a 58-yard effort in the last period. Just to make sure he gave Halas an honest day's work, Lujack kicked the extra point after each of the seven Bears touchdowns.

At least once before, [Lujack] had enjoyed an especially successful outing under the worst kind of conditions. That was in one of his latest appearances as an amateur, on January 2, 1948, in the college East-West Shrine game at Kezar Stadium in San Francisco. They played that one in a driving rainstorm before sixty thousand soaked fans, and when the highly touted Notre Dame boy began to prove the accuracy of his press notices, all the ticket holders were glad they had come. After the West had scored a touchdown in the first four minutes of play, Lujack gathered the Eastern forces for a counterattack. [He] passed for two touchdowns, choked off a West drive by intercepting a pass on his own goal line and running the ball back 32 yards, scored a touchdown on an 8-yard sneak around end, and set up another score with a couple of passes that ate up 37 yards of enemy territory. Lujack did all this working with a wet, slippery ball.

Halas checked out his rookie quarterback himself a few months later. "Papa Bear" hadn't seen Lujack play since 1946 and was eager to see how he had progressed. When he heard that the soon-to-graduate youngster intended to play in the annual Old Timers Game at Notre Dame in the month of May, he decided to take a look.

The Old Timers tussle is an important event on the Notre Dame calendar. Scheduled as the climax to spring practice, it matches the varsity squad against a combination of graduating seniors and alumni in a heavily attended game designed to give the varsity a first-class workout. A few weeks before the game, [Lujack's] pals noticed that he was back in serious training.

"What are you working so hard for?" they kidded him. "Leahy isn't going to bawl you out if you're lousy."

The square Lujack jaw jutted out. He nodded in the direction of Notre Dame Stadium. "Listen," he said, "I never lost a game out there, and I don't intend to start now."

He didn't, either. Aided and abetted by the ferocious line play of the blackbearded "Moose" Connor and the happy-go-lucky "Ziggy" Czarobski, [Lujack] completed 15 of 29, made one savage tackle after another, and directed his pickup team's attack with a calm shrewdness that made the old man, Leahy, smile proudly in defeat. The Old Timers walked off with a 20–14 victory, earned in full view of twenty thousand Notre Dame students and friends. It was the only game that 1948 Irish 11 was destined to lose all year, which gives you an idea of the extent of Lujack's accomplishment.

It was a wonderful farewell scene. In fact, it was so perfect that if you saw it in a movie, you'd razz it. [Lujack] played 52 out of the 60 minutes and was T-quarterback, safety man, and coach all rolled into one. He made Frank Tripucka and Bob Williams, the successors he was leaving behind, look like raw recruits. He invented plays on the spur of the moment as brilliantly as Leahy himself could have done it.

When we talked about that game, his last at Notre Dame, I asked [Lujack] what he thought the difference was between college and pro football. It's a question he must have been asked dozens of times, if not hundreds. But he didn't brush it off. He thought about it carefully. "I guess," he said finally, "that pro football represents another graduating step. They take the best players out of the high schools for college ball, and they take the best players out of the colleges for pro ball. The men you play against are more experienced, they know more about the game, and certainly they're rougher and tougher." He touched his twice dislocated shoulder and grinned. "I can vouch for that," he said.

Recognizing the existence of a point of view which contends that the pros don't try as hard as the college boys, Lujack insisted, "We want to win just as badly as we ever did. Furthermore, because it's our living and because we know our families depend upon how well we play, we have a willingness to learn and a desire to make sacrifices in order to win that is beyond anything we knew in college."

He made one concession to the opposite viewpoint. "Sometimes," he said, "we may be caught on an off day, obviously playing off our game. Well, it could be that we're just plain tired. That's bound to happen now and then. Don't forget, we start playing exhibition games in late August. We don't have that nice nine- or ten-game schedule they have in college. Heck, take last year, for instance. When I played in that All-Pro game at Los Angeles right after New Year's, it was the 24th football game of the season for me."

If the grueling schedule gets Lujack down once in a while, it's hard to spot it from the stands. He's very much a professional, but there's a zestful dash to his play that is something more than ambition; it could come only from a natural love for the game. It's a heritage from his kid days, when he was playing with Val and Allie and Stan on the vacant lots of Connellsville. He shows it in every game he plays.

Like all champions, [Lujack] has a knack of coming up with an outstanding performance when the occasion particularly demands it. Tangling with the highly regarded Doak Walker last November at a time when he and Walker were deadlocked for the league's scoring lead, he personally accounted for 17 points while the Doaker scored only 3 as the Bears roared to a 35–21 win. Lujack sent his team out in front in the opening quarter by diving over from the 2-yard line on a quarterback sneak and then throwing a 39-yard touchdown pass to John Hoffman, one of his favorite receivers. It was easy the rest of the way, and Lujack wound up by scoring two touchdowns and kicking five extra points.

A few weeks earlier, in a battle with the Bears' ancient rivals from Green Bay, Lujack scored 22 points. [Lujack], who did more running last year than at any time during his college or professional career, went over for three touchdowns, including a 25-yard dash on a fake pass play, and kicked all four extra points as the Bears won, 28–14.

Lujack's emergence as a running threat is no surprise to the two men who have coached him since he became a national figure: Leahy and Halas. Leahy knew all along he could do it and passed the word to Halas, who soon found out how true it was. But neither coach felt he could take the risk of sending the invaluable quarterback into the line as a regular thing. Then last year [Lujack] talked the boss into letting him call his own running signal a little more often in order to vary the Chicago attack, and he was so successful—against the Cardinals he carried 10 times and gained 80 yards for an eight-yard average—that he's almost certain to keep it up from now on.

It irritates Lujack to be left out of any part of a football game. He could never be satisfied with just specializing in the art of throwing the ball. He likes to pass, but he also likes to run and block and tackle.

"We use quite a few more plays than the average pro football team," [Lujack] said in discussing the problems of his job. "I'd say we carry about 300 or 350 plays all the time, and believe me, that's a lot to remember. I guess George doesn't think we remember them well enough because we sure spend a lot of time going over them at meetings. During our training camp period, the quarterbacks go over the play book with the coaches at almost every free moment. Then, when the season starts, we have a team meeting every Tuesday, Wednesday, and Friday night." [He] smiled a little wanly. "Thursday," he said, "is the team's day off, and on Thursday the quarterbacks have a special meeting."

The fact is that [Lujack] fully recognizes the need for all those meetings and has no quarrel with them nor with any of the other onerous phases of his job. If he had a different attitude, he never would have become the field leader he is. Leahy once gave this answer to a reporter who wanted to know what made Lujack such a good quarterback: "The quarterback must be keen mentally. He must be able to take orders and to give them, too. But above all, he must have character. He's the leader of the team. And in football, as in anything else, a leader must have character. He must be able to discipline himself and to make sacrifices so that he may become a better football player, and, therefore, more valuable to his team. He must be able to ask the others to make sacrifices—and to get the right response from them. He can't say to his teammates, 'Do this and that,' unless they know that he is doing all the things he asks of them. He can't be the kind of boy at whom the others might point and say, in effect, 'Look who's talking. He's demanding sacrifices of us—and we know he sneaks off at night and goes downtown for his fun.' Lujack is one of the finest boys I've ever known—and one of the greatest quarterbacks."

Something [Leahy] didn't mention, which plays an important part in Lujack's relationship with his teammates, is his exceedingly amiable disposition. [Lujack] likes everybody, and everybody likes him. Because he's such a nice guy, the boys put out a little bit harder for him when he asks them to dig way down. It has been pointed out, perhaps with a good deal of justification, that another reason why the Bears like Lujack so much is that his wicked tackling on defense not only makes him a rare T-quarterback, but also gives him a genuine kinship with the privates who slug it out in the front lines of the ballgame. One thing is certain—the feeling is there and it pays off for everybody.

One of the questions most frequently asked of Lujack is whether he calls the Bears' plays himself or whether most of them are signaled by the bench. [He] says the answer is both. "I call the plays," he says, "with the help of my teammates. I mean, maybe an end or a tackle will come back after a play and say, 'I can trap this guy,' or 'I can take that guy,' and we'll run a play off to take advantage of it. The guys help out a lot that way. You need that particularly on pass plays, because when the passer grabs that ball and goes back with it, he can't see what's going on up ahead. He can use all the information he can get."

That doesn't, of course, mean that the Bears' huddle is a [babble] of voices or anything like it. The players know that Lujack is the boss and they respect his authority completely. The suggestions they make are offered quietly and at the proper time. As far as the coach calling plays is concerned, [Lujack] says merely, "You have plays coming in from the bench off and on during the game." He thought that one over briefly and grinned in a conspiratorial fashion. "Some good," he said, "some bad."

Whenever Lujack is out of the game, he sits on the bench between assistant coaches Clark Shaughnessy, the old T master, and Paddy Driscoll, who maintains telephone communication with Luke Johnsos, Halas' chief aide, who watches the action from upstairs. Strategy is hashed over quickly, and great stress is laid on the observations of Johnsos, who is able to follow the ins and outs of the play much more effectively from his higher perch. The same group has a heart-to-heart talk between the halves, too, with Johnsos again conducting the symposium of play patterns. However, [Lujack] is allowed to have the first five minutes of the intermission for himself. "I just use that to get a good, solid rest," he says, "and to eat a couple of orange halves. Then I'm all set when the coaches yell for the quarterbacks to get together."

"What does Halas do," I asked [him], "while Johnsos is holding this meeting?"

"Same thing I do," Lujack said. "He listens."

[Lujack] is too restless to sleep late on the day of a game. He usually gets up at about 8:00 and goes to church with his wife at 9:00. They eat breakfast after they return from mass, and he leaves for the ballpark at half-past 10:00. "The only thing I can't figure out," he says, "is what I ought to eat for breakfast. I've tried everything. People are always coming up with new suggestions and poor Pat goes out of her mind trying different things, but nothing tastes good to me. Too many butterflies in my stomach."

If that's so, it's the only time on the day of a game when the big man of the Bears is guilty of nervousness. A compact, solid athlete at 189 pounds, 10 more than he weighed when he was in college, he is every inch the skipper when he runs out on the playing field. Watch him as he gets up after a tough play, shakes himself like a puppy coming out of the water, and calmly studies the new situation. Watch him duck into the huddle, give his orders, and move up with crisp confidence to take his place behind the center. Watch him swing into the rhythm of the play after the ball is snapped, handling the ball lovingly, sweeping through the maneuver with a fluid grace that almost deceives you into thinking it's easy. Watch him especially when he throws the ball, the quick movements of his feet as he dodges enemy tacklers, the brazen way he withholds his fire until the last possible second to give his receivers every chance to shake loose, the smooth action of the throw and the long, true arc of the ball's flight to the target. There's nothing nervous or uncertain about [Lujack] then.

"The grimmest assignment in football," according to Leahy of Notre Dame, "belongs to the passer who is getting ready to throw and knows he is going to be smothered as soon as the ball leaves his hand. It takes a man with steel nerves. It is the test of greatness on a football field."

It is a test [Lujack] passes every Sunday afternoon for the Bears and used to pass on Saturday afternoons for Notre Dame—passes with an unbeatable combination of talent and guts.

Jimmy Breslin, *True* Magazine

60-MINUTE LATTNER

The fourth Heisman Trophy winner to wear a Notre Dame uniform, John Lattner could do just about anything on a football field—and his coach, Frank Leahy, often asked as much of him. Jimmy Breslin provided a look at the Chicago native in the September 1953 issue of True *magazine.*

Out at South Bend, Indiana, last spring Frank Leahy was in gloomy midseason form watching his Notre Dame 11 run through [their] paces. The Irish, he said, just don't have the "lads" to play two ways. His sorrow over the death of the two-platoon system was touching but typical. The entire coaching fraternity is worried about finding 11 students who can play 60 minutes of football one day a week.

But the situation is a little different in Leahy's case. For when you watch Notre Dame this fall, you will be watching John Paul Lattner Jr., an All-American who is pretty good proof that they still pour youngsters from the old-time mold—and don't do a bad job of it, either.

Lattner is one of the reasons why warnings about the degeneration of college football this year are not being taken too seriously. The Irish halfback's all-around play last season spoke for itself. A rough-running throwback to the two-way days of the Tommy Harmons and Johnny Lujacks, Lattner was a 60-minute man and lasted it out well enough to receive the coveted Maxwell Award as the best in the business. He is the kind of player one likes to think the game was invented for.

[Lattner] did everything last fall but quote pregame odds for the Irish. Operating from the right halfback slot, the 6'1", 190-pound dynamo averaged close to five yards a carry, caught 17 passes good for 252 yards, scored five touchdowns, and busied himself with other duties such as running back kickoffs and punts, intercepting passes, handling all the punting, and, as an icing on the dessert, throwing two point-producing passes. And when the other team had the ball, Lattner became Notre Dame's official greeter for anybody who broke through the line with a football in his hand.

As spring training at South Bend came to a close, the Irish coaching staff was coming to another conclusion about Lattner's value. They look for him to be just about the roughest fourth-period back in the nation. Last year the hard-hitting Lattner was stacked against fresh platoons of opposition throughout his 60-minute tenure on the field. This time around, the other guy is going to be a lot more tired—but he better not loaf with Lattner around.

"We could see that in practice during the spring," says Charley Callahan, the Irish drum beater. "He seemed stronger than anybody else at the end of practice. That means he's going to be in better shape than the next player in those closing minutes. And that's where he is liable to crack a game wide open. The field is going to come back to him a bit—and he wasn't much behind the two-platoon boys. It looks like he'll have an even better year this time around. Oh, they'll be talking about him as one of the best we've ever had out here before this season is through."

Notre Dame, however, isn't taking any chances despite Lattner's ruggedness. [He] came up with a slight injury during the latter part of the spring workouts and was immediately ensconced on the sideline with the care a Tiffany's official gives a five-carat diamond. He didn't play in the traditional Old Timers Game held on the South Bend campus, and the minor leg injury he suffered was given enough diathermy and liniment to open a medical center. You do not take chances with a player of Lattner's stature.

"Biggie" Munn, coach of Michigan State's all-conquering Spartans, wished Lattner would ease up on him. "He's a great boy . . . and one murderous runner to put up with," Munn says. And he says it despite the three fumbles Lattner committed in last year's game. If there is one big flaw in Lattner's grid makeup, it is a costly habit of losing the ball at times. He partly made up for his fumbles by recovering plenty of loose pigskins last year, but the dropping routine still hurt.

"Don't know what caused it . . . I'd be going along and all of a sudden I wouldn't have the ball. But I'm working on it real hard and I sure hope it pays off," Lattner says. Tenacity is a Lattner forte. "He'll make a mistake, but John does not like to make the same one twice," Leahy points out. And to illustrate this, the Irish go back and tell you about the Oklahoma game—a contest which is still thought of as one of the great wins in Notre Dame history. On the first Okie touchdown, it was Lattner—along with everybody else in the stadium—who was fooled by Eddie Crowder's fake and long pass to Billy Vessels. It was an eye-popping play, and the Sooners smartly saved using it again for a tight spot later on. The spot came in the fourth quarter, and once again Vessels raced downfield into Lattner's territory while Crowder held onto the ball and pranced around like a nervous father. But when he threw the pass, Lattner was running with Vessels—and came through with a big interception. The fumbling is going to be handled the same way, the sideline experts tell you.

The Oklahoma game, which probably was played before the largest audience ever to see a football contest—fifty-eight thousand in the stadium and some 30 million watching in their living rooms—is a good example of what Lattner does in a football suit. The Irish won it, 27–21, in an amazing upset. Lattner set up the second Irish touchdown when he intercepted a pass and ran it back to the Sooner 7. He set up the next Notre Dame score by gathering in a pass and bringing it to the 27. The winning touchdown came after Lattner had barged 17 yards to the Oklahoma 7 for the key gain of the last Irish drive. On defense he made two game-saving tackles, pulling down Billy Vessels and Buddy Leake when it appeared both were in the clear.

In the 7–7 tie with Penn he was even better. He caught a pass good for 21 yards, shook himself loose for dashes of 21 and 22 yards, and then banged center three times to score. With the clock running out in the fourth period, he grabbed two passes from quarterback Ralph Guglielmi, the second one on Penn's 25, and only a desperation lunge by Penn's Ed Bell, the last man in his way, stopped the score.

After that exhibition, the sandy-haired star sat in the dressing room on the verge of tears, quietly demeaning himself. "The way I played today, I shouldn't have been allowed in the game," he said. "On that last one, I played it like a real high school kid. I had the ball and was right on the sideline. I should've stepped out of bounds and we would have had another chance to score. I blew the game, that's all."

The only thing [Lattner] regards as more important than a winning season for the Irish is a B in accounting. He is a serious student. At the end of last season, a Sunday night TV variety show brought in the All-America team, which had been picked by a national magazine. The boys were to put in a personal appearance on the show and then the following Friday were to have their pictures taken by the magazine. It meant a week of fun in New York. But after the show, seen from coast to coast by millions, Lattner could be seen at 5:00 A.M., huddled on a wooden bench in the Chicago terminal of the rail line [that] runs to South Bend. "Had to make that 9:00 class," he explained.

Meeting Lattner on the Notre Dame campus produces the reaction that all the headlines and hoopla devoted to college football heroes is a genuine waste of time and magazine space. When you talk with him, the last subject in the world he wants to bring up is his own play. Here's an example:

That's right, the Oklahoma game was the game I liked to play in the most. The team was really up for that one. No, I didn't find it tough playing both ways last year . . . you just have to pace yourself. I think the rest of the guys will find it the same, too. I looked pretty good in practice today? Thanks. But you ought to be out there when we have a really big game coming up. Everybody makes a lot of noise . . . you know, cheers in the huddle and all that, and we really whoop it up. It's good. We have a good team, and it's fun to play with them. What am I going to do tonight? Guess I'll make an early show . . . got a cowboy movie tonight . . . and then get up early tomorrow and hit the books. They don't go easy with you out here. Gotta keep those marks up. A girl tonight? Huh, I'm going out with Sam Palumbo [210-pound tackle], and if he looks anything like a girl, I don't know. Gee, thanks a lot for coming out here and seeing us. I really appreciate it. I'll see you at the Penn game next year, all right?

There are better runners in the country and better tacklers, but there doesn't appear to be anybody who can do as well in all departments as Lattner. Surprisingly, [he] is not the fastest back on the team, but his well-proportioned frame makes him a hard-hitting power runner who can pass over you if the occasion demands. And he is smart to spot one fault in his offensive style. He admits he runs too high. "Boy, I've found out you can't be a straight-up-and-down man when you try and get through a line like Oklahoma had. You've got to bunch yourself together a little and cut down the target they're shooting for."

When he was in high school Lattner was a well-publicized youngster and for good reason. He played the four backfield positions and filled in at end on defense when the manpower ran thin. That was in the fall. When football ended he was one of the better scorers on the Fenwick High School basketball team. He continued his basketball playing at Notre Dame, and in the 1951–1952 season he got into the traditional NYU game long enough to hit with a shot which beat the Violets, 74–72, with nine seconds left in an overtime period.

Last season, when Notre Dame came back to Madison Square Garden for the game, Lattner was among the missing. He had decided not to play this year, according to Johnny Jordan, Irish hoop coach. But there was more to it than that. After the grid season was over he reported for basketball practice and stayed around long enough to figure out where he fitted in—low man on the Irish 12-man squad. There were four others competing for that last spot on the team, and Johnny was in their same category. One of the four was his cousin, Tommy Sullivan. [Sullivan] was no grid hero, and basketball was his chance to gain some athletic recognition. Lattner realized that if it came to a decision on who should fill that remaining varsity berth, Jordan might naturally lean to him. That would mean Sullivan wouldn't be playing basketball. After three days of practice Lattner stepped out— and the Irish came to town with a Sullivan on the program.

The story seeped into the papers, and, looking it over, it seems on the corny side. That is, if you don't know Lattner. Actually it's a pinpoint example of how he conducts himself in anything. "He's the type of boy who will do things like that all the time," Leahy says. "He's a gentleman all the way." That does not mean, however, that you can stand in front of him on a football field and expect soft treatment. "Oh, he runs pretty hard . . . I guess you could say very hard," Johnny Lujack, now an Irish backfield coach, says.

Lattner, of German-Irish descent, comes from the Windy City's West Side, where he lives with a mother and brother who supports the family. "I never really had anybody who exactly got me hopped up on sports when I was a kid . . . we just played ball all the time in my neighborhood. If it wasn't football, it was basketball or baseball. I began to bowl a lot in high school, and I like to swim, but football was always the big thing," he says. Terry Brennan, a fine climax runner on the 1950 Irish club, was his particular athletic hero.

Lattner's brilliant football record at Fenwick brought college scouts around in clusters, but Leahy had decided to see him in a Notre Dame suit. He had a talk with the boy, pointing out the advantages which Notre Dame offers to a Catholic youth and, if it was a matter of money, why he'd be glad to get the lad a job for the summer. He had just the place, and it was right outside Chicago.

Lattner took the job—and it was the last time a college scout could get within five miles of him. The job was at a top-secret atom bomb plant, and the guards wouldn't let the owners through, much less a college scout.

Lattner's presence on the team might be enough for most coaches making the difficult shift to one-platoon play, but [Lattner] is actually only the brightest star in Notre Dame's backfield constellation. Both of last year's quarterbacks, Guglielmi and Tom Cary, are back, and Lattner will not be a marked man with veterans Joe Heap and Neil Worden around. The consensus around South Bend is that Lattner can't miss making All-America with that kind of supporting cast—plus a big, competent line.

If Lattner does make it, no one will be able to squawk about cheesy opposition. The Irish will again play their traditionally loaded schedule and, with two exceptions, it's the same as last year's. Mighty Michigan State and Texas are missing, but their replacements are Georgia Tech, rated by some as the nation's best last season, and Southern Methodist, hardly a breather.

The lanky Chicagoan's rooters aren't worried about any letdown. They point out that Lattner has been playing the same aggressive brand of all-around football since he pulled on the Kelly-green jersey with the big No. 14. Even as a sophomore he was the team's best ground gainer and was second in scoring. He also led all squad members in minutes played and gave notice of things to come by intercepting five passes and scooping up four fumbles.

When the football season is over, you won't catch Lattner relaxing. He is always in excellent physical condition. He put in five weeks at an ROTC camp this summer and then came back to work on a construction job. This type of off-season activity would appear to be a gilt-edged guarantee that he won't be back on the campus this fall in any condition but the best. Service training and construction work are not calculated to let muscles loosen even a little.

As for the future, [Lattner] would like to give pro football a whirl but Halas and the rest of the National Football League moguls may have to wait a couple of years before they can sign him to a contract. Lattner is tied up in the air force program at Notre Dame and upon graduation will be commissioned a lieutenant, remaining in the air force for two years under present regulations.

"I'll try the pros after that," he says. "You know, it isn't an easy thing to really plan on anything when you're my age. You've got to figure that service time. But if I do wind up playing, I'd use it as a stepping-stone to coaching and teaching. I like that stuff, working with kids. You get a kick out of it . . . and any part of football is fun."

Except, chorus Notre Dame opponents, when you have to play against a guy named Lattner.

Furman Bisher, *The Sporting News*

MIRACLE-WORKER MONTANA

No Notre Dame football player took part in more legendary comebacks than quarterback Joe Montana. It didn't hurt that he helped the Irish to the 1977 national title, either. Furman Bisher, a columnist for the Atlanta Journal-Constitution, *provided this look at Montana for* The Sporting News *late in the 1977 season.*

I'm not sure you're going to believe in Joe Montana any more than some people believe in Santa Claus, the Easter Bunny, and the Bermuda Triangle. I'm just not positive there is one. That he isn't the figment of some vivid Irish imagination, or some leprechaun's conjuration.

Maybe he's some ethereal messenger sent back by the Gipper, who dissolves into the Saturday night air only to reappear again the next time the Notre Dame football team finds itself in desperate need.

I mean, get that name—Joe Montana. C'mon, now, got to be a nom de football. Son of Bull Montana? Son of Flubber? Son of Topper? Why does he specialize only in saving the homestead for Notre Dame? Why doesn't he perform average, everyday quarterbacking like any other college quarterback?

Why does the roof have to be caving in, the dam crumbling, the locomotive bearing down on the maiden tied to the railroad track before Montana can go into his act?

He hasn't even been asked to win one for the Gipper yet. He's winning all these for Dan Devine, who needs them worse.

So here the Fighting Irish were in Lafayette, fighting for their lives, one minute to play in the third quarter, down to Purdue 24–14, when Joe Montana suddenly jells on the greensward.

He had been out of sight for two years, came into the game rated third string, had never been better than second string. But at the sight of his No. 3, the Notre Dame cheering section gave out a mighty roar. The dispenser of sports information at Purdue turned with puzzled expression to Roger Valdiserri, who is the same for Notre Dame, and asked, "What's that all about?"

"It means," [Valdiserri] said roguishly, "you're in trouble. Joe Montana's in the game."

As it turned out, Purdue was indeed in trouble. Notre Dame's first-string quarterback had been able to get little done. The second-string quarterback had come down wounded or Joe wouldn't have been in the game at all.

Now, there he stood, Joe Montana, who hadn't worked a miracle since the season of 1975. And badly in need of one right then was Dan Devine. Notre Dame had beaten Pitt only because Pitt had lost its quarterback, and then had lost to Ole Miss on a trip down South.

Now to lose to territorial enemy Purdue after losing to a bunch of sorghum-soppers and cotton-pluckers would have rendered Dan less than Devine in South Bend.

Joe went to work, as if in physical illustration of the old ego expression, "Have no fear, Montana is here." In no time he presented his coach with two touchdowns, a field goal, and a victory over Purdue, 31–24. Routine. Just Montana saving another day. Any questions?

Montana first came to light two years ago in Chapel Hill, North Carolina, when the Irish were about two minutes away from defeat by North Carolina. He came off the bench, a tender sophomore, threw one pass for a touchdown, followed up by another with a two-point conversion that tied it. Then with the clock almost out of seconds, he threw another 80 yards that won it, 20–14.

The next week found the Irish in even deeper trouble at the Air Force Academy, which would have been a gross upset. Fourth quarter. Down by 30–10. Joe Montana rides to the rescue again, like those insurance knights of the television.

He runs and passes for a touchdown each, then sets up another score by Jerome Heavens, and Notre Dame comes from behind and wins again.

The general impression was that Montana was off fighting famine in some foreign land or trying to save the Alaskan seal from extinction last season. But, actually, he was out with a shoulder separation.

His spring performance this year was fairly ordinary, and in preseason he failed to endear himself to his coaches. Would Rembrandt be inspired painting a fence? Would Sir Edmund Hillary thrill to the challenge of climbing Kennesaw Mountain?

So Montana was in limbo until desperation set in again. After Purdue, his accumulation as a troubleshooting quarterback in the three games were added up and the totals came out thusly: 17 of 26 passes completed for 417 yards, three for touchdowns, another scored on foot, and three games saved all in 15 minutes, 20 seconds of actual playing time.

Well, those days are gone now. Montana played himself out of the game-salvaging business. No more snatching victory from the jaws of defeat. He has played himself into the status of just another average, everyday quarterback who starts games and takes orders from the sideline, with the result that Notre Dame games are not nearly so thrilling anymore. No more of Hairbreadth Harry stuff. Joe wins 'em early and people can leave for the parking lot to beat the traffic, confident all the while they aren't missing the ballgame.

Joe Montana is giving them football in the tradition of the Fighting "Irish" who used to spell their names Melinkovich, Swistowicz, Tripucka, Budynkiewicz, and Vlk—and that's no typographical error.

Joe Montana is a tall, trim, blond-haired son of an Italian–American Indian mating. He comes from Monongahela, Pennsylvania, up the river from Pittsburgh. He has a cinematic smile, a fetching personality, and a kind of a man-to-man appeal that, above all, gets touchdowns on the board.

In his first 17 quarters, he had gained [more than] 800 yards and awakened the echoes that Notre Dame had cocked its ear for this season. And the reason I can assure you he is real: when I telephoned the sports information office, Mrs. Montana answered. His wife works there.

Joe may become the only quarterback who ever came off the bench, out of cold storage, and made All-America. From third string to first cabin. It's a shame, though, that he had to lose his rank as a part-time Merlin and become just another ordinary mortal like Lujack, Guglielmi, Huarte, and all those others.

Rick Reilly, *Sports Illustrated*

MISTER T

Senior flanker Tim Brown graced the cover of Sports Illustrated's 1987 college football preseason issue. A little more than three months later Brown was awarded the Heisman Trophy. The magazine's Rick Reilly came to South Bend that summer to produce this profile.

It's funny, but while he's waiting for the football—turning point-over-point, stripe-over-stripe—Notre Dame's Tim Brown hears like Radar O'Reilly: the band, the cheerleaders, his teammates hollering his name, the "oooohhhh" a crowd makes just before the ball is kicked, and the sudden hush that comes when the people realize a human jet pack like Brown is waiting underneath it. Then, the instant he catches it, his hearing goes dead, as if someone had turned a switch.

Is there any single vignette in sports as rare and tingling as a kickoff returned for a touchdown? A grand slam, perhaps? Last year major leaguers hit 82. Last season in the NFL, seven kickoffs were returned for touchdowns. A triple play? Slightly rarer—five last year in the majors—but a triple play lacks the dulcet anticipation, the stand-on-your-seat-ness of a kickoff. When people see Brown waiting for a kick, they put down their beers and clear off their laps. This is a moment plump with possibility, like being in a room with a piano and Vladimir Horowitz.

Since Anthony Davis brought back six for USC in the early seventies, nobody in college football has returned more kickoffs for touchdowns. In fact, TB has a chance to KO AD's six. He had one his sophomore year, then two last year—95 yards against Air Force and 96 against LSU—plus a 97-yarder against Penn State that was called back because of a clip.

Brown seems to have been born waiting at the goal line. Playing for a high school team in Dallas that won exactly four games in his three years, he returned six kickoffs and three punts for touchdowns and tallied 16 more TDs on runs from scrimmage as a tailback and on receptions. His average touchdown was 45.9 yards, if you can grasp that. The guy scored every 12th time he touched the ball.

Brown runs 40 yards in 4.31 seconds, is as good a bet as any to win the Heisman Trophy—he'd be the first nonback since Irish receiver

Leon Hart in 1949 to claim the prize—and even if he doesn't, he figures to be more fun to watch than the guy who does.

:01

Even under oversized shoulder pads, Brown *looks* 30 mph over the speed limit. His pads are bulkier because Notre Dame used Brown last year the way sportscaster Keith Jackson used the word *hoss*—nearly to exhaustion. He played tailback, wide receiver, flanker, and kick and punt returner. That is still not as many helmets as he wore at Woodrow Wilson High, where he played all those positions plus quarterback, fullback, cornerback, and safety, frequently in the same game, occasionally on consecutive plays. "Put it this way," says his high school coach, Richard Mason. "If Tim Brown didn't get on the bus, I didn't get on the bus."

And now Brown waits for the ball, or rather, doesn't wait for it, which is the secret. Brown gets a running start into the ball (it usually deflects off his face mask, he says). He likes his blockers to get a head start, too, so he hollers, "Go!" before he catches it and then hopes he *does* catch it because otherwise he is all alone with just an odd-hopping ball and 11 angry men. It's a feeling he knows. The first time Brown went back for a kickoff as a freshman he fumbled and lost the ball, setting up a Purdue field goal, which turned out to be the winning margin for the Boilermakers.

If he catches it, Brown and his blockers are already approaching full speed before most return men have planted their first step. The return play called on the sideline tells Brown where his first move is up the field. After that, he's on his own. That's when the fun starts.

:02

Now comes the delicate moment for "T" (so known since the day his pal and former teammate Alvin Miller walked up to him and said, "Man, you're too fast to be called Tim. From now on you're just T"). If the blocking wedge doesn't work, he has to get brilliant quick or get "clicked," as he says. Clicked used to be known as "creamed."

The most clicky bunch are the seldom-used bodies whose only job is to sprint downfield and hurl themselves at Brown in a frenzied stab at human-ballistic heroics. This is one good reason Brown's mother refuses to watch her son play in person. In fact, even if she's in South Bend, she'll stay in their motor home and watch the game on TV, shutting her eyes during the returns. "She never did like football," says [Brown].

Brown's family lives in a small house in lower-middle-class East Dallas. His father, Eugene, is a cement finisher, who has seen five of his six children—Kathryn is only five—go to college. Tim and his friends Brandy Wells (cornerback) and Reggie Ward (another receiver) represent something shiny and modern in sports: talented young athletes who are smart, worldly, and disdainful of drugs. All three were named to the Adidas/Scholastic Coach prep All-America team as high school seniors, and they all exercise their intellects as well as their lats now that they're at the most famous football university in the nation.

Of course, they do sometimes rue the rigid atmosphere at Notre Dame. Girls must be out of the rooms by midnight, students may not have alcohol on campus, and nothing unsavory is allowed. Brown won't be seen in the *Playboy* preseason All-America team picture this year because the current university administration does not want Notre Dame players associated with the magazine.

Politically, players and university are sometimes at odds, too. Notre Dame's refusal to relinquish its investments in South Africa so rankled Brown and his friends that they asked Gerry Faust, their coach until Lou Holtz took over in November 1985, if they could wear black armbands in protest. The university said no.

And then there is drug testing. Notre Dame randomly tests its athletes, but not its other students, for drugs, and Brown wants to know why. "I think it's a matter of my constitutional rights," he says. "If they're going to test me, why not test the guy across the hall? We both go to the same classes. You say I'm a student first, an athlete second. Then why not test him, too?"

No wonder the announcer calls Brown "the deep man."

:03

Because Brown concentrates on his feet when he runs, all he wants to see—needs to see—is a patch of green. If he doesn't see it where it's supposed to be, he takes a guess as to where it might be. "And when you see absolutely nothing," he says, "you just duck your head and hope." When things go wrong, he pays for it.

"You think you're bad?" Penn State players yelled in his face last year after a tackle. "You ain't bad! You ain't——! You run like a little girl!" (The next week against LSU, even though the Irish lost 21–19, Brown rescued the reputations of little girls everywhere by returning that kickoff 96 yards for a touchdown.)

Of course, if, say, six or seven blades of grass side by side do open up, he is through them before daylight can arrive. In his first Irish return for a touchdown, against Michigan State as a sophomore, the hole was supposed to be in the middle, but it wasn't, so he took it left. In the touchdown against Air Force, it was supposed to be right but wasn't, so he took it up the middle. Against LSU and against Penn State, the hole was right where it was supposed to be, in the middle, and Brown jumped on it like it was the San Diego Freeway. "Once I'm past the first wave," he says, "I'm in good shape, especially if nobody's touched me, slowed me up." In the Air Force return, Brown did make it past the wave, but one young cadet grabbed his leg, forcing him to "shift back into first." Not only that, but he also had to run the rest of the way with his sock pulled down. "Ruined the look," he says.

:04

For just a sliver of a second Brown comes gloriously into focus, flying out of sprawled bodies, thighs churning high, the blue-and-gold jersey of Notre Dame glinting with sunlight.

Of course, that jersey was very nearly the red-and-blue of SMU, formerly a practitioner of major college football, but now known mostly for its tennis and track teams. In fact, had it not been for a classic bit of Mustang skullduggery, Tim Brown might have become one of this year's Dallas travelers, knocking on doors, looking for a place to play.

Brown received the SMU pitch from L.A. Rams running back Eric Dickerson himself. "He [Dickerson] said to me, 'Hey, man, when I was here, I got a car, and I got so much money a month. And there's no reason you can't get those things, too.' And that guy, Sherwood Blount [a wealthy SMU alumnus], was right there, not saying anything, just sitting back with his shades on, nodding."

It all sounded fine to Brown. "I could see me there," he says. "I was sold. They were giving 280Zs at the time, and man, I could just see me in one."

Then came the mischief. The night before signing day, Brown was supposed to meet a Notre Dame recruiter. But after basketball practice that day, his high school principal, Wayne Pierce—who happened to operate the 25-second clock at SMU home games—took Brown over to SMU, where Brown went in to see coach Bobby Collins for a quick chat.

"When I got there," Brown recalls, "there was chicken laid out and a bunch of stuff to eat." They were just talking, Collins and Brown, when a minicam truck from a local television station in Dallas showed up for a scheduled interview with Collins. Giving a high school recruit a ride to a campus he had already officially visited and offering him a free meal are borderline no-nos. "They had to hide me," says Brown. And so they did, in a small room, for about an hour, until the TV crew went away. Then Pierce drove [Brown] home.

When Brown got home, the fellow from Notre Dame had left, and older brother Don was so mad the roof tiles were steaming. "SMU's offering you all that stuff, and they're not going to do anything for you down the road!" Don said. "Look! You can go to SMU, but I can't support it, and neither will the family!" Brown signed with Notre Dame the next day. "If it hadn't been for my brother, I'd be at SMU right now," he says.

:05

You are a safety, and coming right at you may be the loneliest moment of your collegiate career. Tim Brown has tripped the light fantastic, danced his way through the masses of humanity, found another free second to kick in the turbo, and is now bearing down on you, one-on-one, a shining vision of speed, grace, and fluidity. In Brown's eyes you can see him thinking, "How bad can I make this guy look in front of his family and friends?"

Pretty bad. An LSU safety stood two yards in front of Brown last year and wound up with a handful of nothing. In the kickoff return against USC, Trojan cornerback Louis Brock Jr., a second-round NFL draft choice, had him eyeball-to-eyeball at the 40 and came up with three fingers on Brown's calf. The move Brown laid on Brock was so mysterious that it is virtually undetectable, even on film. Nonetheless, here is what scientists believe Brown did: facing Brock, Brown began with a stutter step as if to go right, then planted his right foot to go left. Brock didn't buy the first fake but bought this one and lunged that way. Only Brown wasn't going left at all. Dipping low and double-clutching from fourth gear to second, Brown planted his left foot, watched Brock lurch in front of him, and then blew by him on the right as if Brock were a commuter waiting for the next train. "The ultimate juice," said Miller, which means, we think, the ultimate face job.

Brown offers this helpful hint to prospective tacklers: "If I had to try and tackle me, I'd let me commit myself first. I'd let me go where I want to go and *then* tackle. Most guys commit before I ever even make a move."

Of course, that's just the players he sees. Brown has learned to avoid players he *senses*. "It really has to do with peripheral vision," he once said. "If you can't see that guy coming at you from the side, you're going to get nailed. A lot of times I'll be running and see someone coming at me from either side, and I'll just turn and go right at him, and he'll freeze."

Which, of course, is why he's sometimes called Iced T.

:06

Right about now, if you look at films, you can see on the sideline a skinny, bespectacled man about four feet off the ground. He is Lou Holtz, and Brown likes Holtz almost as much as Holtz likes Brown.

Holtz walked off the practice field after his third day at Notre Dame last year and said, "Tim Brown is one of the finest I've ever seen. My wife could've picked out Tim Brown." Holtz wanted to recharge the Irish offense by using multiple formations—everything from the pro-set to the wishbone. But he has never liked shuttling players in and out. He needed a human Kitchen Magician—somebody to play wide receiver, flanker, and tailback, with good hands and a quick mind and big enough to lay a block. "In other words," Holtz said, "we were looking for somebody from Krypton."

So what did Brown do? He set Notre Dame career records for kickoff touchdowns and all-purpose yardage. He averaged more than 20 yards a catch and traveled almost 15 yards every time he touched the ball. And he blew away his *almost mater*, SMU, collecting 235 all-purpose yards and scoring two touchdowns in a 61–29 SMUshing. Brown became so potent as a receiver that Penn State actually used three players to cover him on certain downs last year.

This was a brave new world compared with Brown's Faustian sophomore year, when the game plan was Pinkett, Pinkett, Pinkett, and Punt-it. "They were really, really trying to get [Allen] Pinkett the Heisman," Brown told the *Dallas Morning News*. "They were giving him the ball 40 times a game. I didn't like it. Pinkett didn't like it himself."

The Faust years were worrisome. Indeed, the sight of Brown crying after a pass hit him in the numbers and bounced into a defender's arms in a bitter loss to LSU in 1985 reportedly convinced Faust it was time to resign. "He was a good guy," Brown once said of Faust. "He just got in a little over his head." Or as teammate Wells put it one night, "I remember in the Penn State game, we were behind. We had to get a touchdown fast. Time was running out. And I was standing near Faust, and he's yelling, 'Hey, do we have a bomb play? We have a bomb play, don't we?' Can you imagine that—'Do we have a bomb play?'"

It's a given that Holtz knows a good bomb play or two—the question is whether any of his quarterbacks can throw one. And even if one could, would it be good enough to find Brown in triple coverage? "Tim Brown might end up being more valuable to us this year than last year, yet be less productive," says Holtz. "It's like he's going to have to learn a new role. He was a star in *The Music Man*. All right, now let's see how he does in *Hamlet*."

:07, :08, :09, :10

Now there's only one person left to juke: the lowly, shivering, eminently jukable kicker, who "just sort of dives at your feet," Brown says. When Brown is done with them, kickers sort of resemble hash marks. Which leaves pure Iced T versus any lemon trying to get an angle on him over the last 40 yards. Of course, as Miller says, "There's no such thing as an angle on T." You couldn't get an angle on Brown if you had a phaser gun.

This is when Brown resumes hearing. "When I'm free, I hear all the yelling again," he says. "If you're at home, it's loud, but on the road it's just sort of an 'oooooh.' I get more relaxed. I'm back in second gear."

The sight of Brown gliding in for a 98-yard touchdown is the stuff of 11:00 P.M. sports highlight shows; sports highlight shows make Heismans these days, and Brown wants a Heisman.

"I figure if you're going to go through the whole thing about being a Heisman Trophy candidate, you might as well think in terms of winning the thing," he says.

Win it or not, Denver Broncos director of scouting Reed Johnson figures Brown will be one of the top four or five choices in next year's NFL draft, especially now that a new league rule penalizing out-of-bounds kicks will give the returner more room to do his stuff. All of which means that Brown stands to make a fortune very soon. "I'm going to buy a 928 Porsche for myself and a house for my mom," he says. "And then I'll probably just blow the rest."

You think Mrs. Brown will like football better then?

:11

The warp-speed ballet is over in 11 seconds, but against Michigan State in his sophomore year it took 11.3, of which Brown said, "I must be getting slow."

Anyway, now comes the hard part. He hands the ball to the referee (very Notre Dame) and braces himself to face his inexorable punishment: the celebration. You go to great lengths to run 100 yards in, through, and around very angry, very strong guys without so much as getting a dirty look, only to make it to the end zone and get pulverized by 40 of your dearest friends. "Really, this is the scary part," Brown says. "I just try to get down on my knees and fall *with* 'em. . . . After that, I just walk to the sideline, and I'm standing there, and I just want to scream, 'Yaaaaaaaaaah!'"

After every game, of course, Brown receives hundreds of worshipers. But after the USC game last year, someone came up to him and said something strange.

"Hey, Brown," the man said. "You're almost as good as me."

It was Anthony Davis.

The legendary Knute Rockne was confined to a wheelchair with a leg infection for this 1929 game, a 7–0 victory over Carnegie Institute of Technology.

Section III
THE COACHES

Grantland Rice, *SPORT* Magazine

I REMEMBER ROCKNE

Who better to provide a personal portrait of Knute Rockne than the renowned Grantland Rice? Rice joined SPORT magazine as a consulting editor at the publication's inception in 1946 and put together this piece a year later.

It doesn't seem possible that more than 16 years have passed since Knute Rockne left the scene, killed in an airplane crash over Kansas.

Rockne had such a vivid, vital personality that even the long flow of years has not been enough to wipe away the memory of Notre Dame's great coach, one of football's true immortals. No one who knew Rock closely could ever forget him. In addition to his skill and his all-round ability as a football coach, he had a certain indescribable flame—a physical and mental vitality that few men have possessed. As you consider Knute Rockne's life and career, you must remember that he was a shining star in a game that has always produced top competition, among the coaches as well as the players.

Looking back into the 1880s, there was Walter Camp of Yale, the first of football's brilliant coaches. The Camp system, or the Yale system under Camp, was almost unbeatable for more than a decade. Later on, in the 1890s, we come across such unforgettable personalities as Fielding "Hurry Up" Yost of West Virginia and Lafayette, who, after big years at Nebraska, Kansas, and Stanford, came to the top at Michigan, where his "point-a-minute" machines set new records; John Heisman from Pennsylvania, who wrote football history at Auburn, Clemson, and Georgia Tech; Pop Warner, who left Cornell for Georgia, and then reached the heights at Carlisle, Pittsburgh, and Stanford.

Camp, Yost, Heisman, and Warner were more than masters of gridiron strategy. They were distinct personalities, men who could handle men. They were the kind of human beings you don't forget—pioneers who helped make football what it is today. To a high degree they had brains, character, and color.

Later on we come to Percy Haughton of Harvard, a highly underrated coach who deserves a top place in football coaching's Hall of Fame. And who can leave out Lonnie Stagg of Chicago, still a great coach at 84? Or Bob Zuppke of Illinois, the unforgettable Dutchman? There was Gil Dobie of Cornell's mighty era, the fiery Frank Cavanaugh of Boston College and Fordham, Dan McGuigan of Vanderbilt, Howard Jones of Southern California, Andy Smith of California's "wonder" teams, Bernie Bierman of Tulane and Minnesota, Bill Alexander of Georgia Tech, and Lou Little of Georgetown and Columbia. All these belonged, at least in part, to Rockne's day.

Knute Rockne came along at a time when football coaching was at its peak in both class and color, which makes his own rise to the pinnacle of fame even more remarkable. We have no intention here of trying to tell you that Knute Rockne, judged on his coaching ability alone, was the greatest of all time. Rock, of course, was one of the greatest—but I doubt if there was anyone good enough to wear the undisputed crown. Warner wasn't far away. The great inventor of plays, including the single- and double-wing attacks, for 30 years at Stanford, Warner was always the coach to beat.

But Knute Rockne was more than a great football coach.

Here is just one example. Take yourself back to some big football game in New York—possibly an Army-Navy game, the type of contest that would bring in many outside coaches. I noticed on such occasions that most of them were looking up Rockne. It was always Rockne's room or suite in some hotel where most of the coaches gathered. For here they found cheer, hospitality, an amazing host, and an almost endless span of good stories.

I was talking with Johnny Kieran, the sage of *Information Please*, about Knute Rockne. "Here's an odd angle," Kieran said. "No one questions the fact that Knute Rockne was one of the great football coaches of all time. But Rockne was also the finest scholar I ever met among football coaches. For one thing, Rockne was a fine chemist, and a serious student of chemistry. I recall the night I made a certain Latin quotation. Rockne promptly corrected me on a Latin word—and he was right! I was astonished, until I discovered later that Rockne was an excellent Latin student. How many football coaches have you known who were also Latin scholars? Yes, I know you don't have to be a Latin scholar to be a good football coach. But Rock was well rounded. He knew how to handle men. He was a builder of spirit, the finest spirit the gridiron has ever known."

The fame of Rockne and Notre Dame came together on the football field before Rock had taken the coach's place along the sideline and on the bench. Notre Dame, only fairly well known nationally, was playing a fine Army team at West Point. This was back in 1913. At that time Stagg and Yost in the Midwest, and McGuigan in the South, had used the forward pass effectively. Harvard, Yale, Princeton, and other leading Eastern teams, including Army and Navy, had used the pass only on rare occasions, as a play of last resort.

In this Army–Notre Dame game, Notre Dame had a quarterback and passer named Gus Dorais, now coaching Detroit in the National Football League. And Dorais started throwing passes to a stocky end by the name of Rockne—passes that were good for more than 30 points. A day later Dorais, Rockne, and Notre Dame were famous. This was the game that started one of the dramatic rivalries in football history.

When Knute Rockne moved in as head coach in 1918, Notre Dame became the leading football attraction of a nation that had gone football-woozy. No matter where Notre Dame played—east, west, north, or south—the game was a certain sellout, with the demand for tickets far beyond the capacity of any available stadium.

What Rockne brought to Notre Dame, with the help of a smart and highly human faculty, was a new spirit, the finest spirit football has ever known.

It must be admitted here that, with its rise, Notre Dame got its pick of players from Catholic schools. No such outside aid ever was brought to Holy Cross, Boston College, Georgetown, or other Catholic schools. And Notre Dame in turn rarely played any other Catholic institution.

Outside of this, Notre Dame took on the field—Army, Navy, Southern California, the pick of the Big Nine (later to become the Big Ten), Tulane, Georgia Tech. The Irish met football's best.

There were the days of the Four Horsemen—Harry Stuhldreher, Don Miller, Jim Crowley, and Elmer Layden. Their average weight was 158 pounds. On Sunday mornings after those tough Army games, Rock used to drop in at my apartment to talk things over. He brought along Stuhldreher, a young fellow my wife could never believe was a football player. When he sat in a chair, [Stuhldreher's] feet couldn't reach the floor. He looked like a kid high school player. He weighed 155 pounds, but he could block like a tornado.

Rock told me a story once about one of the smartest plays he had ever seen. "Notre Dame, with the Four Horsemen, was playing a powerful Army team," he said. "Stuhldreher was running the team at quarterback. He called two plays that were broken up. Harry couldn't see just who was doing the damage, so he called the same play again—and never left his position. He merely waited and watched. He saw one of the crack Army backs spoil the play again. Although it was fourth down, Harry again called the same play. But this time he took out that Army back with a terrific block, and we picked up 14 yards. That was my idea of smart football." I readily agreed with him.

The Four Horsemen were the products of speed, spirit, and Rockne's coaching. In front of them they had the Seven Mules, headed by Adam Walsh and Rip Miller.

Rock became famous for his between-halves talks to his teams. I was sitting one night at the Hotel Astor with the Army coaching staff before an Army–Notre Dame game. Novack, the smart Army scout, offered this tip: "Starting the second half," he said, "take the kickoff, if you can. Don't give the ball to Notre Dame. Rock will have them steamed up by that time. They're likely to run wild. Don't give Notre Dame the ball."

But Army kicked off to Notre Dame. On the next play Chris Flanagan of Notre Dame ran 60 or 70 yards to a touchdown. Every Army man was flat on his back. Notre Dame won, 7–0. "That," Rock said later, "was as close to being the perfect play as you ever saw. Eleven of our men did their jobs, and when that happens you get a touchdown."

Everybody knows how Rockne once recalled in a choked voice how Notre Dame's immortal George Gipp had told him: "Some day when things are bad, and the breaks are going against us, ask the boys to go out and win one for the Gipper." They did it, too.

Another Rockne classic was his trick of ignoring his team all during the intermission. He'd sit morosely in a corner with a disgusted look on his face, then finally get up and say, "All right, girls, let's go." On one occasion, when his squad had played badly through the first two periods, he merely opened the door, looked in, and said: "I beg your pardon. I thought this was the Notre Dame team." Then he turned and walked away. The effect was more than successful.

Rockne was a past master at reducing the size of swelling heads. "I had one team," he told me, "that was getting out of control. This team lost a game it should have won. I knew what overconfidence meant, so before the start of their next game I simply distributed newspaper clippings to the bunch. 'Read these,' I said. 'These clippings say you're all All-America. But you couldn't beat a team last week that had no All-Americas. I want you to read these clippings before every play. Either you just aren't that good, or you're yellow.'"

Rockne claimed, "The toughest poison a coach has to face in football is overconfidence. This can wreck any team. That's why coaches rarely predict a victory, even when they expect to win hands down. If your team isn't keyed up, and the other team is, the other team can easily overcome a handicap of two or three touchdowns. Football is that sort of game. You either put out all you have, or you get put out."

I asked Knute once to name the greatest all-round football player he had ever coached. His answer was George Gipp—a great passer, kicker, linebreaker, and open field runner. And a great competitor, although at times the brilliant Gipper was not too easy to handle. I asked Rock who was the gamest man he had ever coached at Notre Dame. His answer: "All Notre Dame men are game, dead game. The star example is Adam Walsh, who played brilliantly at center against a strong Army team although he had five broken bones in his two hands. He never made a bad pass. I didn't think Walsh could last 10 minutes, but he lasted 60 minutes."

We have run into many an argument over the greatest football team that Rockne ever coached at Notre Dame. I talked with Knute about this more than once. In the light of these talks, it is my belief that Rockne's favorite squad consisted of the Four Horsemen and the Seven Mules, but that his greatest squad was his last one—the team of 1930. This squad had the power and the smash that the Four Horsemen lacked.

Many think of Rockne's Notre Dame teams largely in terms of attack—hard, fast running; hard blocking; and timely use of the pass. They overlook the defensive strength that included alertness and rugged tackling. Scoring against Notre Dame was never easy.

Knute Rockne left the gridiron scene more than 16 years ago, but the spirit he brought to the South Bend campus has never faded, and neither has he. His ability, his color, his personality, his stories, and the stories about him are still worth remembering. They'll always be part of American football.

Ed Fitzgerald, *SPORT* Magazine

FRANK LEAHY: THE ENIGMA

Hall of Fame coach Frank Leahy had the pleasure of coaching some of the most talented teams and players anytime in Notre Dame's football history. He won more than his share of games—and more than his share of admirers in Leahy's Lads (as his players termed themselves). Ed Fitzgerald dealt with all that and more in this 1949 piece for SPORT magazine.

This is the core of the Frank Leahy story, these few words, compressed into a couple of nutshells.

1. Leahy is a great coach, the greatest football tactician alive. That establishes his importance, and it can be stated as an unequivocal fact because there is virtually no minority opinion and what there is can be dismissed as overwhelmingly prejudiced.

2. Leahy is a great man, an inspiring and inspired leader of youth, and a tremendous force for good in the world in which he moves. On this point, you can get an argument almost anywhere. Oddly enough, one of the principal breeding grounds of dissension on the subject of the man's character is any gathering of Notre Dame men. There, just as quickly as anywhere else, you can find the anti-Leahys arguing bitterly and combatively with the pro-Leahys. It is always an acrimonious dispute, hardly ever restricted to the bounds of logic and fact, but spilling over almost always into the treacherous pools of emotion, misinformation, and assumption.

It shall be, then, our task to sift the evidence, to study the forces that went into the making of Frank Leahy, to probe the compulsions that shaped the course of his life, to investigate his successes and his failures, and to try to reach an honest conclusion. It should be an absorbing quest, for Leahy is a fabulous, fascinating man. You may like him or not, but you cannot help being interested in him.

When I first called [Leahy], in his room at the Biltmore while he was on a short visit to New York City, he was extremely gracious. "It's very nice of you to call," he said, adding that he had been "looking forward to our meeting." Then, after I asked him what time he wanted me to show up, he carefully explained that "the time element is the only detail about our forthcoming interview that remains to be settled." What all that fancy language meant, in the end, was simply that [Leahy] had another appointment later in the day and wanted to be sure I wouldn't mind if he had to break off the session to make the other date.

At first blush, you might conclude that his careful phraseology was simply grounds for laughter. But after I met him and talked to him for a while, I realized that he had simply been leaning over backward to avoid hurting my feelings. Instead of bluntly telling me that he had another appointment at 6:00, and therefore I wouldn't be able to stay any longer than that, he tried to make it sound as though he wanted to spend all week with me but had to confess that it wouldn't be possible. That's a subtle distinction, perhaps. But to a reporter who is used to meeting all different types of celebrities—the willing, the unwilling, the pleasant, and the rude—Frank Leahy's old-fashioned courtesy is mighty welcome. The cynic might prefer to label it schmooze, but no matter what you call it, it's easy to take.

When I arrived at his room, Leahy was reading a pamphlet titled, "Late, But Not Too Late," written by a Catholic priest named Father Keller. He showed me the publication, [which dealt] with some of the problems that face America today—the rise of Communism, the incidence of crime, the social disease rate, the everlasting problem of illegitimate children. He spoke of the pamphlet's message in awed, grim tones, saying that it made him fearful and humble when he thought of the vast amount of work that had to be done to combat such conditions. He said he was eager to incorporate some of the pamphlet's contents in his talks at banquets and coaching clinics around the country. As if to try out the idea, he asked me if I realized that 1 million children were born out of wedlock in America each year during the war, and that sixty thousand of those were born to girls under 14; that a murder is committed in this country every 40 minutes; and that there are three times as many convicts locked up in American penal institutions as there are students enrolled in all our colleges and universities put together.

Either Leahy was actually deeply stirred by the message he had just finished reading and seriously intended to do what he could to join the fight against the above-mentioned evils, or he is one of the world's finest actors. It is my conviction that he meant every word he was saying. You couldn't sit there and hear the fervor in the man's voice, see the pugnacious set of his square jaw, and not believe him implicitly.

As we began to discuss his phenomenal success at Notre Dame, Leahy quickly showed himself to be tremendously proud of the fact that the university pulls so many promising athletes to its doors solely on the magic of its illustrious name. [He] is emphatic in crediting much of his success to that fortunate circumstance. "This business of going out after the boys and flying them in to look over your campus, and all that sort of thing, may work out all right some times. But you can't count on it. On the whole, it's a poor way to create a winning spirit. Now, every lad who comes to Notre Dame is there because he had a burning desire to come, and I know that the boys are more coachable when they come under those conditions."

Yet, the stories persist that Leahy is not one to sit back idly and merely hope that sufficient material drifts his way to keep his victory mill grinding. Notre Dame men whom I interviewed said that [he] is not at all averse to "selling" the merits of the university to good prospects. In fact, said one informant, when Julie Rykovich, the Illinois star of a few years ago, was taking a wartime Navy V-12 course on the Notre Dame campus, Leahy pulled out all the stops in an unsuccessful effort to get [him] to desert Champaign in favor of South Bend after the war. "Rykovich said no, he wanted to take an agricultural course, and Notre Dame didn't have any," recalled my reporter. "But Leahy said that was nothing. He told Julie he'd get him a private tutor and Rykovich could have the honor of being the first man in history to graduate from an agricultural course at Notre Dame." That was one time the famous Leahy salesmanship failed. Rykovich returned to Illinois after he was discharged and was a great star on the 1946 Rose Bowl team.

There isn't much doubt but that Leahy, who would like to be regarded as above recruiting, quietly sidetracked a group of his protégés who were headed for Boston College after he transferred his own allegiance to Notre Dame. Jim White and John Yonakor are a couple of examples, and [Boston College] rooters who were on the inside writhed in anguish every time they thought how good those players would have looked in the Eagles' uniforms.

Why does Leahy like to pretend that he doesn't go in for such devices, when so much evidence exists that he does? Why does he lay himself open to the charge of double-talking, if not double-dealing? The best guess is that it's because he is a keen, scientific, leave-nothing-to-chance type of football coach who has learned all the tricks of the trade and possibly even thought up a few new dodges of his own, and is now—in his present position of eminence—slightly ashamed that such tactics are necessary. He would, in short, no doubt like to forget a great many things he has had to do and, possibly, still does, in order to win. He would even like to believe that there are more important things in life than winning football games—and he goes around saying so eloquently—but he has never quite been able to bring himself to believe it. Asked by a reporter once what he thought of the ethics of present-day college football, Leahy replied that he rarely had time to think about the subject. "But when I do get time to think of it," he confessed sadly, "it depresses me terribly."

It has been said many times—and quite accurately—that every parish priest in America is an unofficial recruiting sergeant for Notre Dame. But, like so many generalizations, this is only a half-truth. The priests do, in many instances, encourage their young protégés to enroll under the golden statue of Our Lady at South Bend. But in the last analysis it is the great reputation, the glamour, the irresistible appeal of the college itself that mesmerizes so many young men, and not just Catholics. Notre Dame is a nonsectarian institution and is happy to mix young men of all creeds in its student body.

Although he is a deeply religious man, well grounded in Catholic doctrine and seriously interested in it, Leahy himself does not hit you over the head with his faith. It took considerable prodding to get him to talk about his election in January 1949 to the ultra-exclusive clergy-lay group the Knights of Malta. This worldwide organization of Catholic men, each one appointed to membership by the pope of Rome, numbers just 245 members in the entire world. One of these is Frank Leahy, football coach at the University of Notre Dame.

How it happened, [Leahy] does not know. Although he is, of course, by no means ignorant of the international fame he has attained, he professes to be completely astonished by the conferring of such a great honor upon him. As he spoke of it, his tone was awed and humble, his manner almost boyish. "Gee," he said, softly, "I don't know why the pope chose me. I really have no idea because, you know, all the men from this country who are in the organization, men like young Henry Ford and former Postmaster General Frank Walker and Cardinal Spellman of New York, are some of the biggest men in the country."

It would be easy to laugh off such a speech as the work of a man who is trying to sell you a bill of goods, [a man] who is keenly aware of his own importance but thinks it is to his advantage to make you think he holds himself and his honors lightly. Certainly, a great many smart people feel exactly that way about Leahy. Yet, if such is the case, if he is the syrup-tongued double-talker so many critics declare him to be, what is his motive? Nobody has accused him of aspiring to high office and using his Notre Dame glory as a vehicle for rounding up votes. No one has even hinted that he is out for bigger and better jobs in private industry. No one thinks he is in danger of being fired from the post he holds and thus requires all the outside help he can muster. None of these possibilities merits serious consideration. So why should Leahy kid the public? What is he trying to sell?

The answer is—must be—nothing. Nothing, that is, except Notre Dame, which he sells 24 hours a day, 60 seconds a minute, because he just cannot help himself. The answer is, too, that Francis William

Leahy Jr. is that 20th-century rarity, a sincere man equipped with a full measure of faith in what he is doing and conviction that what he is doing is good.

Knowing the man-killing schedule under which Leahy works all year round—a nervous breakdown put him in the Mayo Clinic in 1942—you half expect to see a man with dark circles under his eyes, grave lines etched in his face, and a tired slump to his shoulders. You are hardly prepared for the vigorous fellow who greets you, looking far younger than his 41 years, standing as erect as an Army drill-master, surveying you with a pair of sparkling blue eyes and extending his hand in a strong, confident grip. Even his thick, dark blond hair is just barely tipped with gray. It is possible that Frank Leahy is getting a little weary of the grind, but if so, he certainly manages to conceal it.

[Leahy] wore a conservative brown suit, a plain white shirt, rather gay plaid socks, inconspicuous brown shoes, and suspenders. Taking his ease, he wore no tie and his collar was unbuttoned. It was a warm day, and his first act was to help me remove my coat, hang it carefully in the closet, and suggest that I take off my own tie.

Opening my notebook, I asked, "Do you consider the Arch Ward book on your life a reasonably accurate account?" Ward was sports editor of the *Chicago Tribune*.

Leahy flashed his warm, beaming smile and dropped his eyes with all the modesty of a bashful high school girl being told by an ardent swain that she is very beautiful. "This is going to surprise you," he said, "but, to tell you the truth, I have never read the book. People say so many nice things when they write about you that you always get a quiver reading them, and I hardly ever do. I was reluctant to have the work undertaken in the first place because, of course, I am quite cognizant of the fact that I have never done anything whatever to merit it. But the publishers kept asking Arch to write it and finally he decided he ought to go ahead. He notified me of his decision and advised me that he thought it would be very imprudent of me not to fall in with it. So I agreed, and after the work was completed, Arch sent me a copy. I did read the first few pages, and I blushed. Then I sent the volume along to my mother, and to this day I have not read it."

Leahy speaks in a mellow, soft voice, gaining his effects by underplaying emotions and understating points. His command of the language is impressive and his grammar, on the whole, worthy of a professor of English, although his ordinary conversation is sprinkled with clichés and platitudes. They pop up especially when he is earnestly discussing the need for sincerity and steadfastness of purpose in life, and often they sound as though they sprang straight out of the pages of Horatio Alger. But so earnest is Leahy's manner as he talks, so magnetic are his Irish blue eyes, and so convincing is the friendliness of his smile, that you are absolutely certain you are talking to a man who is on the side of the angels, a man who could not let an insincere word cross his lips. What the great politicians of our time have had, the spellbinders who could rouse the voters to fever pitch merely by appearing before them and talking to them, Frank Leahy has, too.

Leahy is a very modest man—not in a retiring, passive way, but vigorously, aggressively modest. He works at it. He will talk to you at length, eloquently and excitedly, of the great accomplishments of his assistant coaches, of the magnificent loyalty of "the lads" on the squad, and of the almost occult spirit that the University of Notre Dame inspires in its sons. But he not only will never tell you that Frank Leahy is a good football coach, he will not even permit you to say it about him.

Leahy's staff of assistants is headed by Joe McArdle, Johnny Druze, and Bernie Crimmins (McArdle and Druze are former Fordham players, while Crimmins was an All-America at Notre Dame). They in turn are helped by Bill Earley, Bob McBride, and Walter Ziemba, all former Notre Dame players. "Every member of my staff I have coached," said the master with the first note of pride he had allowed to creep into his voice. "And I want to tell you, it's the finest staff in America. Having men of their caliber to work with has been a wonderful break for me. I don't think any head coach can go much farther than his assistants will permit him to go."

Those hostile observers who imply darkly that Leahy is an egomaniac, impossible to work *with* and difficult to work *for*, are stumped when you mention the fact that, of the three assistants he took with him to Boston College and on to Notre Dame, two are still at his side. They are, of course, the two Fordham boys, McArdle and Druze. And the third member of the trio, Ed McKeever, left only because he had a gilt-edged opportunity to better himself.

There were, I knew, other appointments awaiting the busy coach, and I finally suggested that it was time for me to leave. "Only if you're certain you're finished," he said, with considerable concern. "Please don't hurry on my account. I want to be sure that you have all that you need." Later he added, "If you should happen to think of anything you forgot, please don't hesitate to call us at Notre Dame. We'll be only too glad to get you what you need to know." And finally, as I was leaving, he gave me that firm handshake and that big Irish grin again and said, "You should come see us out at Notre Dame. I know you'd like it there, and we'd love to have you. Thanks very much for coming over."

As I walked down the corridor and pushed the button for the elevator, I thought to myself, if I didn't know better, I'd swear I had just done *him* a favor.

If you want a good example of Leahy's formal oratory to contrast with his informal speech, you can't do any better than the address he delivered to the Notre Dame student body upon his arrival at the school in the spring of 1941 as head coach and athletic director. Ward reports the entire speech in his exciting book, *Frank Leahy and the Fighting Irish*. Some of the highlights should serve to illustrate the great coach's forensic technique:

> We are starting out to accept a great challenge, and it is only fitting that together we discuss our plans, our hopes and fears, our aims and objectives. For, together, we should be able to do a representative job.
>
> It is not so long ago, you know, that yours truly was a student here. We do not have to reminisce too deeply into the pages of time to recall how we, too, struggled with the books, the gridiron problems, and the bill collectors. No one ever accused us of being too nifty on our feet on that football field, but when Adler and Livingston came out to try to relieve us of some money which we owed them, we were just as elusive as Steve Juzwik. We always managed to give the aforementioned clothiers the shadow and then we quickly took it away. The thought often came to us that if we had been as clever in avoiding people on the field of play as off it, we might have been another Red Grange instead of a plain, old-fashioned tackle.
>
> We have nothing against tackles, mind you, for they are all right and mighty essential to the welfare of the nation. Food concerns throughout the country would not be operating in the black without a lot of good old heavy-eating tackles to diminish their stocks. Many people have the wrong idea about tackles. Of course, some of us are not too smart, but we tackles always have been noted for telling the truth.
>
> Approximately one month ago, I received the greatest surprise of my entire life. For it was just about four weeks ago that the authorities at the University of Notre Dame saw fit to ask me to coach the football team at my alma mater. My vocabulary lacks the words to describe fittingly the monumental feeling of joy which permeated my entire body and soul.

[Leahy's] inexplicable love for polysyllabic conversation has caused many a newspaperman to view him with dark suspicion. By now, however, most of the working journalists are accustomed to his speech and view it as merely another eccentricity. In fact, they enjoy telling stories of Leahy's peculiar brand of loquacity. Francis Powers, the brilliant football analyst of the *Chicago Daily News*, relayed one of the best ones to me.

Two years ago, Leahy was talking idly with Bert McGrane of [the] *Des Moines Register-Tribune*. The previous spring, Ziggy Czarobski had incurred the coach's anger by blithely skipping spring practice. During his conversation with Leahy, McGrane asked how the coach felt about Czarobski. Said [Leahy], in his most regal manner, "If Zygmont does not return to the campus in the most perfect condition, we shall be obliged to ask him to disassociate himself from our group."

Ziggy, reports Powers, came back in good shape.

The most generally accepted explanation of Leahy's predilection for big words is that he suffered a mild case of stage fright when he first returned to Notre Dame in the role of head coach and undertook to improve his oral delivery by taking courses in English literature and public speaking. But perhaps another sidelight casts more truth on his language quirk.

Talking to me, [Leahy] spoke with considerable awe of his father's accomplishment in acquiring a vast command of the language despite his lack of a formal education. "He would bet anyone that he could define any word in *Webster's Dictionary*," says Leahy, "and I never saw him lose." Maybe [Leahy] is, consciously or unconsciously, merely trying to follow in his father's footsteps, footsteps that he makes abundantly clear he regards with great pride.

Although there is scarcely a college or professional team in the country that Leahy could not coach if he wanted the job, he has been tempted particularly in recent years by two lavish pro offers. One came from the reorganized Detroit Lions of the National Football League, an offer that was undoubtedly pressed to [Leahy] by his old friend Harry Wismer, sports director of the American Broadcasting Company, member by marriage of the mighty Ford Motor empire, and ½ owner of the Lions. The other came from the Washington Redskins, owned and operated by the fabulous Washington laundryman, George Preston Marshall. It is doubtful if either of those offers was for less than $35,000 a year, and it is probable that either club would have gone as high as $50,000 to get Leahy.

It should be remembered that [he] is not being entirely altruistic when he resists pressure to leave the Golden Dome and put his undeniable talents to work in a more commercial atmosphere. As coach of the Fighting Irish, [he] probably earns about $15,000 to $18,000 a year in straight salary. But the lectures, coaching clinics, magazine articles, endorsements, and various other windfalls that come his way because of his connection with Notre Dame raise his annual take to better than $35,000.

With his wife, Floss, and his six children, ranging in age from a few weeks to 13 years, Leahy lives the comfortable life of a country squire in a beautiful, spacious home at Long Beach, Indiana, on the shore of Lake Michigan. Their place has five bedrooms on the second floor, another bedroom on the third floor, and a dormitory that can sleep five or six young boys. It is a commodious establishment. "The closest house to ours is a block away," says [Leahy]. "There is absolutely no traffic, it's way up on a hill, the air is clean and pure, and it's just a wonderful place to bring up the kids. The beach is the finest beach in the Midwest. Oh, I tell you, we're lucky. Very lucky indeed."

But there is more than luck behind the fantastic Leahy success story. This suave, poised man was born on August 27, 1908, a little removed from the genuine Wild West era, but not by much. Around O'Neill, Nebraska, the small town where Frank Leahy Sr. had settled his growing brood, life was real and life was earnest. You worked hard for your daily bread, and you didn't need a permit to carry a gun.

Frank Sr. was never much of a hand for firearms. But he was a big, powerful man who could take care of himself under any circumstances. He especially loved to wrestle. He often matched his strength against the renowned champion, Farmer Burns, his great friend. He was never known to back off from an opportunity to test his wrestling or boxing skill against any man, and he set great store by these manly virtues. It is said of him that he would question young [Leahy] closely as to the last time the boy had had a fight, and when told not recently, would order the youngster gruffly, "Well, don't come home tomorrow until you have one."

When Frank Jr. was only 17, his father encouraged him to get into the ring with a professional boxer just to see what he could do in a tight spot. The boy, his square jaw stuck out almost as far as his left fist, faced his adversary boldly. Slammed off his feet six times in the first round, Leahy climbed up grimly each time, plowing straight ahead after every knockdown. In the third round, he knocked the pro cold.

There was a hunger in Dad Leahy for greener horizons. Not long after his third son (and sixth child) was born, he headed for a pioneer Montana community name of Roundup. Mother Leahy waited with the children until he sent word that he had a place ready for them.

For a number of reasons, chief among them the rarefied air that went with the unusually high altitude, Dad Leahy changed his mind about Roundup after little more than a year. This time he picked out a spot in Tripp County, South Dakota—a brand-new township named Winner by its optimistic settlers.

In the new town, the Leahys had to wait for a livable house to be built. They bivouacked in a canvas tent for a weary stretch of cold months. Then, that first year in Winner, their crops were ruined by brutal climatic conditions. You have to be tough to stand up to hardships like that. But Dad Leahy *was* tough—and so was his pioneer wife, and so were all six little Leahys. Leahy Sr. organized a wagon-freight business and enlisted his oldest boys, Gene and Jack, 12 and 10 years old, respectively, to help him out. It was savagely hard work, and often dangerous, but it was also well paid. Hauling a lot of hard liquor for good prices, Dad Leahy prospered and the family flourished.

Growing up in the midst of such a vigorous family circle, rooted in such a hard-boiled, tobacco-chewing, gun-toting, plain-talking world, it is no wonder that young Frank Leahy developed the strength of character that drove him relentlessly up the ladder of success. It is something of a paradox that the same environment instilled in him a burning desire to gain an education, to speak the language of a gentleman, and to learn the manners of the drawing room. But Frank Leahy is a man of more than one paradox, a man who has accurately been described as the greatest enigma in American sport.

[Leahy] was too young to do much serious work in the family freight business, which was abandoned in favor of a produce enterprise after a half-dozen years. In the new business, however, he was active for a number of his boyhood years, serving usefully as a part-time clerk. "My Dad would buy cream and eggs and cowhides from the neighboring farmers," he explains, "and in exchange would sell them such things as flour, wheat, and grain. I well remember Dad rousing me out of bed at 6:00 in the morning to help lift flour sacks!"

Gene Leahy, who became an insurance agent in Rushville, Nebraska, and one of Notre Dame's most strenuously loyal followers, was the first of the Leahy boys to attain athletic fame. At Creighton University, he established a record that is not likely to be forgotten there. Jack, Frank's other older brother, was interested in no sport except horseback riding, but he has since become an avid football fan. Paralyzed for the last four and a half years as the result of a heart attack—[Leahy] says, "it's an insult to the medical profession that he still lives"—Jack watches every Fighting Irish home game from an ambulance parked behind the end zone.

With Gene's exploits to serve as his example, young [Leahy] gradually switched his affection from boxing and wrestling to football. There is no record that [Leahy] was a star of exceptional brilliance at Winner High, but he must have been a better-than-average player because, in his senior year, a new coach named Earl Walsh marked him as a good prospect for his own alma mater, which happened to be Notre Dame.

Walsh, who had been a great football player at Notre Dame, recommended to Knute Rockne that Leahy be given an athletic scholarship. In order to qualify, however, [he] had to travel to Omaha, Nebraska, to study at the Central High School there [to] pick up some missing scholastic credits. Omaha was the first big city the young country boy had visited, and he enjoyed the experience immensely. While there, he fought several amateur boxing bouts, one of them against Ace Hudkins, who later was to become nationally famous as a professional. He also worked diligently at the high school and had no trouble gaining entrance to Notre Dame in the fall of 1927. The mold of his life was beginning to take shape.

The shy young man from Dakota shook off his early nervousness so quickly, and settled down to the college routine so efficiently, all the while making new friends on every side, that when the freshman elections were held, he was named president of the class.

It would be nice to be able to report that [Leahy] made equally rapid progress on the freshman football squad, but a natural slowness [of foot] held him back, and he only made second-string tackles. But [he] just buckled down and worked harder. His efforts finally paid off when Rockne himself, spending sometime overseeing the freshmen at practice, instructed the frosh coaches to give Leahy a try at center. Just the mere fact that the great coach had singled him out for the smallest mention inspired Leahy to a regular frenzy of effort. The next spring he was awarded the Frank E. Hering Medal as the player having shown the most advancement at center.

It was only natural that Leahy should think he had an excellent chance of becoming at least the number two center on the Irish varsity for 1928, but halfway through the season, after [Leahy] had played only a few minutes as a center replacement, Rockne asked him to switch back to tackle. Leahy's first reaction was that he must have failed miserably at the job he had been trying to do. But, characteristically, he assured the coach that he would do his level best to be a useful tackle. Which he certainly turned out to be, although not that season.

Notre Dame roared back from a miserable 1928 campaign to become undefeated in 1929, and Frank Leahy beat out three other candidates at right tackle. Even an elbow dislocation suffered in the Navy game couldn't stop [him] for more than a few weeks. He was right back in there, winding up the season by playing savagely for half the Southern California game before his painful injury caught up to him and forced him to leave the game.

He didn't suspect it at the time, but that was the end of [his] career as a football player. The bad luck that had started with the injury in the 1929 Navy game was to hound him still more, and finally sweep him out of action altogether with a damaging knee injury in 1930 preseason practice.

After it happened, this twisted cartilage that was to play such an important part in his life, [Leahy] thought the world had fallen around his ears. For the first time since he had entered Notre Dame, he lost that fighting edge. He had been so sure that his senior year would be his best year, so hopeful of getting a good coaching spot after cementing his college reputation. (For there was no doubt in his mind now that he wanted to coach for a living.) Now what was to become of him?

Rockne supplied the answer. He insisted that the boy continue to attend the daily practice sessions, and he included him on all the team rosters for the trips away from home. Furthermore, he gave his tacit approval as [Leahy], too restless to just stand around and watch, began to serve as an assistant coach without portfolio.

Finally—and this, by Leahy's own statement, was the biggest break he ever got in his life—Rockne invited [him] to make a postseason visit with him during the Christmas holidays to the Mayo Clinic in Rochester, Minnesota, where each could have an operation performed. While they were convalescing side by side from their operations, Rockne gave his youthful protégé an advanced course in the art of coaching football that no amount of money could buy, that few students were ever privileged to receive. He did something more, too—he gave back to Leahy the confidence that his tormenting injury had taken from him. He made him see that the future could be whatever [he] wanted it to be.

By way of demonstrating that he wasn't just mouthing words, Rockne dumped a handful of letters in Leahy's lap, each one asking the Rock to recommend a promising graduate for a coaching job, and invited the youth to pick out the one he liked best. Eagerly scanning the letters, Frank noted that his old friend Tommy Mills, who had coached Gene Leahy at Creighton and had been one of Rockne's aides when Frank [Leahy] was a freshman, needed an assistant at Georgetown. "That's it," [he] thought. "That's the one I want." And from that moment on, his outlook brightened, his Irish smile took on its old confidence. Once again, he had something to fight for, a goal to work toward—and that is all Frank Leahy has ever needed.

[Leahy's] new cheerfulness lasted until the bitter day in March 1931 when his idol and benefactor, the great Rockne, was killed in an airplane crash. His tragic passing was a shock that the youthful Leahy was a long time getting over. [He] never did let the inspiration of Rockne's memory fade from his mind. He never will. It is imbedded in him too deeply ever to be removed.

Leahy served only one season as an assistant at Georgetown before Jim Crowley, one of the Four Horsemen, signed Leahy as his line coach at Michigan State and later took him to Fordham University in New York City. It was at Fordham, very much in football's Big Time, that Leahy solidified his reputation. True, when he got his first opportunity to sign as a head coach, at Boston College in 1939, he wasn't well known to the general public, but in the trade he was definitely tabbed as a comer.

One year at Boston College and everybody knew about him. Leahy, taking over a losing team, produced in his first season a football machine that won every game on its schedule but one. He was on the high road now, hitting on all cylinders, working like a slave but working for himself at last. The faith that Rockne had shown in him was being justified every Saturday afternoon. In Frank's second year at [Boston College], 1940, the Eagles ripped through their entire schedule without defeat and went on to restore the prestige of New England football by belting the powerful Volunteers of Tennessee, 19–13, in a tremendous upset in the Sugar Bowl. The day Tennessee fell, Leahy had officially arrived.

Boston College signed him to a new three-year contract but allowed him to stipulate that the document would be forgotten if he ever was offered a chance to return to Notre Dame. The Notre Dame clause wasn't considered especially important by either party to the contract, but it pleased Leahy, and in a few short weeks it was to enable him to accept a bid so wonderful that it left him stunned—an offer to succeed Elmer Layden as head coach of football at Notre Dame.

Like almost all [Notre Dame] men in the coaching field, Leahy had always cherished a secret desire to "go back home." But he had never really thought the chance would come to him, at least not for a long time. When Layden resigned, the school authorities, after weighty deliberation, decided they wanted either Buck Shaw of Santa Clara or Leahy of Boston College. Shaw, approached first, refused. That left Leahy an open track. He said, "I'll take it," and he packed up his assistants—Druze, McKeever, and McArdle—and went back to the Golden Dome. For the kid from Winner, the wheel had turned full circle—and it hadn't taken long to do it, either.

Meanwhile, Leahy's personal life was progressing favorably, too. [He] had met Floss Reilly, a beautiful young colleen, while he was working under Crowley at Fordham. Two years later, on the Fourth of July, 1936, [he] and Floss were married at a small Catholic church in the Bronx. Their union has been both happy and fruitful. They have six handsome children, the youngest of which, a son born during a severe storm last September 1, had to enter the world with just his versatile daddy assisting at a tense candlelight ceremony. After that ordeal, [Leahy] was asked by reporters whether it was a boy or girl. "I think," he said, wearily, "it's a fullback." It was. A boy—Frederick John Leahy.

Although he was laid low by spinal arthritis several times before the war and suffered painful recurrences of the ailment during his navy hitch, Leahy is in excellent health today. That he is, is a tribute to his iron constitution, for no man could drive himself harder. Leahy spends only three nights a week at home during spring practice time. When fall comes, with its accelerated practice routine and the big games themselves, he goes home only on Wednesday and Saturday nights. (When he stays on the campus overnight, he sleeps in a small room reserved for him in one of the college dormitories.)

After the season, the banquets begin, the testimonials, and the coaching conferences. The calls pour in from the alumni and from friends. And when summer comes, and school is out, there are other things. Leahy keenly regrets the long periods of time he has to spend away from home. "The kids are growing up fast," he told me, "and I just know I'm missing a great thrill in not seeing more of them."

When you talk to Leahy about such matters, it's hard to understand how so many people can term him cold-blooded and heartless, a football automaton. He not only answered all my questions about his family courteously and fully, but also volunteered a great many sidelights and anecdotes on his own. In fact, he did everything but reach for pictures of his babies.

For that matter, no observant reporter, digging for information as to why so many of his fellow coaches dislike Leahy either openly or covertly, can fail to agree at least in some measure with the hard-bitten professional coach who, when asked about the matter, commented swiftly, "Why don't they like Leahy? Hell, that's easy. He beats them too often."

That he does. The perfectionist from Winner, South Dakota, wins a whole lot more often than he loses. Under his magic hand, Notre Dame, through 1948, established the amazing record of 50 victories, three defeats, and five ties. The last time a Leahy-coached team lost to a collegiate opponent—this does not count the Great Lakes defeat in 1943—was against Michigan in 1942. Leahy has given Notre Dame *four* undefeated 11s and *three* national championship teams, all of which adds up to quite a record when you consider he only started in 1941 and took two years out for the navy.

To attain such success, Leahy, during the season, generally gets out of bed at about 6:45 A.M., is holding the first conference of the day with his staff by 8:00, and spends the next hour or so looking at movies. Along about 10:00, you'll find him back at his desk checking over his mail and catching up on outgoing correspondence. Every day at noon—following a Rockne tradition—he holds a meeting with his players, either in the Law Building auditorium or in the auditorium of the Engineering Building. After that session, [he] takes time out for a fast sandwich, invariably eaten at his desk and usually washed down with a container of milk. At 3:00, he leaves for the locker room and gets ready for the big two-hour (or longer) practice period.

It is during that outdoor drill that Leahy shows the technique that has made him a great coach. No detail misses the master's eye, no error escapes his scathing—though never profane—tongue. Leahy doesn't have to swear. He can make a poised college senior squirm with such expressions as, "Perhaps you lack the character to see the job through," or "Maybe you are unwilling to make the necessary sacrifice to play for Notre Dame!"

Standing on a 30-foot wooden tower he had constructed in 1946, Leahy supervises all the work being done on the three Notre Dame practice gridirons. This parapet, which gives the appearance of having as many loudspeakers as a destroyer has guns, is in effect Captain Leahy's bridge. Standing up there stiff and stern, Leahy must at times appear to his players to be a reincarnated Captain Bligh. He is after perfection, and it is not easy to get. He knows this, and he fights all the harder for it. Watch one of his swivel-hipped, high-stepping backs explode through the second-string line and race 60 yards downfield in a brilliant exhibition of ball carrying, before being tackled. "You see," Leahy will say bitterly into one of the loudspeakers, "he failed to go all the way."

Talk to Leahy during one of those practice sessions and he will spend all his time discussing the team's weak spots. [He] practically never sees anything to cheer about. But he faces his troubles with equanimity, being a viewer-with-alarm of long experience. To the visitor, he is likely to say, in perfect seriousness, "I will endeavor to obliterate the defects."

Leahy is aware that he is often criticized for working his football candidates excessively hard. He spoke candidly to me on the subject. "Frankly," he said, "we do work them hard . . . awfully hard. We keep after them all the time on the practice field; we find fault with much that they do out there." He turned on the big smile again and forgot to reach for two-syllable words. "We raise a lot of Cain with them," he summed it up.

Then he grew serious again and sat up straight in his chair, chewing off the words slowly and cleanly to make sure I got the full import. "They take it from me," he said, "first, because they know I don't mean it—the growling, that is. And second, because they know that I will pay off for them in the end. I will help place them in the jobs they want. They know I wouldn't fail them there for all the tea in China."

"You mean you get a job for every boy on your squad?" I asked, with some astonishment.

He seemed surprised at my surprise. "Oh, yes," he said, gravely. "Every lad who wins a monogram gets placed. They all know that. That's why they stay with me when I work them hard—that plus their pride in their university." Warming up to his subject, [he] said, "Last June we had 17 lettermen graduating, and by the end of the month I had all but 2 of them placed and I didn't stop until those 2 were taken care of, too."

"You mean they all want football jobs?"

Again there was a slightly surprised look on the master's expressive face. "Oh, no. Some of them want entirely different things. One of the boys last year, for instance, had his heart set on joining the FBI, and he was one of the cases with which I encountered some difficulty. He had no law degree, you see, and that happens to be one of the qualifications for an FBI agent. But I was in Washington in the spring for the Celebrities Golf Tournament and I looked up J. Edgar Hoover to see what I could do. He wasn't in when I called, but I left a message for him describing my problem, and he wrote me at Notre Dame and assured me that the young man would get his wish."

Small wonder, then, that the overwhelming majority of Leahy's "lads" speak of the "slave-driver" with warmth and gratitude. He's a follow-through guy, and even the ones who don't especially like him respect him for that.

In Leahy's favor is the indisputable fact that, if he makes his assistant coaches and his players work hard, he works twice as hard himself. His worst enemy will not deny that, but some of his critics do point out that [his] zeal sometimes leads him to cut a few corners when it comes to observing the letter of the collegiate rulebook.

For instance, Lloyd Lewis, then the sports editor of the *Chicago Daily News*, got on Leahy the very first summer he went out to Notre Dame, in 1941, accusing [him] of holding bootleg summer practice. Lewis knew what he was talking about. One of the boys who was there told me that Leahy had his entire first-string backfield—Angelo Bertelli, Harry Wright, [Fred] "Dippy" Evans, and Steve Juzwik—holding down summer jobs at Notre Dame Stadium and practicing two hours a day from June on. [Leahy] wasn't going to face his first season as Notre Dame coach without doing everything he could in advance to assure himself of success.

No effort is too great for Leahy in an attempt to win a football game. The night before his 1941 club entrained to take on powerful Georgia Tech, [he] sat up in his office until 4:00 A.M., trying to figure out the best possible defense against the Yellowjackets. Finally, he hit upon a novel four-man defensive line with two roving guards. When the team reached Atlanta and settled down in the Biltmore Hotel, he prevailed upon the hotel management to close off the grand ballroom and let him take it over for the evening. Then, all Friday night before the game, he had the boys in that gleaming ballroom, their shoes parked against the wall, running through the brand-new defense in their stockinged feet. To Leahy, that was strictly routine. "We work hard," he will tell you. "We try not to miss any possibilities."

Stop the man in the street and ask him what he thinks is the principal complaint about Leahy's coaching regime at Notre Dame and he will probably tell you that the coach has hurt the old school's schedule. "According to what I read," he would be likely to say, "Leahy has so many people sore at him personally that Notre Dame is having a lot of trouble getting games." That sounds like a serious charge and is certainly worth exploring. Are the Fighting Irish getting the games they want? The answer has to be no.

Because of their geographical location and their high place in football tradition, [Notre Dame] would like to play the cream of the Big Ten schools, both the national service academies, and add spice by including a special rivalry or two with such as Southern California. Big Ten schools like Michigan, Ohio State, Purdue, Illinois, Minnesota, and Northwestern are the opponents Notre Dame covets above all others, excepting only Army and Navy. Yet only Purdue of that select Big Ten core appears on the 1949 schedule of the Fighting Irish.

It is difficult to reach any conclusion other than that the Big Tenners whose friendship is most earnestly desired by Notre Dame are, collectively or individually—and it doesn't matter which—freezing out the Irish. Whether the freeze-out was inspired by Leahy's personality, as many charge, or by the so-called religious angle—the contention that wherever Notre Dame plays, they draw a great many more partisan rooters than the home team does—or by the simple fact that Notre Dame is too tough an opponent, is difficult to tell. It seems reasonable to lay at least part of the blame at Leahy's door. Rockne turned out great teams, too, but he never had any trouble getting the other powers of the Midwest to take him on. During Elmer Layden's hitch at South Bend, he either played or scheduled every team in the Western Conference except Chicago, which was at that time already nosediving. Leahy, on the other hand, has been unable to get anywhere scheduling the best Big Ten clubs. Right now, Notre Dame plays three conference schools—Iowa, Indiana, and Purdue. With Indiana panting to say good-bye to the Irish, only Purdue and Iowa seem safe bets for the future.

Dr. Eddie Anderson, the Iowa coach, is willing to keep Notre Dame on his schedule indefinitely. But part of the reason for his attitude may well be that the Hawkeyes need a big-money game. "Some day we'll come up with a team that will beat Notre Dame," says Anderson, who is a stubborn man.

As for Michigan, the team Notre Dame would rather play than any other, the outlook is darkest of all. There is absolutely no question but that a feud of sizable proportions is raging between Leahy and Fritz Crisler, the former Michigan coach who is now athletic director at Ann Arbor. Neither misses any opportunity to slam the other, even if in genteel terms, and hardly a month goes by that new coals aren't heaped on the fire of disagreement.

After Notre Dame and Michigan ran 1–2 and 2–1, respectively, in the Associated Press national championship polls of 1947 and 1948, there was tremendous public demand for a meeting between the titans. Less than 200 miles apart, the schools are natural rivals by any standard. Until last winter, however, neither Leahy nor Crisler paid any attention to the general clamor. Then, after Michigan was voted national champion in 1948, Leahy began to needle the Wolverines. At every opportunity, he publicly challenged Michigan to a game. He challenged Crisler at banquets, and he challenged him in newspaper interviews. He poured on the pressure, and it must have hurt.

"If Leahy wants a game with Michigan so badly, why doesn't he go to Ann Arbor and talk to Crisler?" stormed angry Wolverine supporters.

I took up this point with [Leahy]. "Have you ever made a formal request of Michigan for a game?" I asked him.

"Not since 1944," he admitted, "when I met Fritz Crisler at a banquet and told him that we would love to play him. Don't worry, they know we want to play them. As we have said, Notre Dame will play Michigan any time, any place, any Saturday!"

Leahy has the more popular side of this battle, beyond any doubt. The team that says, boldly, "We challenge you," always is certain of more support than the team that coyly replies, "No, thank you. We'd rather not."

It is equally difficult for Army's adherents to make Leahy out the villain of their squabble. Notre Dame and Leahy did not want to drop Army. But Army wanted to drop Notre Dame. Certainly [Leahy] never said anything to wound the feelings of the military brass hats—at least, not before the break—but there is no doubt that his teams did a great deal to jab their sensitive natures by inflicting more than one artistic shellacking on the Cadets.

One old Army man blamed Leahy for the cancellation of the big game by saying, "When Rockne was alive, Army seldom beat Notre Dame, but it was different. You didn't hate so to lose. Rock would come up to the Point every spring, stay around two or three days with Biff Jones or whoever was coaching, and renew and strengthen relations. Losing to Leahy is just the same as losing to a concrete mixer."

There, at last, it's out in the open, separated from all the clouds of hokum. Leahy not only wins too often, but he isn't a handshaker.

Perhaps that problem will be solved by the recent appointment of Ed "Moose" Krause to the Notre Dame athletic directorship, a post Leahy resigned in order to devote all his time to coaching the football team and in an attempt to salvage a little more spare time for himself. Perhaps the universally liked [Krause] will display the talent for public relations and general fence-mending that Leahy has proven he lacks. Notre Dame, one suspects, will be satisfied if Leahy just continues to win the football games that Krause schedules.

Certainly no one at the University has ever given the slightest sign that Notre Dame would be happier without its high-powered, high-tension football coach. On the contrary, Father John J. Cavanaugh once said, extolling Leahy's virtues: "A man is a real success when he knows what God wants him to do and has the discipline to do it."

Over and over again, while digging around for information about the Notre Dame genius, you flush charges that Leahy teaches dirty football. "He's not satisfied with all that material," growl these critics. "He's not even satisfied with his own talent for coaching. He can't bear to leave a single thing to chance, so he teaches the boys every dirty trick in the books. And, furthermore, he sees that they use them all."

In this connection, from more than one young college graduate who played football against the South Bend legions, you can hear disturbing stories that the Irish carry things far beyond the "hard play" stage. "They'll give you the knee, they'll hold you, they'll clip you, and they'll belt you with an elbow every chance they get," said one Southern Cal product. "Maybe Leahy doesn't tell them to do it, but he sure as hell doesn't tell them not to do it!"

Yet Stuart Holcomb, the former West Point assistant who is now so successful as head coach at Purdue, is well satisfied with his Notre Dame series even though he had to watch his Boilermakers lose a heartbreaking 28–27 decision to [Notre Dame] last season. "Our game was not rough and it was not dirty," says Holcomb, vigorously. "The only complaint I have is that we had to prepare so strenuously for the game that our players burned out mentally and never recovered."

Asked what Notre Dame does better than other teams, Holcomb said, "They hit harder. Not rougher, but harder. That comes from heavy scrimmaging. Not many teams can afford so much scrimmaging. Army could, in the days of [Felix "Doc"] Blanchard and [Glenn] Davis, and that's one reason why Army was so great."

Marchie Schwartz, Leahy's old Notre Dame teammate and one of the school's brightest gridiron stars, now coaching Stanford, doesn't go around making a whole lot of noise about it, but it's no secret that he hit the ceiling after his Indians played [Notre Dame] in the first game of a scheduled two-game series back in 1942. According to West Coast writers, the Fighting Irish did a little too much fighting in that tussle— most of it off the record. The boys on the Stanford bench were so infuriated that Schwartz had to restrain them from piling off the bench and turning the contest into a gang fight. Stanford never played the second game of that series, and the word is that it never will as long as Leahy is the Notre Dame coach.

Now, how do you figure this one out? Leahy, of course, earnestly denies that his lads engage in any under-the-table tactics. The man's whole approach, his conversation, his speeches, his writings, all belie the employment of *sub rosa* methods. It is my own carefully drawn conclusion that if Leahy is guilty at all (which I seriously doubt), his only guilt in this matter is passive rather than active. I think it is entirely possible that the man's boundless urge to win has, at times, led him to overlook some of the more enthusiastic steps taken in that direction by his "lads." But I simply cannot and do not believe that he goes out of his way to teach his pupils how to behave like roughnecks, though it is entirely possible that, like all good football coaches, he instructs them in the art of self-defense.

Part of the Leahy legend is that [he] delights in plaguing the members of the fourth estate by extensively employing the devious type of answer that is known in some circles as circumlocution and in others as plain, ordinary double-talk. The charge is leveled at Leahy that he has no regard for the job the reporters are trying to do and has no compunction about sending them packing with nothing to show for their time but notebooks filled with meaningless though fancy phrases.

There cannot, of course, be any question that [Leahy] is a Gloomy Gus of the old school. Like the famous Gil Dobie of Cornell, he likes to tell everyone that his ballclub is bound to lose next Saturday's encounter by four or five touchdowns. Coming from almost any coach, that sort of chatter always sounds a trifle silly. Coming from Leahy, the director of a powerhouse that considers it disastrous to lose one game a season, it is downright ridiculous. [He] probably could improve his admittedly shabby press relation a great deal if he would skip the crying-towel act and adopt a more realistic viewpoint in his pregame interviews.

As for the frequent indictment that he refuses to give out any information on his squad unless nailed to the wall—that doesn't seem to hold up. One incident out of many that can be used as rebuttal occurred before the Purdue game last year, a game that Leahy foresaw would be tough and that turned out to be even tougher than he thought. [He] held a press conference on the eve of the contest and drew an audience of about 20 top writers from the East and Midwest.

Without a word about, "This is off the record," or anything like that, he walked to a big blackboard, picked up a piece of chalk, and said, "Gentlemen, when we play Purdue tomorrow, Notre Dame will use a defensive shift. It is the first time we ever have done that, and I want you to know about it so you won't be confused during the game. When Notre Dame is on defense, Leon Hart will shift from right end to right tackle and Bill Fischer will move from left guard to left tackle."

The writers, unaccustomed to such candor and cooperation from coaches with far better reputations in the field of press relations, left the room chattering excitedly among themselves. Obviously, those in the group who were not very familiar with Leahy were speculating thoughtfully about whether or not the picture of the famous coach that had been drawn for them by other reporters was not so distorted as to be actually a caricature.

Gordon Graham, the sports editor of the Lafayette, Indiana, newspaper and a perennial follower of the Purdue team, was not present at the conference. Later in the day, someone remembered that he had been absent and mentioned the fact to Leahy. "Would you," quizzed this writer, "have explained the defensive shift if Graham *had* been there?"

Leahy seemed to be annoyed. "Certainly," he snapped back. "I regard Gordon Graham as an honest newspaperman."

On the other hand, Leahy often makes the mistake of deliberately avoiding the press when the opportunity for some friendly mixing is excellent. On the last two Southern California trips, Midwest sportswriters covering the game never saw Leahy after the Notre Dame train left Chicago. He remained in his master drawing room with his family and Fred Miller, former Notre Dame captain who is now the president of a great brewery. Nor was [Leahy] available to the writers in the hotel before or after the game. In fact, after the 1947 game which clinched the national championship for the Irish, he didn't even go down to the station to see his team start home.

It is impossible to state flatly that [he] does these things deliberately. It would be foolish to make such a statement. No man possessed of Leahy's capacities for tact, courtesy, and friendliness would go out of his way to make people dislike him in that way. It does seem, however, that [he] allows himself to coast now and then, perhaps on the theory that people know he is a busy man and don't expect him to do all the little things a less occupied person is required to do.

That is Leahy's problem. He may be busy, but he is going to have to figure out a way to find time for small talk and pleasantries if he wants the friendship and esteem of his fellow men, as well as their respect. He can get their respect merely by driving his football team to victory after monotonous victory because Americans always respect a winner. But he can get their affection only by breaking out of his shell.

How to sum up Frank Leahy, the enigma of Notre Dame? A difficult assignment. You say he is a great football coach, and you have said only a part of it. You say he is a man of good will, and you have merely touched upon one side of his bewilderingly complex personality. You say he is a living example of morality and all its virtues and rewards, and again you have only touched upon one phase of his character.

The good brothers who teach, and the men and boys who have studied or are studying under the Golden Dome at South Bend, might be inclined to dip into the song and story of the Notre Dame legend for the phrase that is most apt. They probably are closest to the mark when they stand up at one of their reunion banquets or a football rally and shout it out a thousand strong:

"He's a man! He's a man! He's a real Notre Dame man!"

Gary Cartwright, *SPORT* Magazine

PARSEGHIAN: "I HAVE TO KEEP MOVING"

It didn't take Ara Parseghian long to make his way into the winner's circle at Notre Dame once he took over starting in 1964. And it didn't take SPORT *magazine long to decide to publish its own study of what Parseghian had wrought under the Golden Dome. After the Irish won the 1966 national crown, Gary Cartwright (formerly of the* Dallas Morning News*) came by to describe what was happening.*

Ara Parseghian is named for a ninth-century B.C. Armenian king who strangled in his sleep while dreaming he was being chased by a roasted goat. Convenient as the moral seems, it says nothing about Ara Parseghian, the insomniac who hasn't slept more than three hours at a stretch since he was given the job of rebuilding Notre Dame's football dynasty.

[His] mother wanted a girl, not an heir to Knute Rockne. It was a desire she sublimated by keeping her son in pinafore and long curls even after he had learned to tell time and regard it as his natural enemy. When [he] secretly tried out and made his team at South Akron High School, his mother was astonished that he would rather crown a homecoming queen than be one. But like everyone else who has ever known Ara Parseghian, she was overwhelmed by his intensity. So was the editor of his high school yearbook, who blindly predicted, "He will become football coach at Notre Dame."

Ara Parseghian didn't think about it. He was too busy. He didn't think about the future in terms of where he was going, he was merely preoccupied with how long it would take to get there. Time, he has always assumed, is something to be captured, tamed, and put to the best possible use. "It's a funny thing about work, or the definition of work," the 44-year-old piper of the Irish was saying in his office at South Bend a few weeks before the start of the 1967 season. "If you're doing something you enjoy, it really isn't work even though you put in a lot of hours of what people consider work. You think in terms of objective and goal, and what you're trying to beat is time. There is just so much of it. Every minute wasted is a minute lost forever. There was a time not long ago when I couldn't sit still. I was always in a hurry. I don't know where the hell I was going, but I was always in a hurry to get there. I suppose I've slowed down a bit, but . . ."

Ara Parseghian still wears breakaway business suits. His thick black hair is cut short so that he can comb it with his fingers while he adjusts a clip-on tie and snuggles into his faceless loafers.

"I have to keep moving," he says, moving around his office, dark serious eyes reading the intent of each question, thick eyebrows arched in defense, mouth set tight and enclosed in parentheses, words spilling faster as the subject approaches a sensitive area—such as Notre Dame's 10–10 tie with Michigan State in 1966.

On the wall behind his desk is a portrait of Rockne—cocked hat, cocked smile, broken nose spread like an Indiana wheat field across his holy face. On an opposite wall is a clock. Rockne seems to be croaking, "Let's go, girls!" Parseghian looks at the picture, then at the clock, then, as if to break the tie, at his wristwatch.

He has been talking generally of his 1966 national champions, but specifically of today's college football player. He said, "Youngsters today are bigger and faster and more skilled when they get here. They have better medical care from birth. They have much better high school coaching than we had 20–25 years ago. On the other hand, I don't believe today's athlete is as hungry as we were. A nickel or a penny was very important to me. I didn't think of a car. I didn't think of a bicycle. I never owned a bicycle. Youngsters today are getting more, and getting it easier."

He looked at the clock, and at his watch, and he said, "The thing I try to impress on my players—anything of value must be earned. I don't care *what* it is. The things you appreciate in your life are the things you have a right to. Because you've earned that right. You study a situation, analyze it, put it together, sweat over it. Then you say: this is my best, and here it is."

What Ara Parseghian is most proud of in his entire life is being head football coach of the University of Notre Dame. He likes to say it stiffly: *The University of Notre Dame.* The University of Notre Dame job was not handed to him. He hustled it. The University of Notre Dame was a matchless symbol of what he had been in a hurry to reach. It was a national symbol; moreover, its football program was in a state of disgrace. After Frank Leahy resigned in February 1954—two years before Parseghian arrived on the big-time scene as head coach of Northwestern—the Fighting Irish plunged to mediocrity.

Parseghian was aware that his basic problem at Northwestern could not be patched by time. On two occasions the Wildcats were ranked No. 1, but they never had enough players to stay there. In eight years at Northwestern, Parseghian just about broke even, winning 36, losing 35, tying 1. What impressed Notre Dame officials was that Parseghian's Wildcats collected four of those wins at the expense of the Irish.

Contract in hand, Parseghian did something strange, even for Notre Dame. He announced that his objective and goal was to win a national championship. In two seasons (record: 16–3–1) he had the Irish turned in that direction for the first time in 17 years.

Tom Schoen, Notre Dame's excellent senior safetyman, was a member of the first class recruited by Parseghian. He recalls: "My first impression, he was very frank and forward. *Extremely* frank and forward! He outlined what he planned for X number of years (Schoen could not remember the exact number, believes it to be four), and what would be expected of us in return for the privilege [of] attending the university."

Parseghian did not mention that Schoen would be expected to win one for the Gipper.

"I wasn't interested in what had happened," Ara says without defacing tradition, "but rather what would happen. All I was concerned with was the future."

The veterans he inherited were shifted and reshifted until the smorgasbord became an exquisite menu. Meanwhile, Parseghian acquainted himself with the most complicated intelligence system in college football—the loyal, faceless band of fanatics known as the subway alumni.

"There were natural transition problems that you would find at any university," he says. "Things like understanding university policy, finding out who your helpers are, working in a new staff, and assigning staff members certain recruiting territories. The job was further complicated by the fact that Notre Dame is a national institution. I knew that Notre Dame recruited on a national basis, but it was still a great revelation seeing it. It is a staggering experience going through one week's mail."

Not that Parseghian is offended by the doctrine of institutionalism. It seems to fit him. Players refer to him as "God" and assume that there is a cornerstone under the stretch band of his beltless trousers. [He] plays the schedule that was given him—and will until 1973, at which time he will have a voice in selecting opponents. Yet he is uncommon to Notre Dame tradition. He has never claimed to be Catholic, and he holds several colors more dear than blue and gold. He preaches positive thinking, not inspiration. With only traces of Rockne's emotional tremor or Leahy's studied charm, Ara Parseghian may be a better coach than either because his is the doctrine of "total preparation."

He claims that as a football coach today he is primarily a salesman. "Your job," Ara says, "is to convince the boys that the ultimate objective and goal far exceed anything else. A coach must confront different personalities and handle different problems, but there are observations you make on the field under physical and emotional stress. The basic thing in the back of *every* boy's mind who plays for the University of Notre Dame must be 'our objective and goal' and the belief that this exceeds anything else."

Although he did not realize it at the time, Parseghian's career took shape before his junior year at Miami of Ohio. Sid Gillman, now coach and general manager of the San Diego Chargers, was then Miami's head coach. George Blackburn, now head coach at Virginia, was in charge of the backfield. This was not Parseghian's first acquaintance with efficiency and excellence, having played under Paul Brown and Blanton Collier [at] Great Lakes Naval Training Station, but it was his turning point.

In a casual conversation, Gillman told his young pupil that coaches need a degree in education. Parseghian had never thought about coaching. He was studying business administration. What caught his attention was the way Gillman said it: "If you *want* to coach . . ."

Parseghian says now, "Apparently that was enough for me. I changed my major. I didn't know it then, but I had already had a postgraduate course in how to coach a football team. Paul Brown was a great organizer and had a great overall fundamental concept of the game. Blanton Collier had an amazing technical mind, a fantastic grasp of fundamentals. Sid was much like Blanton: vast knowledge, great technician. Sid was also an exceptionally hard worker. I saw the hours that he put in, but there again he never thought of it in terms of work. From Blackburn I learned something about handling players. He showed me that beyond technique and strategy there is an emotional side to the game. He had this rapport with his players."

[He] recalls that Woody Hayes added to his education. Hayes, he says, "was an unusual man. Not so technique-minded as Blanton Collier, but very honest, very realistic in his approach. And there wasn't anything he wouldn't do for his boys. He was much like Blackburn in that respect."

Parseghian was to study again under Brown and Collier with the Cleveland Browns, but after a short, injury-diverted pro career he turned toward his destiny. For a year he coached the Miami of Ohio freshmen under Hayes. When Hayes departed for Ohio State, Parseghian had himself a football team.

Almost immediately he made national headlines when his Miami team upset a Big Ten team, Indiana, 6–0. Parseghian chuckles his weren't-they-good-times? laugh when he remembers that game, or rather the events that led to it. Citizens of Bloomington, Indiana, lured by the curiosity of inspecting a small-college power firsthand, came out to watch Parseghian's men practice the day before the game. [He] had reckoned they would. That is why he fetched along two sets of uniforms, one scraggly and faded, another new and vivid. From the offices of the Salvation Army to the backstreet drugstore where the local bookmaker operated, word spread: [Parseghian] and his boys are in town. Whatever impressions the talk made on the Hoosiers, they played the following afternoon as though the game were shells and dried peas. Miami, on the other hand, put on its new uniforms and played like all Parseghian teams—expertly prepared to get the most out of what they had.

Brown, Collier, Gillman, Blackburn, and Hayes were good mentors, and being head coach at Notre Dame meant being all of them and maybe something more. It meant finding a way to motivate a traditional nonconference, nonbowl team through a 10-game schedule that regularly includes Purdue and Michigan State from the Big Ten, Navy and Pitt from the East, Southern Cal from the West, plus an armada of variety that ranges from Miami Florida to Army to Oklahoma. It meant constant attention from the national press. The thought occurs that had positions been reversed when Notre Dame and Michigan State played their infamous 10–10 tie, the clamor would have been limited, if not in scope at least in duration. This was *The University of Notre Dame* playing for a tie! You may find Joe Louis in the kitchen making fudge, or Toots Shor serving punch to Blue Birds, but never Notre Dame calling for a truce while one Irishman still wiggles.

"I keep hearing all this so-called criticism," [Parseghian] says, "but I can't find people who know what plays were called or why they were called." Reconstructing what 50 million television viewers thought they saw, [he] explained, "You know, we ran a draw play—the greatest play in the world against a team that's expecting a pass. [Then] we ran an option, a run-or-pass option, with Coley O'Brien, only Bubba Smith came in there and knocked him off for a seven-yard loss. The only play we ran (i.e., the only give-up play) was in the final six seconds when O'Brien ran a sneak. There was a great deal of intelligence that went into every call. But that's history."

The institutional dogma that makes Parseghian's job comfortable in the spring makes it almost too hot to handle in the fall. And for the same reason: Notre Dame is a national university. When a sports columnist can't think of anything to say about his local team—or when he finds the subject too daring—he will write about the University of Notre Dame.

There is a theory, for example, that Parseghian is too much for his men, that he cannot share his amazing energy and passion for what lesser men call "work." The charge, in other words, is that he wears out a team. As evidence, critics cite the final game of 1964 when unbeaten Notre Dame blew a 17–0 halftime lead, losing a game to USC and costing them the national championship. They recall, too, how his 1965 team won seven of its first eight games with little to recommend it except a brilliant defense, and then, seemingly on the down side of the hill, finished with a loss and a tie.

No one has actually proved the critics right. But playing for Ara Parseghian is no doubt an emotional and psychological chore, the sort of trip that makes heroes out of great men but leaves others to babble out their troubles to a casual fire hydrant or move to Haight-Ashbury and take up the loom.

Before the showdown at East Lansing, Parseghian had only one short message for his team. "He just told us," recalls Schoen, "that we were about to play 'the biggest game in the nation in a decade.'"

Since Parseghian's objective and goal is a national championship, he regards the criticism as inevitable but shortsighted. Listen to [him] on the suggestion that he emotionally wears down his team: "That's very interesting. Let's review. In 1964 we won our ninth-straight game here against a good Iowa team, 28–0. Then we went to Southern California, went from 11-degree temperatures to 85-degree temperatures. At the half we led, 17–0. After three quarters we led, 17–7. We lost in the last one minute and 33 seconds, 20–17. Well, we won nine games, and we led three quarters and 13⅓ minutes before losing our 10th game. Now if you want to make that criticism valid, there it is.

"The next year, which is a year I'm really proud of because we won seven, lost two, and tied one with a team that really didn't have a passing combination, so we had to play our guts out on defense, this happened: our next to last game, we lost to Michigan State, 12–7, here at the stadium. Michigan State was undefeated and stayed that way (if you don't count its Rose Bowl loss). So that wasn't so bad. The final week we went down to Miami under very similar conditions (to the USC trip of 1964). Hot, humid, a drastic change of climate from the cold Midwest. We played to a tie. Everyone was up in arms because we didn't throw the ball more. We knew we couldn't throw. Because of our personnel we had to play a possession-type game."

Only the most foolish critic has ever considered a Parseghian team timid. Wherever he travels, Parseghian tries to arm himself with an outstanding passing combination. At Northwestern he had Tommy Myers and Paul Flatley. Heisman Trophy winner John Huarte and Jack Snow preceded Terry Hanratty, O'Brien, and Jim Seymour. Navy coach Bill Elias pondered the ways of Ara Parseghian and concluded, "It's probably because his ancestors got practice catching figs that fell out of trees."

There are two things Parseghian cannot abide: dog-pile football and wasted time. Fortunately, one does not appear to follow the other.

For example, consider the case of Notre Dame's comical trip to Norman, Oklahoma, last season to play the University of Oklahoma.

Despite experiences in Los Angeles and Miami, Parseghian likes to keep his team on campus until the last possible minute before a road trip. So the Irish worked on their own practice field that Friday afternoon, then caught a chartered jet at 3:00 P.M.

An hour later the plane made an emergency landing in Chicago.

"You may be familiar with Chicago's air traffic on a Friday afternoon," [Parseghian] says. "It looks like D-day. Anyway, we did get the plane repaired and took off with a nice tailwind. The trouble was, just before we landed the pilot called me up and said we'd have to wait 25 or 30 minutes for a gate at Oklahoma City."

[He] chuckles ("heh heh") then he tells the story: "OK, so we finally get a gate and there are two buses waiting for us. Only one of them won't start. We're already late for our evening meal. I'm going mad. I cram 70 players and our coaches in one bus and leave the other members of the party to wait. When we get to the motel, they give me a suite with no air conditioning. My bedroom is right over the private club. It's hot as blazes, and all night I'm listening to rock 'n' roll music.

"Any coach who says he is not superstitious is . . . well, the trip was planned and organized, but it didn't come off. The game was planned and organized, too. . . . So several other things went wrong. But you know what? We played one hell of a game!"

At [age] 44, Ara Parseghian is at the top. It is a higher plateau than the one Rockne ascended simply because the stairway today is cluttered with more sound teams. The question, then, is what does [he] do for an encore?

Well, for openers Parseghian laughs, then he says, "That's another phase of the game that is damn important. Just because you win one doesn't mean you get tired of winning. First of all, we want to represent the University of Notre Dame in a dignified, high-class manner, and play good, clean football. Then, there is our objective and goal."

And every second a crazed, killer clock to confront.

Paul A. Witteman, *TIME* Magazine

THE FELLA EXPECTS TO WIN

It's not often that a magazine like TIME *devotes a two-page profile to a college athletic figure. But that's the sort of impact Lou Holtz had on Notre Dame and the collegiate culture once he came to South Bend and revved up Irish teams on the field. Paul Witteman provided this look at the Irish coach and his handiwork near the end of the 1989 season.*

Take a peek at the guy in the baseball cap. Short fella. Kinda homely. Ears hanging out there like wind spoilers. Talks with a trace of a lisp. Looks like he'd be at home on the showroom floor of any Sears store in Middle America moving metal. Appliances, that is. Be good at it too. Get you right into that Kenmore 831 series washer when what you were really thinking about was the 701 at 56 bucks less. But oh so politely, so that you later reckon it was your idea in the first place. Bet he loves to fish and swap tall tales. Family man. Churchgoer. Never kicked the dog.

Look again.

The short fella is not so short, not quite so homely. It just seems that way because his 5'10", 148-pound frame is diminished standing, as he is, at the edge of a grove of young Paul Bunyans. He's talking to—no, he's shouting at—one of them. About the option play. How to execute it correctly. As he plants one foot and pivots decisively, moving his hands in a precise pattern that he's repeated thousands of times before, the young man in the football jersey barks, "Yes, sir! Yes, sir!"

The lisp is less evident now, and any thoughts one may have had of this man idling afternoons away over a fishing rod disappear. Abruptly, he turns away from his quarterback and stalks downfield toward the defense. Out of the corners of their eyes, the helmeted giants and his assistant coaches see him coming. Chests tighten. The execution and speed of the defensive drills rev up a notch. The simple reason: no one is eager to receive one-on-one remedial instruction from Louis Leo Holtz on this or any upcoming autumn afternoon.

Just plain Lou Holtz. The name doesn't resonate like Knute Rockne or George Gipp, men around whom the legend of Notre Dame football has been molded. It doesn't sound larger than life, like the Four Horsemen or the Golden Boy, players who subsequently graced the annals of the Fighting Irish. Nor does it seem of sufficient luster to be mentioned in the same sentence with Frank Leahy and Ara Parseghian, coaches who won multiple national championships and were subsequently canonized by fanatic subway alumni. Holtz would be the first to agree with all this. "All I ever wanted was a job in the mill, a car, $5 in my pocket, and a girl," he says with his sly, lopsided grin.

So much for aiming low. In four seasons as coach at the University of Notre Dame, Holtz has returned the school to the pinnacle of college football from which it had fallen in mortification under the earnest but inept Gerry Faust. Last year Holtz drove a young, tentative team to a 12–0 record and a national championship with a variation of the message that ugly ducklings can become beautiful swans if they work hard, love one another, and believe they can be great. Holtz fervently believes that. He also devoutly embraces traditional values, specifically the importance of having on his side God, ferocious linebackers, and halfbacks who, once they are given the football, run like scalded dogs.

This year Notre Dame is 11–0 after last Saturday's 34–23 defeat of Penn State, and two wins away from a second-consecutive national title. The Irish could conceivably stumble this weekend against Miami or on New Year's night against undefeated Big Eight champion Colorado. But the 23 consecutive victories Holtz has directed add up to an achievement unmatched by any of his more illustrious predecessors.

How has this self-described wimp done it? Not with mirrors, although one of Holtz's secondary skills is the ability to perform parlor magic tricks. First and foremost he is a disciplinarian in the Vince Lombardi mold. In his first team meeting in 1985, he looked around and saw players slouching in their seats. He ordered them in no uncertain terms to sit at attention from that point on. Says senior defensive tackle Jeff Alm, who is almost one foot taller and 120 pounds heavier than Holtz, "He's not the biggest guy in the world, but he seems to possess a lot of power." Last month a furious Holtz told the team he would resign if they ever fought again with opposing players as they did before their game against USC. There was a laugh from the back of the room. Holtz cast a withering glance in the direction of the offender, according to someone who was there. "I'll make sure you lose your scholarship first," he rasped.

Holtz is a master salesman. Junior defensive back Todd Lyght was recruited by Michigan, Michigan State, and UCLA when he was a high school senior in Flint, Michigan. But Holtz told Lyght that if he came to Notre Dame he would be part of a national-championship team. "I looked deep into his eyes, and I knew he was telling the truth," says

Lyght. Holtz also persuaded quarterback Tony Rice, tailback Ricky Watters, and flanker Raghib "Rocket" Ismail—players who have been crucial to the Irish success—to enroll at Notre Dame. Not that Notre Dame, with its mystique and a virtual farm team of Catholic high schools providing talent, needs additional help on the recruiting front. Says Beano Cook, the acerbic college football analyst for the ESPN television network, "It's easy to win at Notre Dame. They get enough material to win the AFC West."

Holtz also possesses the ability to make young people believe in themselves. His sharply honed self-deprecation is designed in part to demonstrate to his players that if a 98-pound weakling like him can succeed, surely they can. Holtz likes to tell his coaches, "If you preach something long enough, people are going to believe it. Especially in our case, where it's true."

Then there are his work habits. His days begin with daily mass at 6:00 A.M. and end with paperwork at midnight. He will leave no memo or chart or report unturned that could contribute to victory. On top of all that, Holtz is widely regarded as one of the game's finest technicians, along with Joe Paterno of Penn State and Bobby Bowden of Florida State. Says Bill Walsh, who was viewed as a tactical genius while coaching the San Francisco 49ers, "Lou has great command of game situations and the game itself."

As a result, little Lou Holtz from East Liverpool, Ohio, looms as one of the biggest men on—and well beyond—the Notre Dame campus in South Bend, Indiana. His 35-minute motivational video, *Do Right with Lou Holtz of Notre Dame*, has sold briskly. The living, breathing version of Holtz is totally booked on the lecture circuit through 1990 at an estimated $10,000 per inspirational pop. Moreover, he has his own syndicated cable TV show and a national radio call-in program, and he's featured in magazine ads promoting the Holtz philosophy, paid for by Volkswagen. These things tend to happen when you win.

Ay, there's the rub. A coach is expected to win at Notre Dame. Win a lot—while still putting academics first and observing the NCAA rules of conduct. "If you keep the rules," the Reverend Theodore Hesburgh, then Notre Dame's president, told Holtz at his final prehiring interview, "I will give you five years. If you ever cut corners, you will be out of here by midnight." "We like to win," says the school's current president, the Reverend Edward A. "Monk" Malloy, who as a Notre Dame undergraduate was a varsity basketball player. As a measure of exactly how much Notre Dame likes to win, Malloy describes the 17–9 season the Irish basketball team had during his senior year in the following way: "It wasn't what you would call successful."

Holtz, growing up scrawny along a crook in the Ohio River, where Ohio, West Virginia, and Pennsylvania converge and steel mills and potteries hunker cheek by sooty jowl, was not what you would call successful either. "Everybody felt so sorry for him," says Joe McNicol, a classmate at St. Aloysius Grammar School and a fellow altar boy. "He was always the last person picked for teams." When his uncle Lou Tychonievich started a football team at St. Al's, young [Holtz] learned every position so as to improve his chances of seeing action. He also studied the playbook, such as it was, and occasionally tugged at his uncle's sleeve: "He would try to tell me what play I should call." Sister Mary Roberts, the principal at St. Al's, broadcast Notre Dame's victory march over the loudspeaker each afternoon as school adjourned, perhaps because she belonged to the Order of Notre Dame. No wonder Holtz subsequently told his family that he would someday coach the Fighting Irish.

Holtz avoided a lifetime sentence in the mills and went off to Kent State, where he played as a lightweight and little-noticed linebacker. After graduation he learned his craft as a ubiquitous assistant coach in a succession of schools: Iowa, William and Mary, Connecticut. But it was after accepting a job at the University of South Carolina, only to watch helplessly as the position was temporarily eliminated, that Holtz began to lay out the rest of his life with some purpose. He made a list of 107 things he wished to accomplish, naturally including leading the Fighting Irish and being chosen Coach of the Year (others on the list: having an audience with the pope, landing on an aircraft carrier, scoring a hole in one). To date he has achieved 89 of the 107.

That was in 1966. Four years later, as the young head coach of William and Mary, he took that school to its only bowl game. Seven years after that, he suspended three star players from his Arkansas squad for violating team rules on the eve of an Orange Bowl showdown against heavily favored Oklahoma. Arkansas still managed to win, 31–6, another example of Holtz's turning adversity into unlikely advantage.

The Holtz ability to crack wise, usually at his own expense, has kept his teams loose. But the self-deprecation also allows him to ward off praise, which he feels is the father of complacency. "When it's over, maybe I'll sit down and say, 'Gee, we did something pretty terrific,'" he says. "But it's just not my nature."

"He doesn't really accept compliments," says his son Kevin, a student at Notre Dame law school. When Notre Dame beat Pittsburgh 45–7 in October, Kevin called to congratulate him. What did Dad say in reply? "Kevin, did you see that SMU won 35–9?"

Holtz had even less reason to fear SMU, whom his team eventually trounced 59–6, than he did Pitt. But like most coaches he dreads games against "cupcake" opponents because of the danger that his own heavily favored players might lose concentration and intensity, and hence lose in an upset. Before the Pitt game, he assured reporters that Pitt was only slightly less dangerous than Rommel's panzers. Yet at practice he was telling his players that Pitt was more like the army of Grenada and that he expected the Irish to beat the bejabbers out of them. When this inconsistency is raised, Holtz is only momentarily at a loss. "We just point out the problems to the public and the press," he says. "We tell the players the problems and the solutions."

The 18-hour days that Holtz habitually puts in on the problems and the solutions are beginning to wear on him. In addition, he is doubtless feeling the stress stemming from accusations that he gave money through a third party to a player at his last school, Minnesota. Holtz emphatically denies it. Now one hears the word *burnout* in South Bend. "Football encompasses his whole life. It's everything" says Kevin Holtz. Says Ara Parseghian, who quit, worn out, after 11 successful years, "I told him all summer, 'Please pace yourself.'" When asked what lessons he draws from the experiences of Parseghian and Leahy, who also was totally consumed by the job, Holtz merely says, "I'm a slow learner."

That's because goal-oriented Lou Holtz is on a mission. He wants to win his second-consecutive national championship, although he would never freely admit it. But he quietly asked coaches like Bill Walsh how they tried to avoid a letdown after their teams won championships. How long can he keep it up? His answer is pure Holtz, all deceptive diffidence and then steely follow-through. "I don't think we can win every game," he says carefully. "Just the next one."

David Haugh, *The Sporting News*

THE FALLBACK SPRINGS FORWARD

Tyrone Willingham made believers of more than just Notre Dame foot-
ball players in his very first year on the job in 2002. A 10–2 regular-
season record put the Irish front and center in the minds of college
football fans—but the way in which he went about his job had more to
do with the Sportsman of the Year award he won from The Sporting
News *that year.* South Bend Tribune *columnist David Haugh wrote this*
piece to celebrate the award.

The first of 16 speeches Tyrone Willingham gave on a night back in
June started at 7:00. Charles Lennon, the president of Notre Dame's
alumni association, had heard and read the same things about
Willingham everybody else had: that he rationed his words no matter
how hungry his audience was for information, that Willingham's personality fit the public's demands for being Notre Damn's football
coach as well as a monk with a vow of silence fit the role of talk-radio
host, that Willingham lacked the gravitas required for this particular
position—a college football calling.

But Lennon knew better because Lennon knew Willingham long
before Notre Dame hired him and long before Willingham became the
first college football coach to be named [the Sporting News']
Sportsman of the Year. The two met six years ago when Notre Dame
was playing Stanford and the schools' alumni groups cosponsored a
luncheon on the Palo Alto, California, campus a day before the game.
Lennon and his wife, Joan, parked in the wrong lot and entered the
wrong building. The Lennons were lost until a gentlemanly black man
asked if he could help, even though he was in a hurry. "He just told
Joan and me to follow him," Lennon says.

Of course Willingham did. Leading the way is what he does—then,
now, and back on that warm June night on the Notre Dame campus.
He finished the first speech to an alumni reunion dinner crowd in
about 10 minutes, hopped on a golf cart, and headed to the next. At

each stop, the emcee introduced the man that Domers, still scarred from the previous winter's losing and lying, were desperate to hear. "He talked to 16 different alumni groups that night and said something different each time and got 16 standing ovations," Lennon says.

By 10:00, Willingham had wrapped up the last of his shake-down-the-thunder sermons, this one to the Class of 1977 celebrating its 25-year reunion. Willingham made this his final stop so he could renew old acquaintances with Michael and Cynthia Parseghian, the son and daughter-in-law of Ara, a Notre Dame legend. A few years ago at Stanford, Willingham got to know the Parseghians after quietly sponsoring a charity event to raise money for the Ara Parseghian Medical Research Foundation. The foundation strives to develop a treatment and cure for the rare Niemann-Pick Type C disease that has claimed the lives of two of Mike and Cindy Parseghian's children.

"The only thing I remember Ty saying when he got done talking after his last speech was that he was very emotional about what he had just experienced," Lennon says. "And how happy and proud he was to be able to do it here at Notre Dame."

He compared himself to a Martian. When talking about his impact on college football, Willingham didn't compare himself to past successful Notre Dame coaches such as Ara Parseghian or Lou Holtz. When talking about his social importance off the field, Willingham didn't compare himself to legendary black sports figures such as Eddie Robinson or Jackie Robinson. Instead, Willingham compared himself to a Martian.

"What do we really know about Martians?" Willingham says. "Do they exist? How do they live? Yet I'd say we probably have a bias against them. But if we became more educated about them, we wouldn't have that bias, would we? If we're going to live on Mars, I need to know more about Martians."

Willingham is one of three black head coaches employed by the 117 Division I-A college football programs—he's the Martian in his analogy—and the first in any sport at Notre Dame. According to the Black Coaches Association, only 17 black head coaches have been hired for 348 Division I-A openings since 1982. When Willingham was asked before the Notre Dame–Florida State game about his views on the BCA's proposal that one of every five vacancies be filled by a black head coach, he politely declined. That makes him a focused coach, but hardly a reluctant pioneer.

Willingham grew up in the sixties in Jacksonville, North Carolina, which prepared him for a world that often has different rules for blacks and whites. As a boy, he had to watch *Old Yeller* at the Onslow Theatre from the balcony. He watched Georgetown High, a black school where his mother taught, mysteriously burn to the ground on graduation day. Four years later at Jacksonville High, Willingham beat out a white quarterback for a starting position when the concept of integration was as comfortable as North Carolina's humidity.

Willingham, 48, knows all about racial tension and will talk about it with passion and purpose. Funny how more people than ever on the Notre Dame campus, where 3.2 percent of the undergraduate students are black, have joined the conversation.

"It is a crime," Willingham says of the lack of black head coaches in college football. "Any time we as a people don't allow another person to express their talents based on color, religion, or sexual preference, we deprive someone the ability to reach their potential. It's a crime. It's not just a black thing."

He applauds the BCA's initiative. He longs for the day when men like Willie Jeffries can view the profession with more pride than anger. When Jeffries was hired at Wichita State in 1979, he became the first black head coach in Division I football outside of historically black colleges. "It's racial," Jeffries says. "Most of the athletic directors making $150,000 with perks don't want to go out on a limb, and that's 50 percent of the problem!"

More than half of the solution, Willingham acknowledges, involves winning. He readily acknowledges that without being the first coach in Notre Dame history to win 10 games in his first year, without beating as many top 25 teams (four) as any program in America, without doubling the Irish win total from last season, he still would be considered a work in progress. Not a legend in the making. "When one sees that someone can handle the requirements of a certain job, that is an education," the son of a teacher says. "Education makes it easier for change to occur."

So he educates, one person at a time.

He played with kids during a promotional photo shoot at the Boys and Girls Club in South Bend, the same center where about a dozen Irish players showed up every Monday to play Ping-Pong and video games. Thirty of those children accepted Willingham's invitation to be guests at Notre Dame's final pep rally.

He has spoken to Saint Mary's College students, high school football teams, black church congregations, and mostly white civic groups. People—regardless of race, creed, or color—are hanging on his words like they have hooks. "I don't think we've had a sports leader make the type of impact he has had in this community," says Reverend Donald Alford of the Pentecostal Cathedral Church of God in Christ. "He has united people in the community and begun to change the image of what young football players are today, and even change the image of this community."

Community activism comes naturally for Willingham. His parents, Lilian and Nathaniel, once converted part of their home into a place where at-risk kids could spend time. Lilian, the first black on the local board of education, contributed so much that there is a Jacksonville parkway named after her.

When Tyrone Willingham arrived in South Bend, his definition of needy went far beyond the football depth chart. "It's my belief that this is a great community, but one that has struggled with its own identity," he says. "There were a lot of people saying, 'You shouldn't take that job. You were 25th on the list of 26 candidates.'"

He peeks out his office window. It's 28 degrees and snowing. He arches an eyebrow and grins. "And people in this community, partly because of the weather, say, 'Why would you come to South Bend from Palo Alto?'" he says. "Well, what's wrong with South Bend? There's nothing wrong with South Bend."

The man Notre Dame players call "the Prophet" took a similar tack with his football team: *there's nothing wrong with you.* Willingham didn't worry about coaching the Irish from the shoulders down until August, if then. The first team meeting last January set the tone for an attitude overhaul, which is as responsible for the team's turnaround as quarterback Carlyle Holiday or cornerback Shane Walton. Willingham used a 45-minute PowerPoint presentation that concluded with a single click of the mouse and the word *win* appearing on the screen. The room erupted with hope, which had been destroyed. The program's dysfunction started to dissipate that day.

Almost a year later, Willingham has had such a profound effect on his players that senior wide receiver Arnaz Battle said after his final home game that Willingham is "like a father to me."

"We're all seeking some type of spiritual peace, some type of oneness in the world in which we live," Willingham says. "I do know that those individuals who find their place spiritually find their place in the world. If one is at peace with self, that is an amazing accomplishment. If one can create love, love is frictionless. I've been taught things run smoother the less friction you have."

Each day as Willingham walks out of his office, he walks past a large gray stone on the floor. Engraved in capital letters is the word *INSPIRE.*

They say the eyes are the windows to the soul. Or is it the eyelets? In the Notre Dame locker room on football Saturdays this fall, win or lose, athletic director Kevin White would stare at the ground the instant he saw Tyrone Willingham. White was not looking away from Willingham as much as he was looking inside him.

White would spot the tiny gold circle he was looking for, a medallion about the size of a nickel bearing the likeness of a Catholic saint on the front, handed out at the team's pregame mass. As a matter of routine, Willingham, a devout Methodist, took the Catholic symbol, strung one of the laces on his Adidas through it, and wore it on his shoe during the games as a nod to all the people who call Notre Dame "Our Lady's school."

"To me, that's more than just subscribing to the ideals of this place, that's living it," White says. "Every time I see him with one of those medals in his shoes, I get goose bumps. When I see that, I see how he's bought into Notre Dame—big time."

There was a time, of course, when White wasn't so sure. The first time he met with Willingham about the Notre Dame job was before White hired George O'Leary "straight out of central casting." White wanted to see more outward signs of Willingham's passion for Notre Dame then—wanted to hear how badly Willingham yearned for that calling. It wasn't until after White called Willingham back—after O'Leary resigned for having false information on his résumé—that Willingham boldly declared, "You should have hired me the first time." Had Willingham come on that strong in the initial meeting, who knows?

In White's mind he needed to hire a man with an obvious affection for Notre Dame, partly to show how strong his own is. "My interpretation of Ty [in that first meeting] could have been screened by my own insecurity," White says.

The most rewarding year of Willingham's professional life has been the most trying of White's. The man who brought Willingham to Notre Dame rarely gets credit for doing so because there is a perception White never would have asked if Jon Gruden had a less-confining contract or if Bob Stoops had a less-appreciative employer. Even Willingham has joked that he was either "three, five, seven, or nine," on White's list.

White deflects credit for his hiring power to a higher power. "Divine intervention, that's what it was," he says. "The Notre Dame family prides itself in two personal characteristics: respect and humility. Ty has taken those two ideals to another level. Just by being extremely humble. Just by being himself."

Jerome Willingham has heard from his famous older brother about three or four times this football season—less frequently than when Tyrone was at Stanford. But in those precious few conversations, he heard the excitement within his brother that the public rarely sees. "People think it doesn't affect him," Jerome says. "It has. He tells me about the pep rallies and how there's nothing like it. He's emotional; he just doesn't show it."

Win or lose. Former Notre Dame tailback Allen Pinkett, a radio color commentator for Irish football, will remember this season more for the way Willingham handled losing to Boston College than the way the Irish beat Michigan or Florida State. Pinkett even left a phone message at Willingham's office thanking him for setting such a positive example in handling defeat.

"The poise he's exemplified, that's what we alums want Notre Dame to be," Pinkett says. "It's like he was born to coach at Notre Dame."

Born to lead, he is the Ty that binds.

The unique magic of Notre Dame football is what has separated the Irish from any other program throughout history.

Section IV
THE MYSTIQUE

Bill Furlong, *SPORT* Magazine

WAKING UP THE ECHOES

There's been no bigger turnaround in football at Notre Dame than in 1964, when Ara Parseghian came to town. He took the Irish to within an eyelash of a national championship that first fall, going to 9–1 after a 2–7 record the previous season under interim boss Hugh Devore. It was the start of a glorious era of Ara for Irish football. Bill Furlong wrote about it in the spring of 1965.

"It's dark outside and cold," wrote Father Hesburgh. "There is a strange quiet on campus. . . ." It was the evening after Notre Dame lost to the University of Southern California, 20–17, with 1:34 remaining in the season. "Southern California had done it to us before, and we have done it to them, too, but somehow the world went on, the sun rose again the next morning, and people began to dream of next year. . . ."

—Notre Dame *Scholastic*

Years from now, Notre Dame will look at 1964 as merely an episode in its football history. The season was bizarre, exhilarating, almost stunning in its incredulity, but an episode nevertheless. Its significance is less in its drama than in being the turning point from shadow into sunshine for the Fighting Irish. For years, the shadows had been deepening around Notre Dame football. The Irish had not had a winning season in five years. Not only were they losing regularly, they were losing badly; in defeat Notre Dame could not console itself that it nevertheless offered "excellence" on the football field. The sense on campus was one of mystery: "Where is it now," wrote the 19th-century poet, "the glory and the dream?"

Then in 1964 the sun broke through and Notre Dame was bathed in glory once again. It was more than anybody might have dreamed. [Ara] Parseghian prayed publicly for a 5–5 season and prayed privately for a 6–4 season. When the Irish lost the final game of the season to USC in the final quarter, they wound up with a 9–1 record ("I prefer to think of it as a 9¾–¼ record," says Parseghian). The turnabout was attributed to some mystical, some occult power of Parseghian. If that fades, goes the thinking, Notre Dame fades. But Notre Dame will not fade—at least from excellence. Because the turnabout was due to a number of factors: modest, mundane, meaningful—the artless roots of success. Among them are (1) organization, (2) the proper use of personnel, (3) the uses of strategy, and (4) the stimulus of spirit. Parseghian labored with these tools to build a permanent foundation. His aim was excellence; his result was triumph.

From the very first, his impact on campus was almost electric. Parseghian is an intensely physical man, and he moves in a continuing nimbus of excitement. He wears clip-on ties, shoes without laces, and trousers with elastic waist bands so that he can save a few moments. "Seems like I'm always in a rush," he says. "I'm always in a rush. Don't know where I'm goin', but I'm always in a *rush!*" The feverish excitement of his rush inspired a fever of success at Notre Dame. Yet it was not the style alone but also the substance that created confidence. The men of Notre Dame simply liked the way Parseghian worked.

One of his first moves, for instance, was to ask John Ray and Bernie Crimmins to join his staff. Both had been candidates for the head job. (Ray accepted, Crimmins didn't. "But the thing this tells you about Parseghian is that he's not afraid to hire the men who might succeed him," says one friend.) Parseghian threw open spring practice to everyone in the school, not just to those on football scholarships. He immersed himself in the rough-and-tumble give-and-take of practice. He ran pass patterns, led calisthenics, drove for blocks on the offensive line. "I can't coach from a tower," he says. "I must be in the huddle. I must be in the line. I must be in the action. I must be—I must feel a part of it." By the end of spring training, he'd so inspired his team with the need for never giving up on nailing the ball carrier that Notre Dame men were paraphrasing the Declaration of Independence: "Life, liberty, and the happiness of pursuit!"

The excitement he generated was contagious. Said one player, "The first time I met him, I knew he was a man I could play for." A student wrote in the Notre Dame *Scholastic* that he'd received the news of Parseghian's arrival "in much the same way as I imagine Americans must have received news of V-J day after suffering through World War II." Said one alumnus, "He goes after a weak spot like a surgeon. In many ways he's a better organizer than Leahy. He evaluates talent like a computer." Says the Reverend Edmund P. Joyce, executive vice president of the university, "Ara has certainly won the hearts of everybody down here with his dynamism and his organizational ability."

While Parseghian was stimulating hope and excitement on campus, he was also hiring assistant coaches, organizing his staff, and launching a recruiting drive that would preserve the future. There was no chronological order to all this. Take the matter of recruiting. It had to start the moment Parseghian took the job. It couldn't wait until everything else was tidied up. One immensely important factor was where to place the chief emphasis of recruiting last year. The 1963 freshman team recruited by Hugh Devore, Parseghian's predecessor, was heavily populated with excellent linemen. Devore's success was reflected in last year's defensive team: all four linemen and one first-string linebacker were sophomores.

So Parseghian's problem was finding backs. First of all he had to find replacements for the five passers and fullbacks who would be seniors in 1964. He also sought out halfbacks who were more stream-lined than those recruited by Joe Kuharich, head coach from 1959 through 1962. Kuharich appeared to prefer the huge, heavy halfback. At one point [Kuharich] had in his backfield a pair of running backs—Jim Snowden and Paul Costa—whose combined weight was about 500 pounds. Parseghian much prefers the lighter, faster halfback—the whippet instead of the St. Bernard.

"We like to get the boys who can run and who may put on some muscle and grow up into a little heavier halfback," says Parseghian, "rather than the boy who's already big and still has to learn how to run." The result: one insider estimates "70 to 75 percent of the best prospects on the freshman team last year were backs." And the fresh-man halfbacks ranged from 160 pounds to no more than 190 pounds.

At the same time, Parseghian analyzed the varsity players and their capacity. He discovered a lot of good men were in the wrong jobs. He continued the analysis into the first 2½ weeks of spring training, then undertook the biggest upheaval of player personnel in Notre Dame history. He moved Pete Duranko from fullback to guard and then to linebacker. To guard he moved Dick Arrington, who had been an aggressive but small 5'11" tackle; Arrington is a strong 1965 All-America candidate. Parseghian moved one of the team's fastest half-backs, Nick Rassas, to defensive safety and teamed him up with a couple of aspiring quarterbacks named Tom Carey and Tom Longo. As a unit they picked off 13 passes. Parseghian took a defensive halfback and tight end named Jack Snow and moved him to split end. Snow broke every pass-receiving record in Notre Dame history.

Parseghian's most important decision was at quarterback. The dis-covery of John Huarte was not as sudden as many suppose. When Parseghian arrived, his choice was between Huarte and 5'9" Alex "Sandy" Bonvechio, who lacked Huarte's passing skill and who seemed too short to see over the onrushing linemen. Yet he was Huarte's supe-rior in moving the club and in calling plays. Bonvechio could be an excellent quarterback on a ballclub that emphasized running. But Parseghian wanted to emphasize passing; he wanted somebody who could deliver the ball to a fine receiver like Snow. He chose Huarte, who wound up setting school records with 114 completions and 2,062 yards passing, tying Bobby Williams' record of 16 touchdown passes and becoming Notre Dame's sixth Heisman Trophy winner.

If Notre Dame doesn't score 30 points-plus as often as it did last year, a lack of a passing attack will probably be the big reason. And it might be as difficult to replace Snow as it is Huarte. The loss of fullback Joe Farrell will also be felt in the passing attack.

The leading receiver this year could be tight end Phil Sheridan, who caught 20 passes last season. Halfback Nick Eddy caught 16, and he'll be valuable as a receiver too. With Bill Wolski and Eddy back at halfbacks, the Irish could be devastating on the ground.

Neither line presents much worries, largely because of a virtual talent pool from which Parseghian can draw. But it is the defensive line that is especially potent. All were regulars last year as sophomores—ends Alan Page and Don Gmitter and tackles Kevin Hardy and Tom Regner.

The biggest defensive problem is at linebacker. From Parseghian's four-man linebacker setup only one regular, Jim Lynch, returns. But Gmitter could be shifted. And then there's Duranko, a regular who was injured in the first game last year and lost for the season, and Arunas Vasys, who made 35 tackles in part-time play. The secondary is well set with Carey, Rassas, and Longo.

Notre Dame's success this season will depend mostly on the physical capabilities of its personnel, to be sure. But Parseghian is not one to overlook the matter of "spirit" and all of its many dimensions. Take one dimension—the psychological stimulus—and consider how it alone affects the boys and varies in its usefulness.

Hunger. "This was a hungry team," says Parseghian of the team he inherited in 1964. It hoped to prove mediocrity was not an inevitable part of athletic life at Notre Dame. It hungered after respectability. It got it, and more. As the success of the Irish rose, so did their standards. And yet the ultimate was denied them—the undefeated season, the national championship, the acclaim that comes with being No. 1—all in the last 1:34 of the season. Perhaps this was a blessing, for it gave Notre Dame something to hunger for in 1965.

Momentum. In the first two games last season, Notre Dame received stiff challenges to its purpose and its confidence. Wisconsin rose up in the second half, as it had a year earlier, and threatened to wipe out an Irish lead. But just when the specter of failure was again haunting Notre Dame fans, the Irish line stiffened, Notre Dame seized the initiative, and [the Irish] went on to win, 31–7. The next week against Purdue, the Irish gave up the first touchdown and then failed to score from the 3-yard line. Again the memories of 1963 rose up to haunt Notre Dame fans (a 7–6 loss), and again the Fighting Irish rose up to banish them. It made and exploited its breaks. It intercepted three passes, blocked a punt and turned it into a touchdown, recovered a Purdue fumble on a quick kick and turned it into another touchdown, and went on to a 34–15 win. Now the momentum was built and Notre Dame was moving.

It might not be as easy to build that early momentum this year. Notre Dame plays three of its first four games on the road, and hostile fans always seem a little nastier when the opponent is Notre Dame.

Environment. Just inside the Notre Dame locker room last year was a sign in red letters a foot high. "Pride," it said. On the bulletin board before the Michigan State game were notes mysteriously signed "The Spartan" and "The Phantom." "The Spartan" warned Notre Dame's players of the dire events that would take place when the Irish ventured out against Michigan State's Spartans. "The Phantom" urged Notre Dame to greater efforts.

Parseghian denies categorically that he was either "The Spartan" or "The Phantom." But the important fact is that this type of psychological stimulus tends to wear off. After a while, many players tend to accept them as a normal part of the locker-room decor, like the smell of arnica and the strips of used adhesive tape littering the floor.

Excitability. The legends of Knute Rockne make Notre Dame men uniquely susceptible to as gifted a speaker as Parseghian. Moreover, he has a natural flair; his pep talks are urgent, unstaged, and unpretentious.

Parseghian has an urgency that is almost visceral. "He communicates with his very pores," says one friend. Parseghian may not say much at all. He doesn't have to. An agonizing urgency begins building in the room before a game as Parseghian paces back and forth—pace, pace, pace—a bang of a fist on a table or locker as Parseghian punctuates some private thought—then faster, faster, faster, pace, pace . . . pace. By game time, Parseghian need say only a few words, then a prayer, to get his players to a bone-searing, blood-chilling pitch. When he sends them onto the field, they are ready.

This technique, too, quickly reaches a point of diminishing returns. Most players cannot react to the emotional strain every week; other players simply possess too much sophistication to succumb to it. Parseghian knows this. He knows that the proper psychological climate is not set merely by words or emotional appeals. It is important for the players to see the results of their labor. Parseghian, for instance, designed a practice regimen that pared as much as 20 pounds from some players. This enabled Notre Dame to hit harder than ever. The players and their opponents could see the results. "They hit so hard that I'm thinking of changing my religion," said Stanford coach John Ralston.

Parseghian's type of spirit is durable because it is built also on organization. Literally no detail escapes Parseghian's attention. "How clean is your locker room?" he'll ask. "How well equipped is your training room?" He examines the performance charts after every game to check, among other things, the blocking of linemen. He has the windows of the Notre Dame library scanned before every practice to make sure no enemy scouts are up there.

The spirit of Notre Dame affects the entire campus, not just the football team. "You can't imagine what it meant to the students here," said a graduate student as he walked across the campus this past winter. "In all the years I'd been here, everything seemed a little out of focus. You grow up with the knowledge of Notre Dame and its traditions and legends and all that, and then you come here and we didn't even have a winning team."

For a full decade the Fathers Hesburgh and Joyce, the top two men in Notre Dame's administration, had been the often-abused victims of an unhappy coincidence. They had deliberately directed Notre Dame toward greater academic excellence in the early fifties, and their success was stunning. But that success coincided with the decline in Notre Dame football and led some Notre Dame followers to believe there was a sinister plot afoot to sacrifice football to make Notre Dame a great university.

That was far from the truth. Notre Dame never slackened its recruiting. "We've always limited the number we let in here," Father Joyce says. "It's adjusted up and down, and I do the adjusting, depending on the number of injuries our team has suffered, and so forth," says Father Joyce. The limit is usually around 36 players.

Ultimately, the number of football players admitted to Notre Dame was not the issue; nor, it appears, was their quality. Instead, it appears to have been the way they were taught and the way their skills were used. The significance of 1964 is that, after 10 years of disappointment, they finally succeeded in finding the right coach.

Notre Dame's success is meaningful to all of higher education, but it is imperative to college football. For if Notre Dame can demonstrate it is possible to have excellence in academics and athletics, the notion that academics and athletics are incompatible might gradually disappear.

Can Notre Dame's success endure? In terms of excellence, yes. In terms of games won and lost, a qualified yes. Long unbeaten streaks are pretty much a thing of the past. But a team can win 70 or 80 percent of its games against a tough schedule and maintain its pride.

Out of all this will develop an era that will make 1964 seem more and more like the passing once cited by the poet: "Each age is a dream that is dying—or one that is coming to birth."

Roger Kahn, *SPORT* Magazine

THE NOTRE DAME PHENOMENON

How to represent Notre Dame football—where it's been, where it's going, and what it's all about? Five years into Ara Parseghian's tenure under the Golden Dome, renowned author and Esquire *columnist Roger Kahn set out for South Bend to provide the latest explanation.*

I have been to Notre Dame three times in my life. Once I matriculated at the Cameo Theater and saw Pat O'Brien as *Knute Rockne: All American* in the famous movie where Governor Ronald Reagan, as George Gipp, chewed gum to illustrate the Gipper's libertine ways. You had to like the Notre Dame of that picture, regardless of your religion, race, or favorite sport, and despite the fact that it invariably makes serious Notre Dame historians wince, even these nights when it turns up on the *Late Late Show II*. Long after that, I flew to the real Notre Dame in the wake of what some Irish call the thr'uble. A Notre Dame football team under Terry Brennan had dropped eight out of a possible ten games, including two losses by 40 points each. The question, then, was whether Notre Dame, under its ambitious, intellectual new president, Father Theodore Hesburgh, was going to abandon so-called big-time football.

Now that Ara Parseghian, out of Armenia by way of Akron, had answered that question for the Irish, I was going back for a third time to see how the tradition, the mystique, the Notre Dame phenomenon was surviving. Although the era of Ara has again made Notre Dame everybody's team to beat, new questions extend beyond the football fields. Notre Dame is, after all, a Roman Catholic university, with traditions of rather severe discipline. I remember Paul Hornung talking about the devices a man had to employ to beat the dormitory curfew. But currently academic discipline—and campuses generally—are under attack, and the Roman Catholic Church itself is embroiled in a series of shattering debates. Everything has a frame, and the frame within which the Notre Dame phenomenon developed was an unshakably unified church.

As best I could tell in the hot Hoosier summer of 1969, the Irish tradition is adjusting reasonably smoothly to modern times. Pickets have protested "the lily-white backfield." A number of students put football down as, at the very least, irrelevant. Certain Notre Dame professors resent the image of Notre Dame as a great football school rather than a great educational institution. Still, as you walk the gently rolling campus under statuary and sycamores you know that this is still Old Notre Dame.

The campus sits in pleasant country, without being as striking as Dartmouth, beneath the White Mountains, or Colorado, close against the Rockies. There are adjoining lakes, named, with absolute catholicity, St. Joseph's and St Mary's, and a superb new athletic building, and, when I was there, numerous nuns taking graduate work and reminding one of the changing times by the relatively short skirts that they wore.

Behind the football stadium, where there will be five sellouts this autumn, the new $9 million library tower competes for attention. A gigantic mural covers the wall toward the field and depicts Jesus Christ with both arms upraised. "That," said a university spokesman, "is Christ signaling a Notre Dame touchdown."

Elsewhere one finds a shaded statue of Father William Corby, an early Notre Dame president, depicted as he gave mass absolution to Irish-immigrant soldiers before the Battle of Gettysburg. Father Corby stands with one arm upraised. The students call him "Fair-Catch Corby."

Finally, in these ecumenical days, there is a recent statue of Moses. Bearded and intense, he holds the commandments and points at the sky with the index finger of the other hand. "That's We're-No.-1 Moses," suggested Ted Haracz, of the sports publicity office.

"No," corrected a passing student. "That's Hesburgh saying, 'Follow me, boys.'"

One of the charming, enduring things about Notre Dame is the irreverent quality of the reverence.

The University of Notre Dame is a men's institution of some six thousand undergraduates run by a small religious order called the Congregation of the Holy Cross. It has a substantial endowment for a religious school ($72 million). Scholastically it is one of the two or three finest Catholic universities in the world. It is becoming increasingly liberal. A few years ago, when a Michigan State professor named Samuel Shapiro was dismissed for defending Castro, Notre Dame hired him. Shapiro is as much an Irish Catholic as Parseghian, who is Presbyterian. Many non-Catholics attend Notre Dame, but everyone is required to study theology. Although no one riots, the campus is charged with debate (Eugene McCarthy versus Bob Kennedy, Vietnam), but all this is not, of course, the source of tradition. Sports is what called attention to Notre Dame, and for more years than most people remember. This is the prime case of a university using sports to attain national prominence. Almost as a side product, which no one had anticipated, was the development of Notre Dame as the semi-official U.S. college football team.

"In the first 55 years of the century, Notre Dame football teams went undefeated in 18 seasons," Francis Wallace writes in *Notre Dame: From Rockne to Parseghian.* "In 17 others it lost one game. The 15 campaigns in which two defeats had come were regarded as 'off' years. The year 1934, with three losses, was 'poor.' The three years which had seen *four* defeats (1904, 1928, 1950) were ghastly. The 1933 campaign, the lone *losing* season (3–5–1), was *atrocious.*"

I include Mr. Wallace's italics and inside quotation marks because they demonstrate the passions of a characteristic old grad.

Cheer, cheer for old Notre Dame
A coach who blows two
Gives me a pain . . .

Compare this with the newer Notre Dame approach, as described by the Reverend James Burtchaell, chairman of the department of theology. To Burtchaell, Notre Dame is now dedicated to "creating a community of friendship." It works furiously against "war, racism, hatred." It is contributing "to the birth of a new culture." Notre Dame, Father Burtchaell says proudly, "is a restless Christian College."

Clearly when two Notre Dame men talk about tradition these days, they are not always talking about the same thing.

Ara Parseghian remembers some years ago when he was driving to one high school football banquet after another. He is a restless Christian himself, and his mind worked as he drove. The 1963 football season at Northwestern was over, and he was musing about the limitations of his job. Northwestern's sports structure was not geared to produce a national champion. Parseghian seeks after challenges, and the Northwestern challenge had about run its course.

Driving along, Parseghian was saying to himself, "What is the next step in my life?" Notre Dame abruptly tumbled into his thoughts. Like all sound football men, he knew the old Notre Dame tradition. He remembered the day in 1931 when Knute Rockne died in a plane crash. [Parseghian] was eight years old. A newsboy had come wandering up the oiled, unpaved street where the Parseghians lived in a white two-story house on a hill. "Extra!" the newsboy shouted up Longview Avenue in Akron. "Extra! Rockne killed in plane crash!"

In the car, Parseghian decided that the greatest step he could take would be a stride toward South Bend. He telephoned Father Edmund Joyce Jr., Notre Dame's executive vice president. Hugh Devore was considered to be "interim coach," but Parseghian still chose his words carefully.

"If you are contemplating a change," he told Joyce, "please consider me. And if you aren't, please disregard this call."

"I'm not sure what we're going to do," Joyce said, "but we're going to have to make a decision fairly soon. I'll be in Chicago in a week or so. Would you like to visit with me for a while?"

Taking the same material that had finished 2–7 in 1963, Parseghian won nine straight in 1964. He lost the last game to Southern California in the closing seconds, which caused a wash of tears at the time. But considering the way Notre Dame nipped USC in 1966 (51–0) and the way Parseghian's defense made O. J. Simpson a bottled genie last November, his score with USC seems settled.

It is true that coaches don't kick or pass or, for that matter, fumble on Saturdays. It is also true, as Chet Grant, a notable Notre Dame sports historian suggests, that the winning tradition existed before the days of Rockne. But it is fair to assert that the football coach stands as both the embodiment and the custodian of much Notre Dame tradition. These days he has to live with theologians, respect the English department, obey recruiting rules, understand that there is more to life than scoring or even bottling O.J. But he had better not fail to bottle O.J. either.

Parseghian is a tough, literate, competitive man beautifully organized and dedicated to discipline. For me the tradition of today came alive at 8:00 one morning when I was ushered into Ara's presence, wondering why in the world football coaches had to get up so early in the summer. (He was flying to California later to make a commercial for an automobile company.)

[Parseghian] was putting at a portable hole. His stance is awkward but, one gathers, effective. He has shot a 65 on the Notre Dame golf course.

"Do you want to putt?" he said.

"At this hour a putter is too heavy to lift."

Parseghian grinned, set his teeth, tapped the ball, and—to tell it as it was—missed.

I went into his office, comfortable but unpretentious, and he mentioned that some people functioned best at dawn, others by night. He rang for a secretary who brought coffee.

"Well," I began, "what's a nice Armenian boy like you doing at a place like this?"

He looked at me hard, blinked, and said, "It's nice for any Armenian boy to be anywhere." He was referring to the days when Turks fell to massacring Armenians in an attempt at genocide. He grinned again. We were not in a history seminar. He is a bigger man than one might have guessed, not tall but with a massive, powerful torso.

"To me," he said, "Notre Dame is one of the top college football jobs in the country. It is a successful independent, the most successful, probably. It's all male; you get a spirit comparable to the spirit at military academies. And it's competitive. I'd say a major attraction is the national name of Notre Dame."

"What about the religion?" I said.

"I told Father Joyce that I wasn't Catholic. I suppose then I thought maybe 85 percent of the faculty would be wearing robes. It didn't bother Father Joyce at all. It turns out no more than 15 percent of the faculty are priests. We have exchange students from all over the world. We have negroes on the teaching staff. It's a remarkable open place."

Parseghian has a powerful neck and strong features. His hair is black. Although as we talked over coffee his expression was sunny, one knew that it could darken like a cloud.

"What was it like coming here in the beginning?"

"Well, I came with a respect for what had taken place."

"But there were severe problems. Were you nervous?"

Parseghian thought briefly. "I did feel a great sense of responsibility," he said. "As I came up Notre Dame Avenue, maybe it was something about the school or maybe the memory of individuals, but an electric charge went up my back. Suddenly I was associated with a great history."

Although he was able, in that first year, to turn around losing personnel, his continuing success depended to some degree on his ability to recruit new talent. "I suppose you have to recruit a little," I said.

Parseghian nodded. Coaches discuss recruiting coyly, as maidens discuss virtue.

Well, does the tradition help you there?"

"Notre Dame," Parseghian said, the sunlight gone from his face, "does not tap whom they want. Notre Dame is the only school with a national radio network broadcasting its games, a regular video replay, and all that press. The average athlete is awed by this. In recruiting, the most important thing I have to do is dispel misconceptions."

"What kind of misconceptions?"

"That maybe a boy won't have a chance. That the competition out here is too rough."

"Isn't it?"

"We offer about 30 football scholarships a year. A boy who comes here can break a leg on the first day of practice and never play a game. He still keeps his scholarship for four years—provided he maintains academic standing."

"About the competition."

"What I like to do is show a boy someone from his own area, preferably someone he may have played against, who has made it here. Terry Hanratty came from a small high school in Butler, Pennsylvania. If I was encouraging a boy from that area to come here, I'd tell him about Hanratty." Parseghian's face was quite dark. "What the hell is this going to be, anyway?" he said. "A story about recruiting?"

"No. No. Of course not. Whatever gave you that idea?"

The sunshine reappeared when I asked him to define his role. "We are teachers," he said. "This is not professional football. We have classes that move out, and every class is different from every other. I use modern techniques. Visual aids. Playing football is emotional and spiritual and physical. And there are the technical aspects. The boys have to execute their lessons before sixty thousand people." [Parseghian] was standing, excited by his work as he described it. "The purpose here is to get an education for the whole of life, to go on into law or medicine or whatever. But when they execute what we've been teaching them in football, you really lift off. There's a team sense. It's like man going to the moon." [He] sat down. "Not, of course, that I mean to compare winning a football game with putting a man up there." (And not that he doesn't, either.)

We talked about campus unrest, and he displayed both a lively interest and the essential conservatism one usually finds in men of sport. It is a conservatism that commands respect because it is honestly arrived at.

"In a place this big," I said, "can you get close to the kids? Do they come to you with personal problems?"

"Many times," Parseghian said. He pointed. "I don't know how many problems boys have brought in through that door. And," he said, humbly and also with pride, "we've solved a few of them, too."

Two first-rate football players who came at the tradition from opposite paths talked at length in the afternoon. John Joseph Standring, who answers to Jay, comes from a Chicago family in which a great grandfather, a grandfather, four uncles, and an indeterminate number of cousins attended Notre Dame. "I grew up in Notre Dame T-shirts," says Jay, a defensive halfback of great desire and 190 pounds.

"My father," says Lawrence Charles DiNardo, who is 6'1", 243 pounds, dark, and massive, "is a policeman in New York. I first thought of coming here when I was a sophomore at St. Francis Prep. I don't think I knew the name of the coach [Parseghian was in his first year], but I knew about Notre Dame's reputation. The bad years hadn't dimmed it. As you get better in high school football, you start to think [Notre Dame]."

Standring is light-haired, intent, and rather shy. "I was scared at first practice," he says. "The Notre Dame players were so great. I knew about them as a boy. I thought I never could play here. But the coach sort of helped my determination. He was willing to let me show what I could do."

Standring would like to play professional football when he is through and wishes that he could run faster, jump higher, and had more muscle. He is a serious student who says of campus disruption, "If a student doesn't like the school he's at, he should leave and go somewhere that suits him."

"But suppose a student says no university in the country these days suits him, that the system is wrong?"

[He] thinks and reddens. He has no answer, but he is going to think some more.

DiNardo would like to be a lawyer and looks forward to playing professional football along the way to his first appointment as an assistant district attorney. As a powerful offensive guard, he is sure to go in an early draft round as long as he stays healthy. "I'm an athlete and the son of a policeman," he says, "and I suppose that makes me a conservative. The right to protest is important, but no more than the right to support what we have already. When there's legal protest from radicals, fine. When they're illegal, *crush them.*" A biceps flexes.

At Notre Dame today the education of Jay Standring and Larry DiNardo and the other athletes is the direct responsibility of one Michael DeCicco, who supervises the academic advisors' office. DeCicco, who is also fencing coach, is proud that last year the average student grade was 2.706 and the average athlete's grade was 2.683. "Keeping the athletes that close is something," DeCicco says. "And our offensive line, where DiNardo plays, was a pack of scholars." DeCicco is a strong, roundish man from New Jersey, who occupies a cramped office and speaks across a copy of Edgar Lee Masters' stirring mini-saga, *Spoon River Anthology.* In one corner of the office a foil rests. "That," he says, "applied to the bottom of someone who is not studying, has been known to have an excellent effect."

Before an athlete enrolls at Notre Dame, DeCicco and assistants study his record. A Notre Dame freshman, football player or poet, must take math (including some calculus), a science, a social science, English composition, and theology. By reviewing a boy's high school work and college board scores, DeCicco foresees areas of trouble. He then prepares a tutoring program, tailored to help the athlete stay in school. A standard Notre Dame dialogue at the start of each school year goes like this:

Frosh athlete: "Hey, how come I have to have a math tutor? I haven't even been to math class yet."

DeCicco: "We're playing the percentages, young man."

In his first months at Notre Dame the athlete is required to listen to lectures on how to study, on how to organize a daily schedule—in short, how to pass off the field. From the time Gus Dorais first started throwing to Knute Rockne, passing has been an athletic tradition at Notre Dame.

One needs a certain sense of history. Chet Grant, who was sports editor of the *South Bend Tribune* in 1910 and later enrolled at Notre Dame and played with Gipp, can separate much myth from fantasy. Notre Dame was not, as myth suggests, an unknown cow college when it upset Army on November 1, 1913. It was an established football power; indeed the Army game came after the unbeaten season of 1912 when Notre Dame outscored seven opponents by 389 to 27. Rockne was not a shallow, amiable man. He was deep and troubled and ambitious and hypersensitive, a perfect marvel of complexity. Gipp did not chew gum. At least Grant never saw him chew. As to whiskey, well the Gipper was probably a harder drinker than Ronnie Reagan.

These are important points, but minor in the overall scheme. What is more remarkable than inaccuracies in the Notre Dame legend are the things that actually have happened. Notre Dame was founded in 1842 by a young French priest named Edward Frederick Sorin. The full title is the University of Notre Dame du Lac, which, as any sophomore French student should know, even if untutored, means the university of our lady of the lake. The most famous cathedral in Paris is called Notre Dame, although the French insist on pronouncing the words in an un-American manner: Notre Dahm.

The university played its first football game in 1887, losing to Michigan, 8–0. A touchdown was worth four points at the time. Notre Dame lost to Michigan twice more the following spring, but on December 6, 1888, won its first football game. The victim was the Harvard School of Chicago, not related to the New England Harvards, and the score was 20–0. In 1894 Notre Dame became serious enough to hire a coach, one James L. Morison, and by 1905 was foreshadowing the routs to come. Playing the American Medical School on October 28 that year, Notre Dame won, 142–0. The game was not as close as the score indicates. Notre Dame led, 121–0, at halftime, and the second half was shortened to eight minutes. Notre Dame scored 27 touchdowns, but early rooters were distressed by a glaring weakness: the team missed 20 extra points.

In 1909, four years before the famous Army upset, a Notre Dame team under coach Frank Longmans won seven games over such opponents as Michigan State, Pitt, and Michigan. Almost certainly this was the strongest team in the Midwest. Fielding Yost, the famous Michigan coach, argued, "We are champions. We took on Notre Dame because we needed work, and we got it, all right. But as for any championship claim at Notre Dame, that doesn't go. There are men on the Notre Dame team who have played years beyond the recognized limit, so that bars them."

Photographs survive of the 1909 squad. The boys look reasonably collegiate in dark cardigan sweaters—rugged to be sure, but there is not a gray hair among them. Time has disallowed Yost's claim.

Rockne came as a student in 1910, when he was 22. Eight years later, he became head coach. And seven years after that, he converted to Catholicism in the Log Chapel, a replica of Father Sorin's original Notre Dame building.

Gipp was probably his most famous single football player. Like Rockne, Gipp came to Notre Dame late, after four post–high school years driving a taxi in Michigan. "He had spent a lot of time in pool rooms and bars," Grant remembers, "doing the things young men do in bars and pool rooms. I think he appealed to Rockne as a reclamation project."

Gipp was prelaw, and the Notre Dame athletic department keeps some of his notebooks to this day. In them, one finds notes on personal property and torts and some word play scrawled during some forgotten, uninspired lecture. At the top of a page, Gipp has commented, "Good God Go."

He was a superb kicker, a swift inventive runner, and he was dead on December 14, 1920, at the age of 25. Eight years later Rockne made his "win one for the Gipper" speech, and by 1931 Rockne was prematurely dead, too, at the age of 43. It is difficult to capture a measure of Rockne the man without seeming to exaggerate. His teams won 105 games and lost 12, for a winning percentage of .897. Recently a recording of a Rockne fight speech turned up on South Bend juke boxes and began to match Jefferson Airplane, nickel for nickel.

Rockne belongs with Babe Ruth and Bobby Jones and Jack Dempsey and Bill Tilden in that exclusive group of sports figures who captured America during the impressionable twenties, when sportswriters aspired toward poetry and legions of American Irishmen began to think of themselves as Notre Dame men. These were the subway alumni, more numerous and often louder than men who had actually graduated. It is significant, if anticlimactic, to point out that during the twenties Notre Dame was attacked in an exhaustive and impartial study. The charge was football overemphasis. Repercussions are still felt on the campus.

After Rockne's death in 1930, Heartley "Hunk" Anderson took on the job. In 1934 he was replaced by [Elmer] Layden, who won at a .783 clip. Frank Leahy took over in 1940 and, with time out for wartime service, was head coach until 1953. When stomach disorders plagued Leahy, he resigned, hoping that Father Hesburgh would counter with a request that he go on leave. The president did not. Leahy was bitter for a time and complained to friends that being replaced by a 25-year-old was humiliating.

For two seasons, Terry Brennan was a winning coach. Then came the deluge. According to one analyst, Brennan's weakness was his youth, but not in the way one might suspect. "He was a bright kid," the man says, "and he couldn't take corn seriously. He could never say, 'Win one for the Gipper' or talk like Leahy or shout simple little slogans because he was too close to reacting to that sort of stuff himself. But a coach at Notre Dame can't be afraid to be corny. Corn is a good part of our tradition."

When Parseghian arrived, the Irish swept their first nine games. All around the country, among subway alumni and real graduates, word was that the Rockne spirit was coming back. Then the team flew to Los Angeles for the Southern California game on November 28, 1964. Favored, Notre Dame carried a narrow lead into the final two minutes. The events that followed have been recalled with great freshness in a log kept by Tom Pagna, the offensive backfield coach. With coach Pagna's permission, I use his account here:

Two minutes remained in the game, when [Craig] Fertig of USC hit Fred Hill on a 23-yard pass play. On three ground plays the Trojans gained only two yards. It was now fourth down and eight, with the ball resting on our 15. [Ken] Maglicic came within inches of grabbing Fertig, but the ball was released toward Rod Sherman. Tony Carey (a defensive back) was close by. In the scramble up for the ball Carey fell, Sherman caught, and streaked to the end zone. With 93 seconds left, Southern California had gone out front [20–17]. The rest was comeback gamble football. It was long passes and short outs to Jack Snow. The clock ran out . . . we had lost!

At the moment that Fertig hit Sherman, a *Life* photographer angled onto the field to photograph Ara's agony.

Somehow in that empty moment I sensed his intention and tried to get between him and Ara. I failed and the picture appeared. I had no malice toward a photographer doing his job. I just didn't want the raw and naked image of a crumbled man exposed. I hadn't even time to see Ara's reaction, but I knew what it would be. The actual picture said it all. Heartbreak in the distorted mouth lines. A wrinkled brow burdened by arms brought upward to his head. His body twisted trying to apply "English" or attempt a remote interception. The picture said in a thousand ways, why had we come so close, fought so hard, died so violently?

It was a blurry tunnel to the dressing room, full of tears, full of sobbing young giants. Quietly they suffered. The manly stifled sobs of total despair. My mind turned to one line: "If you can watch the things you gave your life to broken / And stoop . . . to build them up with worn-out tools."

Aside from Father Joyce and a few others always present to console or praise, Ara allowed no one into the locker room.

In his perpetual driving fashion, Ara composed his feelings rapidly. He asked the team to kneel and led them in prayer. The sobs of the men were apparent as Ara fought for tranquility. "Dear God," he said, "give us the strength in our moment of despair to understand and accept that which we have undergone." Then Ara further addressed the players. He told them that there were thousands of things we could say.

There were officials and calls we could blame. But we had won as Notre Dame men, fair, hard, and with humility. To be less at this moment, to cry foul, to alibi, would undo much that the season had done. He asked the players to vent their anger and their tears for the next 10 minutes, when the locker room was Notre Dame's alone. After that period was over, he asked each player to hold his tongue, lift his head high, and in the face of defeat to be a Notre Dame man.

I marveled at the individuals. George Goeddeke, just a sophomore center, was humping his 6' frame over a chair, holding his head and allowing silent tears to moisten his hands. George hadn't gotten into this game but a few plays. He mumbled, "We'll be back here someday."

[Bill] Wolski was disconsolate. He blamed himself for a pitchout that [John] Huarte and he had let misfire. Huarte in turn blamed John Huarte. Bob Meeker was beyond talking to. Bob had been called for holding on Joe Kantor's touchdown that was called back. Kantor, whom I personally knew was made of the toughest fiber, sat dazed and misty-eyed. Kantor, who had practiced in full football gear only 20 days after knee surgery, wouldn't cry if he were hit with a hammer between his eyes. "Joe," I told him, "it may not mean much to you right now, but I'm mighty proud of you!" He thanked me in his quiet way that ran deeper than words can convey.

Tony Carey, who had played a great season, was nearly hysterical. To fans who didn't know football, Tony would be the goat. To himself he was the goat. It had been his lot on the final scoring pass play to miss the tackle. Notre Dame was life itself to Tony, and this event so marked him, that his confidence in justice was nearly destroyed.

It went on and on, each player who had participated blamed himself. It was perhaps the most humble moment we would ever know.

How long can such intensity of college spirit survive? Parseghian says he does not know. DiNardo sees it as fading "eventually." But it is alive now, despite our national obsession with professional football and despite the fact that other shattering disasters of our era— Auschwitz, Hiroshima, Vietnam—make lost college games less consequential than in Rockne's simpler days.

In the balance of things, in our crowded, confusing time, the survival of the Notre Dame spirit is remarkable, and fine.

John Powers, the *Boston Globe*

THOSE FRIGHTENING IRISH

A 1970 Harvard graduate, John Powers had never been to Notre Dame until this stop in 1978. His visit turned into this feature for the Boston Globe, *a look at Irish lore midway through the 1978 campaign.*

Jesus said unto them—"Who do you say that I am?"

And they replied—"You are the eschatological manifestation of the ground of our being, the kerygma in which we find the ultimate meaning of an interpersonal relationship."

And Jesus said unto them—"What?"

—sign on window of the campus ministry

The prophet, bearded and fierce, is cast in bronze outside the library, staring toward the stadium. A sandaled foot rests on the snout of what appears to be a longhorn steer (just the Adversary, in Texas form). The right arm is thrust overhead, index finger pointed at the Indiana sky. We're No. 1, saith Moses.

The library mosaic, easily visible from the press box, presents a delightful Christ, arms stretched out and upward. Touchdown Jesus, they say here. Within punting distance of the quad stands a former president of the university, right hand raised, blessing the Irish Brigade before the Battle of Gettysburg. Fair-Catch Corby is the name.

The university keeps pictures of them on file—color and black and white—and sports information director Roger Valdiserri nods, with mock solemnity, when asked for one. "Just another football factory," he says, winking. It has become a family joke by now, from one good Catholic to another.

And isn't that what we really have here, just another extended Irish-Italo-Polish-Slavic-send-me-your-huddled-masses immigrant Catholic clan?

All that good melting-pot assimilation may have done its work, but Notre Dame somehow keeps alive flickering images of Ellis Island, saloon politics, maiden aunts living in the attic, and the straight Democratic ticket. Just for those who remember How It Was . . . and for those who'd like to.

There is still a trace of the Them vs. Us spirit—not that they won't welcome you happily here as a fellow communicant in the lore. A visitor is overwhelmed with small kindnesses, invited to parties, introduced all around, and wished safe passage home.

Football practices are open—hell, Rockne's were open; why not?—and the players are more than happy to talk, answering the same outsiders' questions about the tradition and the pressures, week after week, with fresh enthusiasm. Are you enjoying it here, they want to know?

But university people will tell you—no, nobody seems to be neutral about Notre Dame. Either you get the shivers when you hear the "Victory March" or . . .

"Clemson," somebody in the athletic department says. You should have been with us at Clemson last year if you wanted to see the other side of it."

Or Lafayette, Indiana, or East Lansing, Michigan, or Austin, Texas, or Tuscaloosa, Alabama, where the mention of Notre Dame brings a curled lip and a curse.

Yeah, yeah, Notre Dame. No. 1 with Jee-zus. Where the halfback is named Heavens and the coach is Devine. Where they go 2–8 and their guy wins the Heisman (1956 and Paul Hornung). Where they play for a tie and win the national championship (1966). Where they only have to win the Cotton Bowl and the damn Eastern mee-dee-a moves 'em up ahead of Arkansas and 'Bama, all the way to No. 1.

Their names are still heavy with clustered consonants, a Heimkreiter and a Martinovich and a Restic for every Foley, Moynihan, and Ryan, but it's still the Fighting Irish, with the balding leprechaun and his cocked fists, peering up at your chin.

They did not conceive that nickname themselves. It was hung on them, scornfully, by Prods and others, along with the Papists and the "Catholic Collegians of Indiana." Finally, in 1927, Matthew Walsh, president of the university, authorized it as a badge of ethnic pride.

Notre Dame was for every Boston cop, every New York fireman, every Chicago hod carrier who couldn't afford college but wanted a place to drink to on Saturday night. The Irish belonged to the big cities and their working classes, who'd heard mick and dago and polack so often they'd become middle names.

Nuns who didn't know a halfback from a touchback listened to Harry Wismer on the Mutual Network and placed a small statue of Our Lady atop the old wooden radio. Even now, now that the cops have fathered lawyer daughters and the firemen's sons are stockbrokers, Notre Dame still has a 350-station national radio network and a

Monday TV replay that is seen in 85 percent of the country. Even in 1978 their people remember where they came from. The subway.

Father Edward Sorin, who arrived in South Bend, Indiana, on horse-back with $300, a letter of credit, and seven religious brothers to build his University of Notre Dame du Lac in 1842, wouldn't know the place. Mandatory mass has been abolished, classes have been fully coeduca-tional for six years, and you can pass an entire afternoon without seeing a rustling cassock on the quad.

From a modest settlement of log cabins and one large brick struc-ture (which burned down from time to time), Notre Dame has grown into a physical plant of nearly 100 buildings worth $240 million. Ninety percent of the faculty are laypersons, and the student body (77 percent come from the top 10 percent of their high school classes) can hold its own academically with Northwestern, Michigan, and the Ivies. And the man in charge (since 1952), Reverend Theodore M. Hesburgh, has been a cover subject for *Time* magazine.

As the church has changed, so has Notre Dame, yet it is still Knute Rockne's place. The Dome, the quad—lushly green, spotted with trees, crisscrossed with walks—the brick-and-limestone stadium where Rockne coached his final season, and the Grotto, with candles ablaze, where the rosary is still said at 6:45 each night. "But just now . . . and just so many times, how I long for the Grotto," a dying Dr. Tom Dooley wrote to Hesburgh from his Hong Kong bed. "Away from the Grotto, Dooley just prays."

Students wander by and gaze out at the lake. "And when things crowd in on me," says Dan Devine, Rockne's latest heir, "I just try to walk across campus, to the four most beautiful places in the world. The Grotto in the winter, just after a snowfall. The Grotto in the spring, when the trees are just beginning to come out. The Grotto in the summer, when it's all green. And the Grotto in the fall, when the leaves are turning."

If you walk along Notre Dame Avenue (Sorin's French-style boule-vard) and into the quad on a September night when rain is expected and the wind shivers the sycamores and the Dome is burning bright and the chimes mark the hour, you can sense the ghosts. Rockne is interred in a small cemetery nearby. George Gipp died here—they say he slept on the steps of Washington Hall the night before he developed the strep throat that buried him at 25, and that his spirit still haunts the building.

It has become so much a part of us now, so much a tangle of truth and Warner Brothers, that the myths merely grow larger with the years.

The images tumble forth on each other. Rockne and Gus Dorais working on crude pass patterns on the summer sand at Cedar Point, planning for All Saints Day and the Army game. Gipp, punting lazily by himself, the undercovered wisecracking rake who'd wring a deathbed promise from Rockne. Johnny "One-Play" O'Brien and Jack Chevigny scoring the two touchdowns against Army and winning it for the Gipper in 1928—and both of them dying violently within 20 years, O'Brien in a car crash, Chevigny at Iwo Jima. The Kansas farmer running for the old crank phone as Rockne's plane falls out of the sky. Leahy, the master, with the dark suits and the parted hair and the elaborate Victorian sentences, telling center Jim Schrader he'd burn in hell for missing an extra point in 1952. Brennan, Hornung, Hanratty, Seymour, Joe Theismann, Ara. The jerseys, now blue, now green, and the gold helmets glistening. The most famous sporting lead of the century—"Outlined against a blue-gray October sky, the Four Horsemen"—was written about a Notre Dame varsity. And they say that American POWs, forbidden by their Vietnamese captors to sing patriotic songs, used the "Victory March" instead to keep up morale.

They will say that you can make too much of all the lore. "Someone told me that Luther Bradley (last year's All-American defensive back) had never heard of George Gipp," Devine will say, dryly.

But Devine would also bring down Pat O'Brien (the Hollywood Rockne) and interrupt a movie before a game at Southern Cal to do the Gipper speech.

"I flicked the lights on, and I introduced this little old man," Devine remembers. "And he started off talking about how he'd lived with the Rocknes before the movie was made. And he imitated the way Rockne stood, with the bad back. And then he went into the locker-room speech. Here were 40 skeptics . . . and in four minutes, Pat had them in the palm of his hand. Every one of our kids jumped to his feet and gave him a standing ovation. And Willie Fry had tears coming down his cheeks."

The lore endures, to be summoned forth and pumped directly into the adrenal glands. "I don't believe in ghosts," says quarterback Joe Montana, the second most important man in the Catholic church, by some estimates. "But I think you recall all those things and use them to motivate you."

Montana will tell you how, growing up in western Pennsylvania, he'd listen to the games on Saturday afternoon, then get up to watch the TV highlights Sunday morning. "And then a friend and I would go out into the yard and play catch, and I'd be Hanratty and he'd be Seymour, and every play would go for a touchdown."

And last month at the Friday night pep rally before the Michigan game, with rolls of toilet paper sailing overhead and the "Victory March" booming, Hanratty would be talking on stage, and he would turn around and wink at Montana, introducing him as the best quarterback in the country.

The corner office has been freshly decorated with green carpeting and blue-green-gold plaid wallpaper and, behind the desk, you can see a mounted photograph of Dan Devine, grinning hugely, wearing a heavy knitted sweater. One hand is holding a telephone receiver, and the other is giving the news, index finger pointed. We're No. 1.

Devine is sitting at the desk now, wearing the same sweater, and he is saying no, no, the feeling wasn't vindication. Just happiness. There had been nine straight victories to finish up the season, after all, and then the shocking 38–10 demolition of Texas in the Cotton Bowl and then the phone call, confirming another national championship. Just happiness.

He said that last January and he'll say it now, but Devine is being diplomatic. It *was* vindication. Devine was on his way out, they'd been whispering, until he beat Texas. Those two 8–3 seasons and the loss to Mississippi with all that material and . . .

Devine has been here for nearly four years, and for four years he has heard the muttering and the rumors, just as you have, and most of them have him on the next train out. In a sense, he is just as embattled at Notre Dame as he was in Green Bay (although nobody's killed the family dog here), and he has come, quickly, to understand the horrible, unspoken pressures that gnawed at Leahy and Parseghian and anybody who has ever tried to deal with the legend.

"Notre Dame is the only place where they get ready for you a week before they play you," Devine says, asking an assistant to fetch a clipping from an Ann Arbor newspaper as evidence. "Here's the quote from Ron Simpkins [a Michigan player], before they played us. 'We've been getting ready for them since the beginning of the season. The coaches put the two games [Illinois and Notre Dame] together.'"

Devine smiles wryly, shaking his head, "I was astounded when I came into Boston in 1975 (for his Notre Dame coaching debut), and one of the Boston papers ran a headline saying, Biggest Day in BC History. Well, in 1941, I think they went undefeated and beat a good Tennessee team in the Sugar Bowl. If I were on that 1941 team, I'd feel kind of funny. Just the fact that Notre Dame being in town is the most important day . . ."

Parseghian, who walked away from the job after 11 years and 95 victories, had told Devine how it would be. "The demands on your time," Devine says. "The speaking engagements. There was a week where I was in Phoenix one day, St. Louis the next, Boston the next, Charlotte the next, and Columbus the next. And it was all university business."

It is the best coaching job in America, they say. The name is magic for recruiting. The national exposure with the radio network, the Sunday replays, and the NCAA package appearances (53 national and regional since 1952) on Saturday. The Bowl games. The guaranteed sellouts at home, where the atmosphere is captivating and eternal. Notre Dame sells itself, which is part of the problem. Devine has to convince people that they don't have to be Hanratty or Gipp to play in the shadow of the Dome. "That's one of the great recruiting devices used against Notre Dame," he admits. "That you'll never play here. I probably used it when I was recruiting at Missouri."

Yet the academics are frequently the tougher challenge. Athletes at Notre Dame receive no special privileges, and Devine frequently finds himself conducting his late-afternoon practices without a starter or two. "Labs," he shrugs. "People come here expecting to see a football factory. But every year the board scores of the incoming freshman class go up."

Devine tells a story about punter Joe Restic (who could have played for his father at Harvard or gone to Yale) going with a recruiting prospect to an evening movie, then leaving to study at 11:00. "And we lost that kid because he said he didn't want to go to a school where you had to go study at 11:00."

This is still Father Sorin's university (wasn't Rockne originally hired as a chemistry instructor?), the Catholic educational beacon shining through the Indiana sycamores. But it will always belong, too, to Rockne and Gipp and Leahy and Parseghian and Warner Brothers, with national championships and All-Americas (94 since 1913) and Heisman Trophy winners (six) not so much celebrated as assumed.

There will always be the lore, and the pressures that go along with it, and the urge, for Devine and his successors, to walk across campus, past Touchdown Jesus and Moses and Fair-Catch Corby, to the Grotto and a moment's escape.

"Has it come true, everything Ara told you?" Devine was asked one bright September afternoon this year.

Devine smiled, "Only 99 and $^{44}/_{100}$ percent of it."

John Underwood, *Sports Illustrated*

CASTING A SPECIAL LIGHT

Notre Dame's executive vice president, Father Ned Joyce, came to be good friends with John Underwood while Underwood was a primary college football writer for Sports Illustrated. *Joyce gave Underwood an open invitation to come to South Bend and write a story about how athletics at Notre Dame worked—and he promised to open any file and answer every question. Underwood took Joyce up on his offer, and this piece in the January 10, 1983, issue was the result.*

The challenge came by mail from a valued friend who, over the years, had favored me with a sporadic correspondence, mainly in the form of gentle but well-aimed critiques of things I'd written. This time, apparently, I'd gone too far. He said he had read the things I had done on the recurring failures of intercollegiate sport. Failures to curb the big-money madness. Failures to relieve the pressure on coaches to win—pressure that has led to desperate conduct on and off the playing field and court, the cheating and the gratuitous violence. Worst of all, that pressure had led to the academic derelictions that have scandalized America in recent years.

Although granting that my stories—notably "The Writing Is on the Wall" (*SI*, May 19, 1980)—called attention to "inexcusable acts," my correspondent thought them on the whole too negative, too likely to rally only the cynics. There is indeed another side, he said, and he was living it every day. He wrote, "As I read [your words] I say to myself, 'Not the slightest tinge of this scenario is applicable to Notre Dame. It simply doesn't describe the athletic picture as I know it.'"

Then, taking both sides of a lively little morality skit, he asked rhetorically if Notre Dame might be unique in the high values and integrity it demanded of its athletic program. "I trust not," he answered. He encouraged me to make an appraisal, promising "full access" to records and personnel, and reminded me (unnecessarily) that this wasn't a self-serving suggestion, that, after all, Notre Dame really didn't need any more publicity. But he thought some good could come from it because college administrators were more troubled than ever that the system might be fundamentally flawed.

He polished off the challenge with best wishes and signed it with a flourish, right above the typed signature and title, "Edmund P. Joyce, C.S.C., Executive Vice President."

The letter sat around for some time, but not passively. Like dough rising under a baker's towel. It expanded in my consciousness even as the system's breakdowns made their ugly marks in increasing number on the nation's sports pages and TV screens. I'm neither Irish nor Catholic, not a Notre Dame fan. Not an alumnus. Not even especially fond of the place or its famous "Victory March" ("On Brave Old Army Team" has always struck me as a more inspiring number), but I had nonetheless come to include myself in that legion of admirers who harbor a vague conviction that Notre Dame is doing something right, that it possesses something that, if transmittable, might very well deserve parceling around.

Shortly after that, I was in the company of a coaching friend whom I happened to know once lusted for a football job at Notre Dame. A tyrannical pragmatism cured him of that itch—needing to eat, he took a job elsewhere. I asked him if he thought there were things to learn from Notre Dame, if in its success in football and other sports and its upgraded academic status in recent years, there were patterns to be found and followed.

The coach is a combustible conversationalist. When he gets on a subject he stomps around and waves his arms. Immediately he was into the verbal equivalent of top gear. "Learn? What's to learn?" he shouted. "That's Utopia! You can't even *compare* Notre Dame with us. Some of us try to run first-class programs within the rules. Some of us succeed, some don't. Notre Dame doesn't worry about it because it doesn't *have* to cheat. Father Joyce brags about not allowing transfer students or junior college graduates into Notre Dame and not red-shirting players. Notre Dame doesn't *need* to do those things, you get the picture?" He paused to allow the picture to be gotten.

"Notre Dame doesn't recruit, Notre Dame *gathers*," he said. "You say 'Notre Dame' to a high school football player, and it's like saying 'free lunch' to a starving man. Half the top players in the country tell you they've been *dreaming* about going there since they were little kids. Nobody tells you they've been dreaming about going to Louisville or Memphis State.

"What do you learn from a place where a coach loses 12 games in 13 years? You want to know? OK. One, tradition. Notre Dame has fantastic tradition. Two, it has Rockne. He's dead, but he'll live forever. Twelve losses in 13 years! Three, it has a great common denominator, Catholicism. Four, it has a great fight song. Five, it has a golden dome that blinds you to the fact that in the winter the campus looks like a penitentiary. But number one, it has great tradition, and you can't get that anymore because college presidents fire you if you don't win, and the program has to start all over again every time that happens.

"Educationally, I think Notre Dame is overrated, but for overall prestige in academics *and* athletics, it's in a class by itself. I think it's great that intercollegiate sport has an example like Notre Dame. But it's not the real world. It's Utopia."

Prejudices aside, Notre Dame undoubtedly is neither the dream world my coaching friend thinks it to be, nor the model for every school that other administrators should rush to imitate, as Joyce appeared to suggest. But, upon evaluation, Joyce would seem closer to the mark. Certainly, Notre Dame has great football tradition, but so do other schools. There's no doubt, for example, that emerging O.J.s all over Southern California dream of playing for USC. Like Notre Dame (and a goodly number of other schools), Southern Cal doesn't "*have* to cheat," but evidentially it does—since 1956 the school has been on NCAA probation three times.

Notre Dame had Knute Rockne, but Alabama had the Bear, and Penn State *has* Joe. Notre Dame has Catholicism going for it, but Nebraska and Oklahoma and a lot of other schools have the religion of statewide football obsessions going for them. In short, Notre Dame may have more tradition and mystique and social forces working for it than any other football school, but its lead over its rivals in such things is nowhere near what a lot of them would have you believe.

Rather, the Irish's success in blending big-time football—and basketball—with integrity may be just as easily rooted in more mundane factors that other universities *can* copy to one degree or another. Joyce himself is the embodiment of perhaps the most significant of these factors: a consistent leadership.

Joyce has been one of Notre Dame's two major influences—the other, of course, having been the school's president, Father Theodore M. Hesburgh, C.S.C.—for an incredibly long time. Every person hired for a key position at Notre Dame in the last 30 years has been hired by Joyce or Hesburgh; they have been in charge that long. In the harsh realm of higher education, where leaders burn out quickly or get routed, no other major institution has been granted such consistency at the top. None comes close: the national average for time in rank for college presidents is seven years.

The tall, graying, icy-eyed Joyce comes across as a solid and caring administrator, comfortable in his role as a highly visible second banana to Hesburgh. For three decades he has played archconservative to Hesburgh's flamboyant liberalism. "It's Father Joyce," says one official in the Notre Dame administration, "who keeps Hesburgh from bankrupting the place." Working companions for 33 years, Hesburgh and Joyce have, among other accomplishments, performed a notable balancing act in keeping the monster of Notre Dame football both healthy and under control. Philosophically, they accept football's clout as a kind of astral benefit, like a prevailing wind, and refuse to be embarrassed or intimidated by it, although Hesburgh went through an early period of "putting it in its place."

At his first off-campus press conference as school president in 1952, Hesburgh was asked to hike his cassock and crouch over a football for the photographers. "Would you ask the president of Yale to do that?" he replied testily and refused to pose. And he still revels in his in-house victories over coach Frank Leahy on the issue of strict interpretation of eligibility standards for football players. These triumphs helped Hesburgh establish his power base in the fifties.

"Intercollegiate athletics are important in the life of an institution, but not *all*-important," Hesburgh said at the 1981 Notre Dame football banquet, commemorating, ironically, the Irish's first losing season in 19 years. He once wrote in this magazine (September 27, 1954) that those who "favor intercollegiate athletics praise them out of all proportion to their merits." But those who deny them "are quite blind to the values" they possess. He says he wouldn't want to be at a university that didn't participate in major competitive sports, as long as those sports were honest. He also says he has his statement of priorities whittled down to a two-minute speech he gives new coaches: "The one I gave Gerry Faust is the same one I gave Ara Parseghian and Digger Phelps and Dan Devine. I say, 'You've got five years. We won't say boo to you if you lose. I think you'll have the tools here to win more than you lose; it seems to work that way, but if you don't, you won't hear from me. You *will* hear from me if you cheat. If you cheat, you'll be out of here before midnight.'"

Joyce defends the same hallowed ground in his own speeches and writing, and both he and Hesburgh regularly reaffirm their view that Notre Dame exists not to provide the civilized world with first-rate football teams, but with a place to go for a first-rate Catholic education. The football teams just happen to make it a more attractive place to go. That's what they say. I don't doubt they believe it.

It's instructive to point out, however, if only to give schools that have run afoul of the rules proof that fanaticism can raise its ugly head in the best of circles, that in the twenties another Notre Dame president, the late John Francis O'Hara, proclaimed Notre Dame football to be "a new crusade" that "kills prejudice and stimulates faith," and blatantly promoted the sport on and off campus.

And the poor coaches who succeeded Rockne and Leahy—but without their predecessors' success—felt the wrath of the administration and wound up unemployed. Heartley "Hunk" Anderson (1931–1933), who followed Rockne, and Terry Brennan (1954–1958), who succeeded Leahy (1941–1943, 1946–1953), were sacrificed just as surely as they would have been at LSU or Texas A&M.

In the Brennan case, it was Hesburgh himself, with Joyce's backing as chairman of the athletic board, who yielded to the dark attraction college administrators seem always to have to firing football coaches. While bringing Notre Dame into the 20th century academically, an achievement for which he may well deserve sainthood, Hesburgh had taken on Leahy's victory machine—four national championships, in 1943, 1946, 1947, and 1949—and some highly dubious coaching ethics, and by 1953 had cut that eccentric genius down to size with restrictions that, in Leahy's eyes, if not Hesburgh's, amounted to de-emphasis. The number of scholarships was cut from 40 to 20 for a year, and the football department was made to adhere to strict eligibility rules.

Then, in 1954, Hesburgh helped ease Leahy, only 45 but suffering from ileitis, into retirement. "We made no effort to keep him," Joyce admits now. Four years later, Hesburgh had to scuttle Brennan, his personal choice as Leahy's replacement, when it became obvious that Brennan wasn't going to win enough games under those same restrictions.

The experiment in de-emphasis was over. It had done precious little for Notre Dame's spiritual or financial needs. Recalls an alumnus who has remained close to his alma mater for 40 years, "Fund-raisers were not mad. They were furious." It's not likely that Hesburgh will make such a mistake again. For one thing, he's too alert to fiscal needs. Notre Dame's endowment was $8.5 million in 1952: it's now more than $200 million and in the top 20 nationally.

In recent years, Hesburgh and Joyce have been outspoken critics of those abuses that have fouled college sport. Just last month, at the National Football Foundation and [College] Hall of Fame dinner, Hesburgh called for a stricter code of academic standards—and struck fear in several university comptrollers' hearts by saying that Notre Dame might refuse to schedule schools that don't abide such a code. There is some risk in this crusading business, especially if your own laundry isn't clean. But Joyce and Hesburgh can speak with confidence that their school has been obeying the letter—and even the spirit—of the rules.

Evidence: a private survey of the National Football League two years ago showed that of the 31 former Notre Damers then playing in the NFL, 30 had their degrees. When he passed on the survey to me, Joyce said that No. 31, New York Giant offensive tackle Jeff Weston, not wanting to be the lone ranger, was returning to school to get his diploma, which he has since done.

In the 18 years that Mike DeCicco, the Notre Dame athletic department's liaison with academe, who doubles as the Irish fencing coach, has kept such records, only five Notre Dame football players have completed their eligibility without getting their degrees. Since 1971, all 41 basketball players who have completed their eligibility have earned degrees. Every single one.

Moreover, it must be noted that Notre Dame doesn't offer any of those "life science" majors or have any other apparent means of shielding an athlete from exposure to at least some of the rigors of scholarship. At all schools there are a few professors who grade athletes with affection—like the beloved "88" O'Grady, who taught philosophy at Notre Dame from 1936 to 1956—but there's no such thing as a jock curriculum in South Bend.

There's no athletic dormitory at Notre Dame, either. Notre Dame doesn't believe in segregating athletes. Says Joyce, "We expect our athletes to be full-time members of the student body, no more, no less." In the dorms, the jocks get no perks, no favors, no fancy hideaways for watching color television. There is no special training table, except during the season of an athlete's sport when he has no choice but to dine late (after practice). Even then he eats the same food as everyone else in one of the two campus dining halls. The athlete, in sum, benefits from having lived a "complete" college experience, rather than tunneling through a narrow corridor to the pros.

Seventy-five percent of the scholarship athletes in football and basketball are liberal arts or business majors; the other 25 percent divide into engineering, premed, and prelaw. They, like other students involved in extracurricular activities, are granted one privilege in their academics: a priority in arranging their class schedules so that they can be free by 3:00 P.M. to practice. But even this isn't always possible, and when laboratories run to 4:00 or 5:00 P.M., as they often do, it's the coaches, not the athletes, who must make an accommodation.

Neither does Notre Dame believe in redshirting, and allows it only in cases of injury, never to "season" a player for later service. It pushes its athletes to graduate in four years. Most do. If one fails or drops a course, he must make it up in summer school. If his grade point average falls below the required 2.0 or he's lagging in the credits he needs (30 a year) for normal progress toward a degree, same thing— summer school. The salutary results can be charted: of the 28 players who were given football scholarships in 1978, 25 graduated on time in 1982. Two are still in school and will get their degrees. Only one dropped out.

What good could possibly accrue to the athletic program in terms of successful teams under such academic orthodoxy? Economics professor William Leahy says the Notre Dame faculty is "more appreciative" of its athletes—a subtle bonus. "They're not privileged characters, and we see it."

Equally illuminating is Notre Dame's police record with the NCAA. Great success attracts underminers who try to bring greatness down. Undermining is tacitly approved by the NCAA because its policing process calls for "cooperative enforcement," which means members are encouraged to snitch on each other when rules are believed to be broken. Currently 20 of the 788 member schools are on some kind of probation, and 30 to 40 more are under investigation. Since 1952, 261 public penalties have been handed down. It would seem only natural that with its high profile Notre Dame would have gotten nabbed at one time or another. And it has. Twice: in 1952, when it was "reprimanded" for illegal tryouts, and in 1971, when it was "reprimanded" for a minor technicality involving the grant-in-aid forms of several football players.

But that's it. Two misdemeanors—reprimands are the NCAA equivalent of parking tickets—in 62 years of big-time football and basketball. When I asked NCAA Director of the Public Relations David E. Cawood, he said, "The astonishing thing our enforcement people find is that they get so few complaints [about Notre Dame]. For a school that attracts so much envy, and even hate, you would expect it would be defending itself all the time. But nobody points a finger."

Last winter the reverse occurred. Digger Phelps, Notre Dame's basketball coach for 11 years, pointed the finger at certain unnamed programs in his sport that he said were paying star players $10,000 a year under the table. The interesting thing about the charge wasn't that Phelps made it—he has been saying as much privately for years—but that he aroused no *counter* charges. Not one rival coach was heard to say that Phelps should clean up his own act before implicating others. To the contrary, the integrity of Notre Dame's program was never questioned.

The ability of Notre Dame's leadership to see the ways as well as the values of staying clean in an increasingly dirty world must be considered a reason that the school's reputation for rectitude goes unchallenged. Over the last couple of decades Hesburgh and Joyce have skillfully avoided the pitfalls that others so willingly leap into. There are, for example, no Notre Dame booster clubs, those rabid alumni-and-friends groups, [that] at other schools create so many of the embarrassments (under-the-table payoffs, recruiting misdeeds, etc.) that result in penalties.

This isn't to say that Notre Dame discourages financial support. It generates millions through the 164 alumni clubs that Hesburgh shamelessly plies for funds. But not one penny of any contribution can be earmarked for athletes or athletics. All donations go into the university's general fund. Therefore, no direct influence can be exerted by old grads on the athletic program. Notre Dame alumni clubs are notorious for complaining about the Irish football coach's won-lost record—and consistent in getting nowhere with their complaints.

Two football seasons ago, Joyce hired Gerry Faust from a Catholic high school in Cincinnati to succeed Dan Devine as football coach even though Faust had never coached a day at the college level or ever recruited a college player. An ominous murmur could be heard from the direction of the alumni clubs. This apparent lapse in good sense should be carefully examined because it will tell us more about Notre Dame than meets the eye.

Six months earlier, Joyce had announced that for the first time in Notre Dame history an athletic endowment fund was being established, with a goal of $10 million. In justifying this new endowment program, which would be administered by the office of development, *not* the athletic department, Joyce had cited soaring expenses, which had cut the "advantage" football and basketball revenues traditionally gained, as well as the need to expand the athletic program for women. Revenues in 1980 had reached an all-time high ($4.3 million), but expenditures were so large that the net had been only $29,000. By contrast, over a 50-year period—from back in Rockne's day to 1980—Notre Dame's athletic department showed an average annual profit of $250,000.

An essential ingredient in Notre Dame's rise to glory has been the keen eye its leadership has always had for the bottom line. The power of profits has never been lost on the school. It's a pragmatism that comes directly from Rockne and is best illustrated by one example. In Depression-wracked 1930, when the entire nation seemed on the verge of disintegrating, Notre Dame was *building*. It was building two dormitories, the law school, the engineering school, the commerce building, and the new football stadium, mainly because Rockne's football teams had gained a national constituency through as slick a packaging job as spectator sport has ever seen. The Irish were a box-office smash year after year. And always, the profits were pumped back into the general fund. After financing the rest of the athletic program, Rockne's undefeated 1930 team *netted* $689,000. Says Francis Johns, class of 1929, a South Bend attorney and intimate of his alma mater's administrators and athletes, "Notre Dame has *never* had a depression."

That being the case, what did the hiring, at this critical fiscal juncture, of a high school coach represent? One editorialist suggested that it amounted to bringing in a local car dealer to run General Motors. But it strikes me that there are two ways to look at the chance taken in hiring Faust. One, it was a gamble not inconsistent with others taken during the Hesburgh-Joyce era. Parseghian, for example, turned out to be the *beau idéal* of all Notre Dame coaches, but his previous coaching success was limited to several above-average seasons at Northwestern. He was no sure thing. To this day, neither Joyce nor Hesburgh admits to understanding why Devine (1975–1980) wasn't beloved by the Irish faithful. He arrived in South Bend with a distinguished record, and he gave the fans good teams and even a national championship. When he could no longer handle the alumni charges that he somehow "didn't fit," Devine quit. He wouldn't have been fired.

Any coaching job carries within itself seeds of an abrupt termination, but last winter, after his 5–6 inaugural season, there wasn't—and there still isn't—any movement by the university toward ending Faust's employment at Notre Dame. The jury of public opinion may still be out, but Joyce and Hesburgh don't answer to juries. Or alumni clubs.

Which brings us to the second, or more idealistic, way of looking at the Faust hiring. It represented a kind of *Dei gratia* stand for right-eousness at Notre Dame, and never mind the business risk. Faust was more than just a successful high school coach. He was a devout, stand-up Catholic who made a lasting positive impression on his players. "We have a short motto," says Joyce. "'What's good for the boy is good for Notre Dame.' I think Gerry Faust will be good for the boys." In effect, the Faust hiring put Notre Dame's actions where its mouth has always been. But not [where it] always was. A South Bend man who was close to Leahy recalls his installation in 1941. "Leahy asked Father So-and-so, 'What do they want?' Father So-and-so said, 'They want to win, and they don't care how.'"

Certainly, the hiring of Faust was more in line with what Notre Dame now sees itself to be, and that's almost as important as what it is. To be good, you must aspire to goodness. It doesn't come naturally.

In answering Joyce's challenge, I've now heard many voices giving many impressions of Notre Dame. Not all the voices were admiring ones. One rival coach denounced the school's "bullying" ways, especially at Notre Dame Stadium, and the "smugness" of its leadership in not taking "certain types of athletes."

Even some of those who were intimately connected don't feel that the bricks of Notre Dame were laid by angels. Alan Page, an All-America on the 1966 team, says that the place "never had a mythical effect on me." He says it was different "only in that it was smaller and you couldn't get lost in the classes the way you might at Minnesota." Page says he has "no nostalgia for Notre Dame."

Perceptions randomly given are, of course, imperfect barometers. It is, rather, the weight of evidence between the extremes that make the larger truth. In sorting out an accumulation of viewpoints, I found that the majority of those who have played at Notre Dame have an unusual affection for the place, even more deeply felt than I had imagined. Many of them talk in terms of the bond they forged, the kind you find among participants in a great mutual undertaking, like a war or a social crusade. They are not, however, of one mind.

The earlier ones speak almost exclusively of the football experience, how inspiring that was. Johnny Lujack quarterbacked the national championship teams of 1946 and 1947. He remembers his first visit to the Notre Dame campus as a high school senior. "I got to meet the coach [Leahy], to see the Notre Dame team, to be in the locker room after the game," he says. "Everything was the way I'd imagined it. Hell, if God had taken me then, I'd have thought I'd had a full life, and I was 17 years old."

Those whose experience is more recent seem to see Notre Dame in broader measure, as if in recognition of the greater breadth Hesburgh has brought to virtually all aspects of the university. In the pre-Hesburgh days. Notre Dame was considered academically a limited, sectarian institution and not necessarily even the best of the nation's Catholic schools. Today it's a well-regarded, "national" university that, while certainly no Harvard, ranks comfortably within the top 100 of the nation's 2,500 colleges.

Michael Oriard, a walk-on center who cocaptained the 1969 team, recalls that of the 10 or 12 people "I really lived with" in the dorm at Notre Dame, only he played football. "Four of the others are now doctors, three are lawyers, two are engineers," he says. "They were guys who got great educations. But you know, they never missed a football game." Oriard is now an English professor at Oregon State.

And among the contemporary players, there is unmistakable pride in being honorable at a time when honor seems to be in short supply. Standout senior defensive back Dave Duerson was, of course, recruited by other schools. Duerson says one recruiter in the South told him, "When you take a test here, all you have to do is put your jersey number on top of the paper. That'll get you your grade." Duerson says the suggestion turned him off: "I had a 3.75 average in high school. I didn't need any free passes."

What these statements of devotion—especially the ones from more recent players—say is that the experience of being at Notre Dame is enhanced by the way football is integrated into the very marrow of university life. Football isn't a matter of survival at Notre Dame—it hasn't been that since the twenties when Rockne put the school on the map—it's a matter of enrichment. The game has greatly enhanced the school and continues to do so.

Why is it important to accept football's eminence in Notre Dame's life? Does doing so not admit that Notre Dame is, after all, a "football factory," just like a lot of other big-time schools? Of course it does, but the point is this: Notre Dame has a leadership that knows how to appreciate football as much as it knows how to control it. That's a combination that has led to an integrity of purpose that didn't spring from some bygone miracle but has been an evolutionary thing brought about mainly by good people doing a good job. Notre Dame's special quality when it comes to athletics isn't a superior morality, but a superior and deeply involved leadership.

Says Hesburgh, "No coach can ever say he wasn't aware of our policies." Joyce, who, with Hesburgh's blessing, runs Notre Dame athletics as a sort of autonomous fiefdom, says he "constantly reminds people that integrity is our top priority here. I do that personally, not through an intermediary. . . . Many schools fail in athletics because of a lack of control at the top. We will never have that here."

Like all human institutions, Notre Dame isn't "pure" and never has been. It's not above reproach and never has been. But it strives mightily to attain purity and be above reproach. The heart of the matter is that Notre Dame is proud of being righteous. This creates a perpetuating kind of morality. In a way, this makes obeying the rules easier. When you build for yourself a glass house, you watch what you wear to the breakfast table.

All the testimony supports this trust. When Anthony Lewis, one of the first blacks to play for Notre Dame and now a vice president of F. W. Woolworth Co. in New York, says, "The quality of the education, the quality of the people, the integrity, the honesty—they must never change," he means that Notre Dame is obligated to this. Parseghian says that he's proudest of the fact that he achieved what he did "without ever cheating." He says Notre Dame has an "obligation" to set this example. "People have a need to idolize, to look up to something. Notre Dame provides that."

It got to that only in time, however. Early on, Notre Dame was holier-than-thou, but not always so holy. Only in recent times has the reality come close to living up to the reputation. There's some irony in this, too. As its outside image became more liberal, Notre Dame's inner commitment to scrupulous behavior—at least in its athletics— became more conservative.

Notre Dame doesn't cheat in recruiting. At least there's no evidence that it does, and the prospect of having the man at the top intervene if it did is surely a reason for coaches not being tempted to cut corners. The leadership rides equally hard on academic matters. Joyce gets monthly progress reports from DeCicco, who gets them from deans and professors. Admissions are gone over with a fine-tooth comb. Notre Dame requires an incoming freshman athlete to have a combined score of at least 900 on his SATs, rate in the top third of his high school graduating class, and be credited with 16 units of English, foreign language, social studies, science, and math at a minimum 2.0 average. There are no special admissions.

Notre Dame doesn't take junior college or transfer athletes ostensibly because it doesn't want to be in the business of "prepping" players for big-time football or basketball, but also because it doesn't want to risk trusting the entrance criteria or normal progress rules of other institutions.

Those are guidelines. In point of fact, circumstances can warrant making exceptions—and two such cases were on the football team last fall. Fullback Larry Moriarity, whose grandfather and brother played at Notre Dame, came in from Santa Barbara City College. Tight end Rick Gray transferred from Clemson to nearby Holy Cross Junior College, and then to Notre Dame. Both cases had to go to the athletic faculty board, whose chairman is Joyce. The rationales for their acceptances were that it had made sense for Moriarity to attend a college near his home while recovering from the trauma caused by a traffic accident and, later, a near-fatal case of spinal meningitis, while Gray had been previously accepted by Notre Dame's admissions committee. Nevertheless, I have to think a considerable soul-searching was involved on Joyce's part.

It's simply not accurate to believe, moreover, that Notre Dame doesn't make academic allowances when competing for athletes. It suffers its share of coaches lobbying director of admissions John Goldrick for special consideration. Goldrick doesn't always turn a deaf ear. The difference is that his gray areas for admissions are just not as broad as those at numerous other schools, and the scrutiny—primarily Goldrick's, but Joyce's too—is so keen that a coach would be ill-advised to try pulling a fast one with, say, a recruit's transcript. DeCicco says that only 3 of the 27 football players brought in on scholarship last year were under the standards, and "any more than that would have the admissions department screaming, not to mention Father Joyce."

The halfback who can run a 4.4 40 or the quarterback who can throw a 60-yard spiral into a water bucket might get in with 14 credits or a combined SAT score of 850 or a "predicted" GPA of 2.0 (the NCAA's minimum), "but never a combination of the three," DeCicco adds.

Willie Fry, a defensive end (class of 1978), came in with only two years of math, but high grades in other subjects made him a worthwhile risk and he graduated on schedule. Halfback Jerome Heavens (1979) raised some eyebrows at Notre Dame when he was accepted there. His average, says DeCicco, was barely over 2.0, and he "generally didn't have the numbers in other areas." In such instances, Notre Dame tries hardest of all. "With Heavens we went on red alert," DeCicco says. We had him tutored in English, math, and science, and we kept waiting for the other shoe to drop. He majored in economics and graduated in 3½ years."

It would be naïve to believe that this devotion to scholarship has always been so scrupulous at Notre Dame, or that it would be so if the leadership qualities weren't as strong in the coach's offices as they are in the administrators'. Notre Dame has been blessed by many things, and more than anything, it has been blessed by the presence of three extraordinary football coaches: Rockne, Leahy, and Parseghian. The fact is, however, that by Hesburgh-Joyce standards, only Parseghian would measure up as exemplary. Rockne was a football original—a brilliant coach, a spellbinding orator, and an entrepreneurial genius. Notre Dame was lucky he came along. But he was also a shameless huckster who played loose with the truth, and there is more than casual evidence that his dedication to the academic side of his players' lives was not as rigorous as some have made it out to be. Leahy had the Irish good looks of a movie idol. He was capable of eloquent, impassioned speeches and was a tactical genius. But Leahy was also a practice-field martinet obsessed with winning, and he brought more than a casual shame on old Notre Dame by his devious on-field tactics—for example, the notorious sucker shifts and fake-injury plays.

As for Parseghian there is no evidence that he recruited illegally or that he pampered or paid his athletes or that he played loose with the rules. He wasn't even paid like a big-time coach at least at the start. He came to Notre Dame for $20,000 a year, a $2,000 raise from his salary at Northwestern. He didn't ask for or get a car or a house. In the end, of course, he became rich and famous. It could be argued that it was justified all around.

Along with Notre Dame's administration, Parseghian believed, as does Faust, that big-time athletics and meaningful education are compatible, that you can compete and still have your athletes graduate in four years, and not be segregated in jock dorms, and not be bribed as recruits or babied as undergraduates, and not be paid a penny beyond the costs of their education. But as long as Notre Dame's leadership clings to the fable that "football is only a game, no more, no less," a statement Hesburgh made at the 1981 football banquet, it will come up short of being an athletic paragon.

To show that that statement has the heavy odor of baloney, one need only compare the treatment afforded Notre Dame's football and basketball programs with that given its other varsity sports. Football and basketball get a ton of support and attention, not because they are better character builders or better examples of manliness or anything else. They get it because they represent money and interest. And the chance to make more money and get more interest. You don't concoct a $1.9 million budget for a sport that is "only" a sport. The practical consideration is as important as the idealistic one. As long as this isn't acknowledged, the inconsistencies will jump out every time the lid is off.

It is fiction that Notre Dame is successful in all 18 varsity sports. There are now only four full-time head coaches at Notre Dame—in football, basketball, hockey, and women's basketball (as a concession to Title IX legislation). Other head coaches must perform other duties. Of the 160 athletes now on scholarship, 95 (the NCAA limit) are football players, 18 are hockey players, 13 are basketball players. The other sports divide and subdivide—by giving "partials"—the rest: track gets eleven, women's basketball eight, baseball four, tennis two, golf one, etc.

The results speak for themselves. The Notre Dame baseball team had eight losing seasons in the 10-year period from 1971 through 1980. Since 1958, swimming has been .538. The tennis team had six undefeated seasons and won two NCAA titles, but those came over a 60-year period and it doesn't do very well anymore. DeCicco's fencing team is a notable exception: with no scholarships and a tiny budget ($45,000), it has achieved a 369–36 record in 21 years.

The rationale is practical and understandable: football and basketball make money, the others don't. Phelps' teams have sold out every home game for 10 years, and the basketball budget benefits accordingly. After expenses of $455,000 (including salaries of $107,000 and grants-in-aid of $90,000), the 1981–1982 basketball team made $160,000. Football in 1981–1982 had expenses of $1,900,000, including $339,000 in salaries, $651,000 in grants, $148,000 in travel, and $101,000 in recruiting. It spent $36,000 on film, $19,000 on laundry, and $19,000 on long-distance telephone calls. And it made a profit of $577,000.

Joyce says he's sympathetic to the idea that increased support could make other sports do better and perhaps make more money, but he's not inclined to wait too long for it to happen. In 1980 hockey was promoted heavily for the first lime and it drew nice crowds. But at the end of the year it had nevertheless lost $123,000, and in 1981 its wings were clipped. The Notre Dame hockey team now competes in a "bus league," in which it doesn't have to fly to away games. Joyce is hopeful that women's basketball "will prove revenue-producing," and in 1980 granted $220,000 a year to run that program. But he admits if it were field hockey "such an expense would be unconscionable."

Joyce is correct, of course, when he says a university can have a "satisfactory athletic program without being expensive." He's justifiably proud that Notre Dame supports 28 intramural sports and 11 club sports. These are never revenue-producing. The profits from varsity football cover the expense. Moreover, it wouldn't be very practical to throw fistfuls of money into sports that might color the bottom line red. You have to call a halt somewhere. Lavishly endowed Ivy League schools "can afford a million-dollar loss in athletics," says Joyce, "but Notre Dame can't."

Notre Dame doesn't have to. Its football team has been on network television 71 times. It has been the subject of more than 50 books. Its appeal has been instrumental in the foundation of 164 Notre Dame alumni clubs. It continues to be the linchpin for the entire Notre Dame athletic program and the promulgator of the Notre Dame image that makes the school's endowment drives so much easier.

Notre Dame? Father Joyce was right in issuing his challenge. It tells us something worth listening to. I remember a full-page ad from *Time* magazine that ran midway through the second decade of the Hesburgh-Joyce administration. Taking up half the ad was a picture of a football. Under the football was a caption: "If that's all you know about Notre Dame, you have a lot to learn." That is clearly the truth.

Eric Zorn, *Notre Dame Magazine*

FOOTBALL WEEKEND

Experiencing all that's involved in a football weekend at Notre Dame is no easy task. It requires a mountain of energy, at minimum. So, Eric Zorn, a Chicago Tribune *columnist, experienced one for himself in 1992 and then wrote about it for* Notre Dame Magazine.

Friday, Noon

What in the world possesses these people?

No, not those people—not the 2,400 people dressed in green and gold and blue spread out at an endless expanse of round tables on the floor of the Joyce Athletic and Convocation Center [JACC] Fieldhouse here on the Notre Dame campus. We know what possesses them: they are members of the Quarterback Club, here to eat a roast beef lunch with other very serious football fans and then to push back from their tables and listen to a round of comforting gridiron platitudes.

I mean these people way back here: this genial, middle-aged couple sitting on the top row of the bleachers that rise in the rear of the great hall, on beyond the tables, on beyond a high green curtain, well across the hockey rink—100 yards or so from the dais at which Lou Holtz will soon hold forth. What possesses them?

"I'm not sure," admits Carl Hieber, taking his eyes off the distant scene for just a moment when he is pressed on the point. "I didn't go to this school. And," he adds after a moment's puzzled reflection, "I'm Lutheran."

But here he is—having taken two days off from work and driven nearly 10 hours from his home in Williamsport, Pennsylvania—sitting with his wife, Beverly, in the cheapest of cheap seats just to gaze upon the Quarterback Club luncheon. It is the first official event of the elaborate, multifaceted carnival that is a football weekend at Notre Dame, and even though the lunch has long been sold out at $11 a plate and the only seats available are in this distant spectator's gallery, the Hiebers have arrived well before the speeches and are now simply watching other people eat.

Oh, sure, Notre Dame has a fine football program and all, but why don't the Hiebers get nutty for a team closer to home, like Pitt? Penn State? Temple? Rutgers? Even Slippery Rock State?

"I've been for Notre Dame since I was a kid," says Carl. "I guess because I could always get their games on the radio."

Beverly Hieber, who also did not go to school here, adds happily, "I just like the excitement of being on campus."

Good thing, too. She has more than 24 hours to kill before kickoff, and the lucky people way down there at the luncheon have yet to start on dessert. You can't see from here, but it's brownies and cookies.

12:15 P.M.

Several souvenir stands on the perimeter are loaded up and ready to go. They offer Notre Dame golf umbrellas, $42. Notre Dame baby jerseys, six-month size, $15. Notre Dame hand towels, $12. Notre Dame boxer shorts, $9. A limited-edition, framed set of the historical trilogy paintings featuring such great moments in Notre Dame football history as Joe Montana leading the comeback in the 1979 Cotton Bowl, $6,000.

Twenty such paintings are available at a total price of $29,800 if purchased individually, or $13,000 if you buy the full set right now. They are, quite deliberately and unapologetically, icons. Artist Steven Csorba has hand-painted these football images onto a flat, weathered, gold background sharply reminiscent of ancient religious art. Faces and quotations appear on tablets. What rumpus room is really complete without a graven image of Lou Holtz over such words as, "The only reason a person should exist is to be the best he can"?

12:30 P.M.

"I am always amazed," says Lou Holtz in the flesh, having stepped up to the dais, "with the great way, the articulate way, that our athletes get up here and talk about their experiences at Notre Dame. We give them no thoughts, no ideas whatsoever. We just say, 'Get up and speak from your heart.'"

"I'd like to share a few things with you from my heart," begins senior tight end Irv Smith after Holtz concludes his introduction. "Because of what coach Holtz has instilled in each and every one of us, I've been able to grow through each of my four years, and it's given me the opportunity to be the best human being I possibly can be."

Holtz returns to the podium at the end of Smith's brief remarks. The amateur magician is a crisp emcee, his sentences even, quick, and regular, with a predictable rise at the beginning and fall at the end.

"We have an unbelievable student body," he says. "Their enthusiasm, their love of life are just an inspiration to me, and I say that sincerely."

1:20 P.M.

Holtz's final words to the Quarterback Club serve as a preamble for this weekend and for every home football weekend at Notre Dame.

"I love being at Notre Dame," he says with that matter-of-fact passion of his. "The only thing I truly regret is that more people can't experience what Notre Dame is all about on a weekend. Not the game, but going into Sacred Heart, going down by the Grotto, coming to the luncheon, walking on campus, seeing the people, visiting with the students, etc. The Notre Dame football team is not the most important thing—the most important thing is really and truly being part of the Notre Dame spirit."

1:25 P.M.

Bill Schafer [class of 1949] flew yesterday from his home in Riverside, California, to Chicago, where he rented a car and drove two more hours to South Bend. He carried in his wallet the ticket stub from the first Notre Dame football game he ever attended, on November 23, 1935. He was wearing his "ND Fighting Irish" sweater, and he is, at this moment, gazing delightedly at his own tiny, blurry image in a 360-degree photographic panorama from the 1989 Fiesta Bowl.

If you were in the class of 1949 and don't recognize Schafer's name, don't worry—it wasn't the Notre Dame class of 1949; it was the DePaul University class of 1949. Schafer, the Hiebers, and literally thousands of others now crawling over the campus are the notorious "subway alumni." And yes, reports the Alumni Association, many of them do actually donate money to their un–alma mater.

1:50 P.M.

"I just want to look," begs Jim Harty, a 34-year-old fan. "Please. Just one picture?"

Security guard Tom Boykins says no, no, no, no, sorry, but no. He's standing watch outside stadium Gate 1, and Harty is one in a stream of fans who approach him, trying to wheedle their way in. They tell him how long they have been following the Irish ("Since I was a little kid," says Harty), how far they have come ("We're all the way from Jamestown, North Dakota," says Harty), and how humble their request really is ("We'll just peek at the field for a second"). But Boykins remains unmoved.

Serious work is taking place inside the stadium. Telephone and television crews are laying cable and plugging things into other things. At the 50-yard line, veteran groundskeeper Galen Berger fusses over the numbers on the field with a product called Pioneer Brite Stripe. "I'm touching up the zeros," he explains. "From one angle they look fine, but because of the way the grass is lying, they look bad from the other angle."

2:30 P.M.

It is a peaceful afternoon in the recreational vehicle parking area south of the JACC. The first of the RVs began arriving very early this morning, and by now at least 100 of them have staked out territory in what is quickly becoming a thriving little community.

"We rent this thing for five days for $900," explains Ed Small, 25, a Philadelphian in a Gumby T-shirt, of his 30-foot Winnebago camper. He is here with eight friends. "We've got our roller blades and our kegs," he says. "We're planning to drink all day here, go to the pep rally, then party all night."

Outside a nearby 35-foot Crown Imperial camper, five guys in their fifties from the East Coast are polluting the immediate air with smelly cigars while blasting the Notre Dame Glee Club's *Shake Down the Thunder* album from the stereo. "It's the buildup we love, not so much the game," says Harold Weber of Seneca Falls, New York. "The whole point is to socialize with all the other animals," adds Dennis Coggins of Pittsford, New York.

Did they bring their wives or girlfriends along? Don Plourde of Lancaster, Pennsylvania, almost swallows his cheroot. "What's your next silly question?" he demands.

3:00 P.M.

Grown men and women in gaudy clothing they'd be embarrassed to wear anywhere else are strolling the campus in groups of two, three, and four. They point out buildings to one another. They read the hand-painted banners hanging from dormitory windows—"The Best Defense Is a Great Offense" dangling from a window on Cavanaugh Hall, for instance. They sit on benches by the Clarke Memorial Fountain near Nieuwland Science Hall and experience again—or perhaps for the first time—a sense of belonging at Notre Dame. At the Hammes Bookstore, the line to get in at this moment is 30 yards long. Even sportscaster-provocateur Dick Vitale isn't getting cuts.

"I'm a fan," says Ward Mahoney, 70, of Struthers, Ohio, who is near the back of the line, "But she"—he thumbs to his wife—"is a nut." Helen "Nunchie" Mahoney, wearing a green visor and an "Irish Fever, Catch It" T-shirt, accepts this assessment as a compliment.

3:30 P.M.

Inside the jammed bookstore, Jay Mondry, 61, a district court judge from Park Rapids, Minnesota, is shouldering down the aisles with arm-loads of merchandise and insatiably looking for more.

"A Notre Dame cap, $15," he says, showing it off. "It's always nice to have some extras around. And here's a Notre Dame flag, $19. I had one before, but gave it away."

And? "Notre Dame golf shirt for myself, $33. Two little Notre Dame shirts for my grandchildren, $11 each. A double-X Notre Dame T-shirt for me, $15, a Notre Dame sweatshirt, $34, and a Notre Dame, what would you call this—warm-up undershirt?—$33."

A district court judge, mind you. One hesitates to estimate the purchasing habits of less sober and restrained individuals, and the Hammes Bookstore management refuses to release even a rough approximation of how many extra tens of thousands of dollars they'll see on a weekend like this.

4:00 P.M.
A man wearing a sandwich board walks slowly through the crowd outside the bookstore. "ND '63 grad, drove from Dallas," the sign reads. "Needs two tickets. Go Irish."

Another man has fastened a "Need 4" sign to the front of his T-shirt with duct tape. Others simply hold their signs and rely on the sales pitch—"Need 2 tickets for the Gipper. Will pay best price for 2." And simply, "Please."

Action is very slow. The going rate, report the needy, is still $150 a ticket—steep because tomorrow's opponent happens to be highly ranked Michigan, and the winner stands to end up No. 1 in the early season polls.

Halfway across campus, the football players carry their equipment from the locker room at Loftus Sports Center over to the stadium.

4:30 P.M.
A man in bright green pants and a 1992 Sugar Bowl, "ND-39, Florida-28" T-shirt is lighting a candle at the Grotto of Our Lady of Lourdes. For world peace? For a departed family member? For a smashing victory tomorrow? He keeps his secret.

As he gets up from the kneeler to leave, marching band members can be heard in the distance warming up with a Scott Joplin rag. A small ensemble will make a circuit of the campus while the rest of the band meets on Green Field for a rehearsal.

5:00 P.M.
Well, of course, wouldn't you know the hot water heater would break on this day of all days?

Notre Dame senior Justin Jakovac, 22, from Allegany, New York, has emerged from a brief, tepid shower and is standing in the living room of his off-campus apartment consulting with one of his roommates, James Ashburn, 21, from McMinnville, Tennessee, on plans for their pregame party tonight. Who will buy the steaks? Who will pick up the beer? Who's going to stay behind during the pep rally to greet early guests?

At least the apartment is relatively clean. Justin and James have stuffed as much furniture as possible into the bedroom occupied by their third roommate, Matt Helminiak, 20, from Sykesville, Maryland, and pushed everything else flush to the wall. This exposes great, unappetizing expanses of brown carpeting bearing sticky, discolored reminders of previous soirées.

This apartment is an anthropological specimen—the habitat of *homo collegiatus*: a two-bedroom, two-story, $545-a-month unit in the Turtle Creek Apartments complex just east of campus, decorated with posters celebrating beer, music, and football, as well as scores of photographs of fashion models clipped from magazines. One prominent sign reads, "To survive you need four things—food, sex, shelter, guitars. Make that two things."

A set of cardboard tablets in the corner states the Ten Commandments by which these young men live. Many of them are in-jokes, but the first two are simple enough:

I. Notre Dame is thy school. Thou shalt have no other schools before it.
II. Keep holy football Saturdays.

Football is a unifying element on campus, a common cause, a social catalyst. It is not, however, what drew Justin to Notre Dame— not exactly. What he liked when he visited here in March of his senior high school year, he says, was "the aura, the mystique, and the tradition" of the place, some of which is intertwined, even confused with football. "It sure wasn't the weather," he adds.

6:00 P.M.
The boys expect 90 guests tonight, so Justin buys three kegs of Budweiser at Citywide Liquors. Each $40 keg holds the equivalent of 216 12-ounce glasses of beer—seven beers per guest. He also buys four bags of ice and several stacks of plastic cups, which he and his roommates will later "sell" to guests for $2 to help cover the cost of the party.

Justin and an employee of Citywide load the kegs into the back of the truck, and Justin drives back to the apartment. The day has been a good one so far—a diverting study of Anglo-Saxon poetry in his British Lit class in DeBartolo Hall, then a workout in the weight room at Rockne Memorial.

The literature classes are something new for Justin. Over last summer, he dropped engineering and switched to English, a change of majors that did not go over well with his family, he says. He drew a cartoon for the *Scholastic* about the conversation he had with his father. "I can get a job with an English degree," the character representing

Justin says. "Yeah, right," says the father's character. "Look, I'll put you through school. But when I see you on a street in 10 years begging quarters from passers by, I'll kick the bottle of Night Train out of your hands and laugh my ass off."

6:15 P.M.

Justin and James unload the kegs, and James stays behind while Justin heads toward campus to catch Zahm Hall's 23rd annual freshman initiation conducted on the evening before the first home football game.

"The male-female ratio here is always a problem," he says sadly. "They say it's improving, and I guess it is. But last year we were at a party where there were six guys to every girl, and we said, 'Hey, we're doing all right!'"

Of the three roommates, only Justin is unencumbered by entangling alliances. James has a serious long-distance girlfriend, and Matt has an on-campus steady with whom he is puzzling out the future.

6:30 P.M.

At the Hesburgh Library, some 100 men dressed in bedsheet togas are wading disconsolately into the chilly reflecting pool in two parallel lines, their heads down.

"All hail Odin," they chant. Each year, an elder dorm resident is selected to play Odin, a wise and all-knowing Nordic god. He dresses in lordly regalia and leads the initiates in ritual debasement.

"On your knees," commands Odin, played this year by junior Doug Scholer in a flowing robe and warrior's hat. The freshmen comply.

Odin's foot soldiers wade up and down the line, liberally applying shaving cream to the heads of the initiates. "And now," Odin thunders, "we will sing 'Twinkle, Twinkle, Little Star!' I know you all know it."

This draws a laugh from the rapidly growing crowd of students and alumni standing three and four deep around the pool. The song begins, tentatively, pathetically, and Odin forces up the volume with repeated cries of "I can't hear you!"

When they are done Odin commands the initiates to proceed double-time to the mud pit. So the freshmen run east, crossing Juniper Road at exactly the same moment that the marching band is crossing in the other direction a hundred yards north, drums rattling, children following behind, on their circuitous way to the pep rally.

The men in robes end their mad dash behind the Band Building, where a sprinkler has turned a 30-foot long patch of naked soil into swamp. Two by two they scream "I love Zahm" and dive—mostly head first—then come up gasping for air, swallowing slop.

"What a beautiful display," says Justin, who stands just far enough back to avoid getting spattered.

7:00 P.M.

The pep rally crowd fills the basketball arena in the JACC—the muddy men of Zahm Hall take a block of seats close to the back row, far from the floor where the team members, cheerleaders, and marching band are assembling. Justin is interested to hear that such pep rallies are not common at other universities anymore—for big games, yes, from time to time, but routinely, with such vigor? No.

The band plays the "Victory March," the leprechaun dances, and the crowd claps. Paul Hornung, 1957, is the first to speak: "I guarantee you these kids will play the game of their lives tomorrow," he says.

The other remarks echo those heard earlier in the day at the Quarterback Club: "We'll come through for you," promises defensive tackle Bryant Young. "I hope you all wear your green tomorrow and get fired up for us," says quarterback Rick Mirer.

The muddy men of Zahm interrupt Mirer to begin the chant. "We are (clap, clap) ND (clap, clap). We are (clap, clap) ND (clap, clap)." It spreads through the arena.

8:00 P.M.

"Aww, I miss this," says Mark Donahue, 1992, one of nine young men in Justin Jakovic's apartment when he returns from the rally. "Notre Dame was the best four years of my life." He is now a first-year medical student at the University of Cincinnati and is back for a football weekend.

"It's very weird," he says. "I walk around campus and these annoying alumni come up because they think I'm a student and want to ask me what I think about Demetrius DuBose or Rick Mirer. I have to tell them, 'Sorry. I graduated.'" Mark makes a face; "I'm one of you now."

Justin's roommate James, who is clearly the rudder to the ship of this apartment, is serving "steak dinners to everyone." "Steak dinner," in the lexicon of male college seniors, is a piece of meat on a clean plate. No garnish. No vegetable. No bread. No soup. No napkin.

Ben Moore and Chris Queensbury are among the dinner guests who will also be spending the weekend flopped somewhere in the apartment. The two are roommates in Kill Devil Hills, North Carolina. Ben's grandfather attended Notre Dame, and [Ben] once worked with Justin's sister. Even with this thin connection, the two are welcomed like family.

8:30 P.M.

The first women begin to arrive at the party. Among them is Erin Kenny, Matt's girlfriend. She has brought along her father, of all people, but nobody minds because they all agree that ol' Charlie Kenny, 1963, is the coolest dad there is.

His daughter is at Notre Dame because he went to Notre Dame, and he went to Notre Dame because, in 1927, his father saw the Irish play in Yankee Stadium. "He was so impressed," Kenny says. "He told everyone, 'If I ever have a son, he's got to go to Notre Dame.' He was like a lot of people. And the reason this university is so important to them is because it represents the American dream and the American ideal to most of the nation. Harvard?"—he laughs—"You don't want your kid to go to Harvard. Harvard represents godlessness, which is absolutely antithetical to the values of Notre Dame. At Notre Dame you learn that you are special without being better than other people. Does that make sense?"

9:00 P.M.

More and more girls are arriving in groups of three and four, and although no one is dancing yet, the party is about to reach critical mass.

A card game has broken out around the dining room table. The name of the game is "Beeramid," and it begins with 10 cards laid out in a pyramid formation. No skill is required. The point is to take the number of sips of beer that corresponds with the face value of the cards that are turning up.

9:20 P.M.

Renee Street, a lively, dark-haired sophomore from Mount Vernon, Ohio, who is studying anthropology and psychology, quits Beeramid after a losing streak (or is that a winning streak?) and repairs to the kitchen where the conversation turns to what football weekends mean to students.

"One good thing is that you can walk around with open cans of beer and nobody bothers you because nobody knows who's a student and who isn't, and they don't want to make people mad," she says. "Another is that it puts everyone into a good mood. Like this afternoon I had a fight with my rectress and I thought, 'I hate this school,' but then I went to the pep rally and I was like, 'God, I love this school.' And also, the food is a lot better. They know the parents are coming in, so like, tonight they had sirloin tips and spinach and cheese tortellini. You never get that on a regular day."

But with the tortellini, as sort of an unwanted side dish, comes tighter enforcement of the male-female visitation rules, Renee says. The thinking is that parents like to see virtue as well as good nutrition. Hence the popularity of these off-campus parties, where it remains easy to "scam" and "hook up."

These are very important terms to know, Renee says. To scam someone is not, as an older person might assume, to offer to repave his driveway for a ridiculously low price, then simply coat it with thin black oil. Rather, to scam is to pursue, to circle, to flirt, to put the moves on.

Hooking up is about what you might guess.

10:00 P.M.

Marlene Zloza, 1975, is at home at this hour in rural Lowell, Indiana, 80 miles west of South Bend. She is chopping vegetables and slicing cheese into neat squares to get a head start on tomorrow. She is an editor and reporter for the weekly *Lowell Tribune*, and she's missed only one Notre Dame home game since graduation. But going to the game involves more than just hopping in the car and heading to South Bend; it means joining in an elaborate pilgrimage that includes friends and food and requires careful planning and preparation.

Her mother and housemate, Elsie, made the dip while Marlene was out covering a high school football game this evening. Now the two are jamming the soda pop into the refrigerator and loading the trunk of the car with folding tables and coolers.

It will be an early morning tomorrow.

11:30 P.M.

On the 10th floor of Flanner Hall, a small party is cranking in room 1016. A boy and a girl, each holding cans of Miller High Life, are kissing passionately to "Jumpin' Jack Flash" by the Rolling Stones on the stereo. Others are giving their intimacy a wide berth, though they are heedless of their surroundings, defiantly, proudly affectionate, sloppy, goofy, giggly.

It looks like fun, to tell you the truth. It looks like the kind of time everyone should have at least once, the kind of time you can have only when you're young enough that desire can totally eclipse reason, block out your surroundings, turn you into a spectacle, and you don't even care.

Saturday, Midnight

Rick Bowen, a 40-year-old welder from nearby Bremen, Indiana, knows himself well enough to shut down the compressor that operates his air horn when the clock strikes 12 in the RV parking lot.

"I have a tendency to get a little wasted, start blowing it loud, and really irritating people," he says, speaking up to be heard over the sound of Eric Clapton's "Hand Jive" slamming out of his 1,200-watt stereo system. His custom-built RV is 22 feet long with a sweeping awning out front, a buzzing blue neon ND sign, and a distinctive observation tower thrusting 20 feet into the air. Bowen does not have tickets for tomorrow's game, but the TV is ready and, when the time comes, the air horn will be too.

Just down the row from Bowen, Notre Dame police officer Cori Bair is refereeing a dispute between a group of frisky young revelers and a woman wearing an "I (Heart) My Grandchildren" T-shirt. The young people have been running pass patterns in the lot, every so often hitting the side of the woman's RV with an errant ball. "Partying is one thing," the woman snarls, "but being rowdy is something else."

"Figure it out," Bair says to the kids. "Are you partying all night, or are you sleeping? If you're partying, go down there." He points toward Rick Bowen's stately pleasure dome.

When the disputing factions have drifted off, Bair adds, "You'd think there'd be some way to arrange this so the sleepers aren't mixed in with partiers. I mean, we'll be running around out here all night."

1:00 A.M.

The lights in the living room at Turtle Creek go down at last. "You Make Me Feel Like Dancing" causes the cluster of young men and women caught between the speakers to begin bobbing up and down with mild abandon.

Justin seems to have narrowed his scamming for the evening down to one girl, Jenny, a friend of a friend. She now has his full attention, which isn't saying a lot because he is experiencing what wags used to call the Heineken Uncertainty Principle—he can't be sure how many beers he has had tonight.

1:30 A.M.

The left speaker has blown. "Cecelia" by Simon and Garfunkle, which was a hit in 1970 when most of these kids weren't even born, is at full volume on the right speaker and, at last, putting this party over the top.

Everyone sings along. Then they start in with "Brown-Eyed Girl" (1967) and "American Pie" (1972)—all the words, not just the choruses.

"The players tried to take the field, but the marching band refused to yield . . ."

"Everyone plays this song at every [Notre Dame] party," Matt says as it ends. "This and 'Only the Good Die Young' by Billy Joel. People just don't like that much from today."

3:00 A.M.

The third keg offers up its last beer and a desultory game of darts ends inconclusively. Renee and the other remaining guests stumble for the door, while those who are left behind begin to maneuver for floor and couch space.

5:45 A.M.

At just under seven hours before kickoff, Marlene Zloza's alarm clock shatters the predawn darkness back in Lowell. She showers, puts on her Notre Dame sesquicentennial T-shirt and her leprechaun earrings, then unfurls the Notre Dame flag on the front porch.

She wakes her mother, and they make a final review of a 40-item checklist: chairs, cups, paper towels, camera, Triscuits, forks, lunch meat. . . . They improve on the list as they go along. Tortilla chips, shrimp and cocktail sauce, Vlasic pickles.

Check, check, check, check. Tailgate picnicking is equal parts science and art. Forget the decorative flags or the mayonnaise, and the entire business is compromised.

7:15 A.M.

At the Plymouth Holiday Inn, the wake-up call goes out to the Notre Dame football players. In 45 minutes they must be showered and ready to leave for the North Dining Hall for the pregame meal.

9:00 A.M.

At about the time the Zloza car reaches the Indiana Toll Road for the long final leg of the journey, James rolls over in his bed in the Turtle Creek apartment and says his first words of the day: "I can't believe we didn't get busted last night!"

When the South Bend police never even stop by to ask you to turn down the volume, then your party is, in some respects, a failure. But a look around at the morning-after entropy suggests the event was not a total bust—five other people are asleep in James and Justin's room, four have crashed in Matt's room, and three more are sprawled in the living room,

Mark Donahue, the medical student, walks bleary-eyed to the VCR and sticks in a tape that consists of nothing but old episodes of *The Simpsons*. It will serve as background entertainment most of the morning.

At this same hour, the Notre Dame Alumni baseball game is getting under way at Jake Kline Field, and the alumni hospitality center is opening its doors in the JACC. All classes of Notre Dame, Saint Mary's, and Holy Cross are welcome, though 1942, 1954, and 1986 are holding special reunions this weekend.

In the North Dining Hall, a breakfast briefing is ending for approximately 300 state, county, city, and university law enforcement officers. They'll be keeping order and directing traffic all day.

9:30 A.M.

It is a tradition that every home football Saturday, the boys in the Turtle Creek apartment start the morning with "kegs and eggs"—beer and omelets. But with the kegs having run dry, they are having to substitute wine for beer. "It's pretty bad," says Mark, his mouth half full. Matt is skipping eggs and eating dry Quaker Instant Oatmeal directly out of the pouch.

10:00 A.M.

As usual—of course, no really big deal—Marlene and Elsie Zloza and the relatives and friends they have picked up along the way are caught in a traffic jam entering South Bend. U.S. Highway 33 is one-way

inbound for three hours before the game to accommodate the four-
teen thousand vehicles that converge on the stadium, but even now
the cars are crawling and the ticket-seekers are hoping to take advantage of the situation. "Need two," "Need two," the signs say. No one
seems to be selling.

In Keenan Hall on the campus, the players are beginning the
pregame mass.

10:15 A.M.

Justin cannot stand to see tradition despoiled, so to salvage kegs and
eggs he takes a short walk through the apartment complex to Belmont
Beverages. A policeman stands outside the front doors, carding cus-
tomers even before they enter the store so as to speed the action at the
register.

10:45 A.M.

The Irish arrive at the stadium in their street clothes.

11:00 A.M.

The Zloza car finally takes its place among four thousand other cars in
the red field parking lot. The passes to this prime lot are prized like
heirlooms and nearly impossible to get—the Zlozas have one only
because Elsie knew someone at the university who was able to grease
the way for her application back in the early seventies. Other people
have been waiting 30 years and more.

Their picnic tables unfold out of impressively small briefcases. A
blue tablecloth goes on one, yellow on the other. The centerpiece is a
bouquet of yellow and blue flowers that is actually a clever arrangement of boutonnieres and corsages, each with tiny plastic footballs in
the middle.

As soon as they are set up and ready to eat, Marlene heads over to
the stadium to rendezvous at Gate 10 with Dennis Casey, 1976, from
Chicago, and his friend Dorn Deans. Dorn, a Michigan grad, will
become the party's token member of the opposition; he has taken the
red-eye flight in from Los Angeles to catch the game, a 12-year tradition he and Dennis share, even though it means he is missing his son's
first organized soccer game.

Notre Dame people are nice to the Dorn Deans who now
inhabit their world. Obscene anti-Michigan T-shirts here and there
notwithstanding, the rivalry is friendly and the teasing incessant
but good-natured.

Most students today are wearing the green T-shirt featuring a mock-
up of Mount Rushmore with former Notre Dame coaches Rockne,
Parseghian, Devine, and Leahy carved in the stone. The image of Lou
Holtz is in the foreground with the legend, "The tradition continues."

Many students and faculty make a pregame stop at the Grotto—in her undergraduate days, Marlene Zloza used to go there before every game to pray that no player would be hurt.

Justin's group, which includes his roommates, several assorted girlfriends, and a handful of hangers-on, joins in the stream of students flowing toward the stadium. They are looking for a tailgate party, any old tailgate party. Very few of these picnics literally use the tailgates of station wagons as tables these days—in fact, several of the picnics are not assembled around any vehicle at all. Justin is adamant that one can throw a tailgater inside an apartment if one is so inclined.

11:30 A.M.

The teams are limbering up, practicing field goals and such on the stadium field. The TV blimp is putt-putting overhead. Outside the stadium, a giant barbecue kettle with dozens of hotdogs smokes furiously. A dog wears a custom-tailored Notre Dame T-shirt. A potato chip bowl looks like a Notre Dame helmet—the dip is in the mouthguard. A proud sign on an RV reads, "Foleys—1915, 1950, 1974." There are six-foot submarine sandwiches sliced into dozens of pieces, candelabras, cloth napkins. Little children sell candy for the Kiwanis.

Justin's group ends up in the red lot at a three-table tailgate party hosted by the parents of his friend Amy Shawl, a junior from South Bend. They are within 100 yards of Marlene and Elsie Zloza's tailgater, but, of course, so are hundreds of others, so they never meet or even see one another.

To the spread of Oreo cookies, Cheez Whiz, Tastibuddy pretzels, Sociable crackers, burgers, and bratwurst, Justin, James, and Matt contribute their remaining cans of Miller Genuine Draft. The conversation is desultory and has very little to do with football. Football is what brings everyone here, true, but it is not, in a larger sense, why they are here.

Noon

With a little more than half an hour left until kickoff, the tailgate parties are breaking down. Marlene and Elsie stow the grub back in the trunk and disassemble the centerpiece.

Elsie slips her hand into a football-player hand puppet and puts on her lucky hat, a fishermen's cap festooned with souvenir pins such as "Notre Dame Mom" and "1988 National Champs."

Not far away, James leads the Turtle Creek crew in song: "Head 'em up, move 'em out, Rawhide!" he cried, and they are out of there.

12:23 P.M.

The alumni and faculty seating sections of the stadium are calm, uneventful, quietly anticipatory as the clock blinks down toward game

time. But the students who fill the northeast corner are already standing, clapping, and chanting.

Justin, James, and Matt shoulder their way into row 49 of section
28, which is kind of, sort of, where their tickets say they should be. The
fact is, no one in the student section pays the least bit of attention to
the numbers painted on the seats. This allows friends to stay together
and a certain exciting density to develop, though the informality tends
to confuse some older folks who have bought tickets from students
and were clearly hoping for a peaceful vantage point.

Fat chance. They are right on the 40-yard line, where the humanity is densest and the expectations are highest. "Let's go I-rish, let's go
I-rish!"

12:37 P.M.

It's here: game time. The fans stand, whirl their fingers in the air, and
drone "Go-ooooooooooooooooo" as Notre Dame kicks off. When the
kicker's foot meets the ball they shout "Irish!" in a disorganized splash
of sound.

12:48 P.M.

Michigan has turned the ball over, and the Irish have possession at
midfield, third-and-seven. This is the game's first key play, and the students take their keys out of their pockets and shake them overhead.
Many of them, like Justin, carry only the two or three keys a college kid
needs, so the noise is hardly deafening. It's a nice tradition, harmless,
and somewhat clever, but Notre Dame students are not in the vanguard
of college-crowd hijinks. They almost never pass students up the rows
overhead or throw food at each other during games (marshmallows are
a favorite at many schools), and touchdowns do not prompt a white
cloudburst of toilet tissue. They are not given to swearing in unison.

They can't get a wave going in the stadium to save themselves, not
that the freshmen don't try from time to time. "We used to get so mad
at the seniors," says Justin. "They'd never keep our waves going.
Course now that we're seniors we just look at them and say, 'Naaaah.'"

12:50 P.M.

Nicholas Mester, the captain of the ushers, is eating a hot dog and
watching the game from his vantage point in the press box. He grew up
in South Bend and has been a fan all his 72 years—has copies of all the
game programs, home and away, dating back to 1930.

He was a banker when he started ushering in 1952 and worked his
way up to the press box in the midsixties. His job now is basically to
make sure no one is in the press box who shouldn't be there.

"Touchdown!" he yells suddenly as senior tailback Reggie Brooks
slips into the end zone after shedding no fewer than five Michigan

tacklers. "You can't beat the excitement! I get so wound up it takes me several hours afterward to wind down."

12:55 P.M.
Justin, James, Matt, Erin, and 30 or 40 other seniors have discovered something very interesting. Movie star Julia Roberts and her movie star boyfriend Jason Patric are somewhat discreetly trying to blend into the crowd one row behind them and four seats away. Roberts, the better known of the two, is wearing sunglasses, an ND cap, and very understated makeup; Patric has on a weathered Notre Dame sweatshirt. Neither are Notre Dame grads. He is cheering and swearing with the best of them, while she is politely following the action.

The students are very cool about this, but some of them invent excuses to squeeze past the famous couple on the way to the concession stand, and one or two ask for their autographs, but the prevailing attitude is to allow them their privacy and allow them to enjoy the game as though they were ordinary fans.

And, to be perfectly honest, Julia Roberts is not a starlet whose bathwater Justin would be proud to drink—he has scores of photographs of beautiful women clipped from magazines taped to the walls around his desk and bed, and Roberts is not among them.

"I mean, she's all right . . ." he says. Then he looks at her again.

1:05 P.M.
As the quarter winds down, the first banner appears overhead being pulled behind an airplane circling the stadium. The planes take off from the Michiana Airport about six miles away, and advertisers pay Gary's Banners, Inc., up to $300 for six laps. Arby's is today's first customer, and as the game goes on we will hear from GMC trucks, Kickers Sports Bar, the Wharf, the Heartland Club, on and on, around and around.

2:00 P.M.
Halftime. Tie score. The students decide to sit down at last, but when they do, the word about Julia Roberts and Jason Patric flashes through the entire section. Ten rows, 20 rows, 30 rows down, people stand, turn around, and stare.

This is very uncool, so Justin, James, Matt, and several of the others who are sitting close to the stars decide to do the gallant thing: they stand to form a human shield that blocks the view of the curious.

2:40 P.M.
The third quarter of a football game often has a lazy quality when you're in the stands—the initial bloom of excitement has faded, halftime has left the fans well fed and contemplative, and it's still a little

early to begin to build to the final crescendo. But if it's contemplation you want, try the library. Here in the huge reference and study area on the second floor, two lonely students are bent over their books. "I was going to go to the game," says sophomore Michael Gayles, who is prepping for a biology exam on Wednesday. "But last night I changed my mind. I didn't even try to sell my tickets, they make it so hard to do."

His companion, sophomore Eboni Price, is studying for a physics exam. "I love football," she says. "But I skipped one game at the end of last season to study and it really paid off."

Gayles nods purposefully. "It's a sacrifice," he says.

No one shushes them.

3:20 P.M.

Just over 11 minutes left in the game, and the student section is rollicking after a pass interference call against Michigan keeps a critical Irish catch-up drive alive. Justin leaps sideways into the air, heedless of where he will land, touches a high-five with Matt, then crumples harmlessly into an unsteady, delirious throng. The scene repeats with twice the energy two minutes later when a Notre Dame touchdown narrows Michigan's lead to three. The air is filled with flying plastic souvenir cups, most of them empty.

3:23 P.M.

And now for the moment Justin has been waiting for—the safe-driving warning from the Indiana State Police. Retired trooper Tim McCarthy has been writing and delivering these warnings for 20 years or more, and each week they seem to get cornier—a brush with the law can be a hair-raising experience, and like that. You can't beat it for entertainment, even when the game is close.

"Remember," McCarthy booms now. "Not using a shade of caution could be curtains." The lusty cheer drips with sarcasm.

3:30 P.M.

The palpable shift in the momentum of the game is playing well out in the parking lots, where hundreds of ticketless fans are happy to be watching the action on TV.

A group from Decatur, Michigan, has created a living-room atmosphere by hauling down two full-sized couches in a bus and placing them out on the asphalt in front of a TV set. Joel Stambeck and his mother, Emma, are part owners of the bus, which has made nearly every home game in the past four years. No matter what the Irish do on the field, Emma is always the big winner in the parking lot because she charges viewers a dollar for every F-word she hears.

3:38 P.M.
Julia Roberts finally sits down for a rest. She misses seeing the Irish interception that leads to the field goal that ties the game with 5:28 to go.

4:00 P.M.
Too quickly, the game is over, the first tie here since a game against Southern Cal in 1969. No one seems to know how to react—on one hand, the tie was lucky, given the way Michigan had been moving the ball in the last few minutes; on the other hand, the Irish made a lackluster effort after intercepting with 1:05 to go in the game, so . . .

"I feel empty," says James, hanging his hands to his sides.

"Do we clap or boo?" asks Marlene in her seats directly across the field.

5:20 P.M.
The parking lot is emptying out. Smoke from bottle rockets and barbecues hangs in the still air. From a distance, with the flags, debris, and little clouds, the scene suggests a Civil War battlefield at dusk.

Downtown South Bend is a ghost town, but crowds are starting to form at the Sunny Italy restaurant across the river on Niles Avenue. The Zloza crew has just barely beaten the dinner rush at this popular alumni hangout, and the hostess tells them their table will be ready any minute.

6:15 P.M.
It looks as though someone has fired a canister of nerve gas into the Turtle Creek apartment. Six young men are sprawled out asleep in front of the television set, no covers, no pillows: Ben Moore, Chris Queensbury, Mark Donahue, Justin, Dave Anderson (a recent grad who's been sleeping on the couch here, on and off, for a couple of weeks), and another guy who apparently is a stranger to these parts.

8:00 P.M.
After dinner at Sunny Italy, Marlene and Elsie have one more stop—the Grotto. "I have to drop her off at Badin," Elsie lies to the guard at the campus gate, gesturing to her 39-year-old daughter. The guard buys it and waves them through.

So many visitors have come by to light candles today that the Grotto seems aglow from a distance, an impressive sight. Marlene pays 50 cents for a small candle for her father, who died 16 years ago; Elsie lights the large $2 candle.

8:30 P.M.
Restored by his nap, Justin is vertical again and doing the accumulated dishes from the weekend. The U.S. Open tennis tournament is on the TV, but no one is really watching. Tonight feels unfocused, drab.

10:45 P.M.
Marlene and Elsie arrive home in Lowell just as Justin, showered and dressed, heads out the door to check out the action at Senior Bar. As he walks briskly across the now-vacant parking field near his house, he passes the first reminder he's seen all weekend of a real world beyond this charmed milieu: Carl Jones, a 66-year-old raggedy man in a torn coat, an unlit cigarette hanging from his lips, is picking up aluminum cans and stuffing them into a canvas sack.

"I'm just passing time," Jones says evasively. He'll get 16 cents a pound for the cans (about 25 cans to the pound) when he takes them to the recyclers. He'll walk because he doesn't own a car.

11:05 P.M.
The dance floor at the Alumni-Senior Bar south of the stadium is muddy from dirty shoes and slopped beer. People are packed in here, screaming to be heard above the Bachman-Turner Overdrive on the speakers. The beer garden outside is far less crowded and noisy, so Justin repairs there for a second beer.

"If Julia Roberts hadn't been with her boyfriend today, I'd have asked her out," Justin says. "I'd have just gone up to her and said, 'Will you go to dinner with me?' I know it's a one-in-a-million chance, but why not?"

Sunday, Midnight
The littered parking lot is still dotted with quietly humming RVs, but the parties have nearly collapsed. At Turtle Creek apartment, Erin is taking chocolate cake out of the oven. "It's not very good," she warns Justin.

4:20 A.M.
Two voices in the darkness of Justin and James' very crowded bedroom:
"Hey, where can we crash?"
"Who's sleeping where?"
"Any spot for us in here?"

6:30 A.M.
Justin is fully clothed as is a friend of Renee's who is nestled sweetly in his arms on his single bed. They are both asleep, as are the five other people who have staked out territory in the room.

In this moment of repose, the light seems to fall for the first time on Justin's academic schedule, posted over his desk. Fifteen credit hours: world literature; British literary traditions; American literary traditions; elementary French; and war, law, and ethics. No one has spoken of these things since Friday, but they will seem important and dreadful again soon enough.

Terri Frei, *The Sporting News*

THE MYSTIQUE OF NOTRE DAME, THE MYTHS, THE LEGENDS, THE TRADITIONS

When The Sporting News *decided to rank Notre Dame first in its 1994 preseason poll, it also sent Terry Frei to campus to take a stab at explaining what football at Notre Dame is all about. This is the result.*

Lou Holtz would prefer that this story was about another football program. Florida State. Michigan. Even William and Mary, where Holtz had his first head coaching job. *The Sporting News*, in its College Football Yearbook and now in its weekly pages, has made Notre Dame its preseason choice as the No. 1 team in the nation.

"I don't want to insult you starting off, but I've never seen a greater display of ignorance than you all have displayed this preseason," says Holtz, otherwise affable during our conversation in the Joyce Athletic and Convocation Center. "I mean that sincerely. I wish somebody could explain it to me. I wish someone could explain to me how you picked us No. 1."

Holtz runs down his list of doubts. They include, but are not limited to (woe is Lou): going into the season with an untested quarterback, Ron Powlus; losing seven defensive and six offensive starters and a total of 10 players to the NFL from last season's 11–1 team; and replacing four assistant coaches, including offensive coordinator Dave Roberts and defensive coordinator Bob Davie.

So the coach who was lobbying for No. 1 after last season is indulging in his characteristic late-summer pastime. Notre Dame? Who, us?

"What you all try to do each and every year is to put tremendous pressure on us hoping we won't live up to the expectations of people," Holtz says. "That's the only logical explanation."

Well, if we talked about that at a [*Sporting News*] strategy meeting, I must have been out at the copying machine. There are other explanations.

"Even though people graduated, I think this year we can be as good as anybody," senior linebacker Justin Goheen says. "When I was a freshman and sophomore, we had guys like Rick [Mirer] and Jerome Bettis, these huge superstars. And when they graduated, we were all looking around at each other, wondering what would happen. Then we all just stepped up and played. We all came to this school for the same reason they did—to win."

That's the most basic, easily qualified Notre Dame football tradition. The Irish win. From Knute Rockne to Holtz, they've won 11 consensus national championships and seven Heisman Trophies and become the lightning rod for fervent affection and acrid hatred. They've had the television deals, from the DuMont Network in the black-and-white days of television's infancy in 1951; to the Sunday morning replay deal that had Lindsey Nelson saying, "After an exchange of punts, we move to further action in the third quarter . . ."; to the current sweetheart arrangement with NBC that brings the Irish consistent home kickoff times, $37.5 million (primarily targeted, the university emphasizes, for general "need" scholarships and doctoral fellowships)—and still considerable resentment from other members of the College Football Association.

Even now, the intriguing mix of mystique and myth continues to be played out on the campus of the small Catholic university to the north of South Bend, Indiana.

Cocaptain and defensive end Brian Hamilton, a native of Chicago and a Catholic who attended parochial schools from day one, says he "knew a little bit" about the Notre Dame tradition when he arrived on campus. "Then, when I was a sophomore, we were going out to USC and coach Holtz gave all the freshmen a test about Notre Dame and said they had to pass before they could go out to California. Now he gives it to the freshmen every year."

More than with any other program in the country, in any sport, the past is part of the present at Notre Dame. However, the past quite often has been so polished in the retelling, it has evolved from fascinating American social history into myth. Myth and mystique seem inexorably linked to the program, and sometimes they're hard to separate.

The truth—warts and all—is compelling enough.

Mystique: "Notre Dame Victory March"

No contest. Notre Dame has the best fight song in America.

In 1945, James Riehle arrived on the Notre Dame campus as a freshman. Nearly 50 years later, after his short career as a salesman, after his ordination as a priest, after his long service to Notre Dame in a variety of administrative and spiritual roles, one annual moment still can choke up the Reverend James Riehle, C.S.C.

"The band comes back before school starts and before the season," says Riehle, who is in his 19th season as the athletic department chaplain. "They start practicing, just like the football team."

Riehle gestures toward the center of campus. "The first time they walk across the campus, the first time they play that 'Victory March,' I get a tingle. Still. Every year."

> Cheer, cheer for old Notre Dame,
> Wake up the echoes cheering her name,
> Send a volley cheer on high,
> Shake down the thunder from the sky.
> What though the odds be great or small,
> Old Notre Dame will win overall,
> While her loyal sons are marching
> Onward to victory
>
> —chorus, "Notre Dame Victory March"

Simple. Stirring. Hummable in the shower. Adaptable, which means generations of high school players have run through butcher-paper pep banners as sophomore flutists butcher the song.

Like many Notre Dame stories, the origin of the "Victory March"—credited to the Notre Dame graduate/brother team of Michael (music) and John (lyrics) Shea—has gone through considerable permutation. The most credible and seriously researched book about the early days of Notre Dame football—Indiana University professor Murray Sperber's impressive *Shake Down the Thunder*, released in 1993—concludes that Michael Shea almost certainly wrote not only the music but also most of the words. Michael, a priest, eventually was a prominent church musician, for a time playing the organ at St. Patrick's Cathedral in Manhattan. John, who copyrighted the song in his name, became a politician in Massachusetts and seemed to claim more credit for the "Victory March" every year.

Myth: The "Unavailable" Tickets

Notre Dame Stadium seats 59,075—and the demand is so high, university officials finally have given in to the inevitable and are planning an expansion to about 80,000 seats.

The visiting team is allotted five thousand tickets. Students at Notre Dame and adjacent St. Mary's get 10,500. Older alumni are guaranteed the right to buy two tickets to a designated game; so are the parents of current students. Some tickets change hands and are available.

For a price.

A call to one national firm's 800 number was educational. For the Michigan game September 10, I was told I still could get seats in the end zone or corners for $250 each.

Mystique: The Fightin' Irish

At least until the Political Correctness Police protest that the nickname presents an unfair stereotype of Irish Americans as bellicose—and perhaps point out the theory that the nickname first was a derisive term used by anti-Catholic fans of the opposition—the Notre Dame nickname will remain.

Irish? Interestingly, the first native language of the campus was French. Notre Dame du Lac was founded in 1842 by a French priest, Edward Sorin. His religious order—the *Congregatio a Sancta Cruce* (C.S.C.), or the Congregation of Holy Cross—wasn't recognized by the Vatican until 15 years after Notre Dame opened. In the early days, Notre Dame didn't turn away any men who wanted to attend the school as long as they could work off or barter away their tuition, and that brought working-class men to the campus, many of them from immigrant families.

Given the occasional historical enmity between Irish Americans and Italian Americans, who both were battling anti-Catholic prejudice and often each other, it's surprising that Italians neither rebelled against the Irish nickname nor adopted another school. But to this day, Italian Americans are fond of pointing out that they have contributed many of the Irish's stars.

The Holy Cross order also founded other schools, including the University of Portland [Oregon]; St. Edward's in Austin, Texas; and St. Mary's, the one-time women-only school adjacent to Notre Dame. If somebody offers to bet you that tiny St. Edward's of Texas has a better football team on its campus than its sister school, Notre Dame, and you think you're about to claim some easy money, don't rise to the bait. The Dallas Cowboys hold their training camp at St. Edward's.

Myth: Saint Knute

Listen to the legends, and you reach the conclusion that Knute Rockne was a saint—and not because he coached the Irish to three consensus national championships in his 13-season reign. No, Rockne is supposed to be a saint because he scrupulously ran a clean, exemplary, and high–moral ground football program.

As Edward Sorin might have said, *"Au contraire."*

Rockne was a great coach and innovator and certainly a superb— if highly inventive—motivator. But he constantly was pushing the envelope of even the looser collegiate football standards of the twenties, when Notre Dame's mandate to Rockne was to abide by Western Conference (Big Ten) guidelines in an attempt to gain admission.

(That's a myth within a myth. Notre Dame was not a feisty independent by choice; it repeatedly was rejected by the Big Ten before settling in as a contented independent with a national schedule.)

From 1918 to 1930, Rockne oversaw a system under which Notre Dame football players got the majority of on-campus jobs to "pay" their way in an era when "full rides" were against the rules and birddog alumni financially sponsored talented recruits. Rockne chafed against academic eligibility restraints and tried to circumvent them whenever possible. He ruthlessly manipulated newspapermen, for years hiring influential sportswriters to officiate Irish games while they also wrote about the team. Walter Eckersall of the *Chicago Tribune* was a Rockne referee/writer favorite. (Seems incredible, but that was part of the system in those days, and Rockne was by far the best at using it to his advantage.) He also, in essence, bribed writers by supplying them valuable complimentary tickets, at times by the dozen, knowing they would be scalped. He even was known to skip Notre Dame games to make money as a print commentator at other big college games. A Notre Dame man forever? He talked with other schools, including Columbia—with which he even signed a contract—and Southern California.

Rockne was a master of artfully (or otherwise) stretching the truth. Knute's "Win One for the Gipper" speech for the 1928 Army game was bunk; there is no indication that George Gipp ever made such a request, or that Rockne was even in position to hear it from a dying Gipp in 1920. Moreover, the words used in *Knute Rockne: All American* apparently were the invention of Rockne's ghostwriter for his autobiographical articles in *Collier's* magazine—which were turned into a book after his death. But hand this to Rockne: Notre Dame upset Army, 12–6, in that 1928 game, in part because Eckersall—the journalist/referee— whistled the game over with Army on the 1-foot line. That game was played the Saturday after Herbert Hoover routed Al Smith, the Catholic governor of New York, in the 1928 presidential election. To many, the election showed that an America in which the Ku Klux Klan was powerful wasn't ready to jettison ridiculous and hateful anti-Catholic prejudice. So Rockne's speech came when Catholics needed a boost.

After Rockne's fatal 1931 plane crash, university officials tightened the reins on subsequent coaches, worked harder to dispel the image that the university was a football factory, and created what Sperber labels the "Fortress Notre Dame" concept of trying to operate not only under national rules, but under more stringent standards.

So the change began: the Irish, once portrayed as renegades and "Ramblers" under Rockne because they seemed to be on the road more often than the St. Louis Browns, evolved into the program that drew resentment because it had higher standards—and [wasn't] afraid to brag about them.

Mystique: The Game Weekend

Before every game, team managers mix gold dust, lacquer, and lacquer thinner and repaint the helmets. The helmets are a tribute to the famed Golden Dome on top of the administration building, which was built after an 1879 fire destroyed most campus buildings. Sorin, the university founder, said, "Tomorrow we will begin again and build it bigger, and when it is built, we will put a gold dome on top with a golden statue of the Mother of God so that everyone who comes this way will know to whom we owe whatever great future this place has."

On the day of games, Riehle conducts mass for the players and team personnel. All the players are required to attend. In the Catholic Church, only members of the church are supposed to take communion, and Riehle estimates that half of the players do so at the game-day masses. The football team is far from all-Catholic.

"After the mass, the captain leads the team in the litany of the Blessed Virgin Mary," Riehle says. "And I give them all a medal, a different medal for every single game. I have a relic of the true cross, and each player comes up and kisses that relic, and the manager gives them the medal."

At Notre Dame Stadium, the feel and appearance hasn't changed much since the days of Rockne. The locker room is not plush, and the stairway/tunnel down to field level is a chamber of memories, complete with the listing of the Irish national championship teams.

Says Lee Becton, the fullback who has an outside chance at the Heisman, "I got chills and things like that. It's so much more than that. You feel nauseated, you feel weak, but you're fine."

Mystique/Myth: Hooray for Hollywood

Last month, Rudy Ruettiger was signing copies of his book in the campus bookstore. Normally Hollywood wouldn't have touched a script for a fact-based film about a walk-on football player. But somebody said the magic words—*Notre Dame*—and next thing we knew, *Rudy* was in a theater near us.

Rudy was the only movie filmed on campus and with university cooperation since *Knute Rockne: All-American.* Various attempts to do another Rockne/George Gipp movie have failed over the years, perhaps in part because America would be so reluctant to see the truth about Gipp and Rockne.

Gipp was an indifferent student, once expelled but reinstated when the administration gave in to alumni and football staff pressures; was a professional gambler who played pool, bet on his own team, and acted as the squad bookie; and was a hard driver who might have brought on his fatal illness—most probably strep throat—with a three-day bender. Wonder what would have happened to American political history if the screenwriters hadn't so bent the truth, partially because Rockne's widow, Bonnie, insisted on a sanitized, glamorized story? Portrayed accurately, the Gipp role might not have been so, well, presidential.

Mystique: Four Men on Horses ... or in a Poster

On a summer afternoon, Holtz pulls up to the parking gate outside the Fightin' Irish locker room, gets out, and joins the four 1994 captains. Becton, Goheen, Hamilton, and tackle Ryan Leahy (Frank's grandson) are in uniforms for the captains poster set up by the sports information department.

It fits in with tradition.

Seventy years ago, the school set up another camera session with four Irish players—Don Miller, Elmer Layden, Jim Crowley, and Harry Stuhldreher. They were the Four Horsemen, astride livery stable horses lined up by student sports publicist George Strickler. It was Strickler's baby all the way since he planted the "Four Horsemen" idea in the head of *New York Herald-Tribune* sportswriter Grantland Rice with an offhand remark in the press box during the 1924 Army–Notre Dame game in the Polo Grounds. Strickler had just seen the silent-movie version of the Vicente Blasco Ibanez novel, "The Four Horsemen of the Apocalypse."

The Four Horsemen were great college players. But this was Rice hyperbolic prose at its best or worst—depending on your perspective of an era of gushing sportswriting:

> Outlined against a blue, gray October sky the Four Horsemen rode again.
>
> In dramatic lore they are known as famine, pestilence, destruction, and death. These are only aliases. Their real names are Stuhldreher, Miller, Crowley, and Layden. They formed the crest of the South Bend cyclone before which another fighting Army team was swept over the precipice. . . .

Rice wrote that this "set of backfield stars . . . ripped and rushed through a strong Army defense with more speed and power than the warring Cadets could meet."

So this mighty Notre Dame offense/cyclone must have blown away the Cadets, right? Notre Dame won, 13–7. What would Rice have written had the Irish cracked 20 points?

Mystique/Myth: Holier than Thou

Why is it that we can't throw out that accusation when a coach at, say, Your State U. says his program is going to do it "right"—make players go to class, point them toward graduation, recruit within the rules, keep the boosters under control, the whole package?

Every once in a while, though, Notre Dame leans into the "holier-than-thou" punches.

Notre Dame trumpets that it doesn't have an athletic dormitory where players are isolated and kingly. That's the right approach, but it does get a little tiresome in the sense that many schools—in the Pacific 10 and Big Ten, for example—don't have athletic dorms, either . . . and don't brag about it.

The Irish don't redshirt their entire freshman class but have red-shirted on a limited scale for years. They still target players for gradu-ation after four years and try to have eligible fifth-year seniors taking graduate-school courses or going after a second bachelor's degree. Although there's nothing illegal or even morally questionable about redshirting, the Irish's past anti-redshirting rhetoric perhaps has left them hypersensitive about the concessions. Brian Hamilton, a 1994 cocaptain, played briefly in only one game—against Purdue—as a freshman in 1990. He was listed as a senior by Notre Dame last season but is back as a fifth-year senior this fall. Interestingly, the 1993 Notre Dame press guide listed Hamilton as appearing in that one 1990 game; the [1994] press guide has dispatched that to computer heaven.

The Notre Dame reality should be impressive enough. This is as close to the noble collegiate model as a national power can be in 1994. Part of the reason is that Notre Dame can afford to be that way and still win, which again can especially rankle some of the resentful.

"We're not perfect," Riehle says. "We're dealing with human beings here."

A few of the players have gotten into trouble. But keep in mind that you don't read about it when the lead in the student production of *My Fair Lady* fouls up. (That applies at any school, by the way.)

At Notre Dame, Holtz frequently has gotten carried away in his coaching demeanor, but there isn't a college coach in the business—no matter how beloved—who causes everyone to be laudatory and loyal after leaving the program. Coaches make friends for life; they also inevitably make enemies. It's unavoidable.

With its very selective admissions policy, Notre Dame has been known to reject valedictorians, but it accepts football players who are not threats to be Academic All-Americans. But even major public schools allow "special admittance" for a limited number of athletes who don't otherwise pass muster at the admissions office. Notre Dame still rejects, or doesn't even bother to approach, football players who easily gain entrance elsewhere. Notre Dame recruits good players it can get into school, and sometimes does it with the basic underlying knowledge familiar to every school: a roster full of future Nobel Prize winners couldn't beat anybody in I-A.

The Irish standards have been tightened again after some internal dissension following the admittance of Tony Rice, a Proposition 48 student who eventually quarterbacked the Irish to a national championship. In a way, that was too bad: Rice is a decent young man who didn't deserve to be labeled some kind of academic freak.

Clearly some Notre Dame players were caught up in the steroid craze of the eighties—and despite one of the most rigorous testing programs in the country, the Irish sent mixed messages by hiring strength coaches in the eighties from the steroid-plagued Nebraska weight room.

You'll notice we haven't brought up athletes' graduation rates. Here's why: they're overrated. By no means is this an indictment of Notre Dame, which routinely has one of the highest graduation rates for football players in the country. Getting players degrees, at Notre Dame or anywhere else, isn't always a sign of academic commitment but can be the product of nursing some students through the system—regardless of whether they deserve it.

Is Notre Dame perfect?

Of course not.

Never has been, despite the myths.

Never will be, despite the recruiting advantage of the mystique.

But above all, Notre Dame claims to be different. And that's undeniable.

Jeff Gordon, *Lindy's Football Annual*

FOOTBALL UNDER THE GOLDEN DOME

Lou Holtz used to like to tell people that coaching at Notre Dame indeed was different. "The team isn't really yours," he'd say. "You're just taking care of it for a while." Jeff Gordon heard all that and more as he put together his own look at what makes Irish football tick.

It always amazes Notre Dame coach Lou Holtz when one of those pre-season polls puts his rebuilding Irish at or near the top. A spring football writer's poll rated them No. 2, despite the loss of six starters on each side of the ball and four assistant coaches.

"They picked us second in the preseason last year," Holtz said. "They have as much business picking us No. 2 this year as they did last year."

But hey, Notre Dame is Notre Dame. The school isn't merely at the top [of] college football, it *is* college football. The Irish usually deliver, as they showed last season while finishing a close second to Florida State. They will always be near the top of somebody's preseason poll.

"It says a lot about Notre Dame," Holtz said. "When I really realized how big Notre Dame football really was came after I watched that doggone place-kick six thousand times since the Boston College game."

That kick, of course, was David Gordon's game-winning field goal that upset the Irish at Notre Dame Stadium and ultimately denied them another national title. They will have to try a little harder this season.

"You sort of feel an obligation to make sure Notre Dame is one of the better schools, not only on the field but with the conduct of the athletes and their academics," Holtz said. "It's a very, very special thing to be part of Notre Dame."

It's not just a college football team, it's a big part of the American sports culture.

The History

When exploring the Irish mystique, where do you start? The 18 bowl games since the Irish started attending them in 1970? The 11 national titles? The seven Heisman Trophies won by Irish players? Legendary coaches like Knute Rockne, Frank Leahy, Ara Parseghian, Dan Devine, and yes, Holtz? The Four Horsemen? George Gipp? Rudy?

"There is a special feeling about Notre Dame," Holtz once said. "It's like feeling God."

Devine had a different sensation when he came aboard. "It was like you suddenly found yourself in King Arthur's chair and found out those people really lived," he said.

Parseghian was blown away by his first day. "I remember driving down Notre Dame Avenue, toward the Golden Dome, when I first came in and it hit me that I was the head coach now," he said. "Chills went up my back. I went to a basketball game where I was introduced to the students and I was cheered for 15 minutes. There was a pep rally in January and about three thousand people showed up. The spirit was just amazing. I felt it immediately."

It's only appropriate that the College Football Hall of Fame move to South Bend. The Notre Dame campus is a shrine, with Touchdown Jesus and the Golden Dome. The Hall will only add depth to the scenery.

ESPN commentator Lee Corso, a former college coach, said Notre Dame has no peer in the football community. "When they have an experienced head coach in there, their football is the best," he said. "No one's better. Notre Dame *is* the epitome of college football."

The Popularity

Even under poor Gerry Faust, Notre Dame football was huge. From coast to coast, the "subway alumni" gave the program a tremendous national fan base. But since Holtz began rebuilding the Irish in 1986, the popularity has soared to new heights.

After going 5–6 in his first season, Holtz has rung up 8–4, 12–0, 12–1, 9–3, 10–3, 10–1–1, and 11–1 records and has gone 5–2 in bowl games. His 1988 national title brought the program all the way back.

Larry Michael, sports director at the Mutual Radio Network, quantified the enthusiasm Holtz restored. "We have 325 stations carrying Notre Dame," Michael said. "There is no other college coach that has his own national call-in show."

In Faust's disappointing 30–28–1 tenure, Michael said, "The number of stations dropped down below 200—it was down to about 175. As the program got stronger, it picked back up. What we have now is more than 300 quality stations. When you think of college football, you think of Notre Dame. It's the only one of its kind. There is nothing else like it."

Indeed, NBC-TV struck a five-year deal with Notre Dame (starting in 1991) to televise Irish home games. Obviously, this was the first time in modern college history that an individual school signed its own network deal. Before college football telecasts were deregulated—creating noon to midnight coverage—four of the five highest-rated college football games of all time involved the Irish.

"If Notre Dame didn't exist," sports commentator Beano Cook once observed, "the NCAA's television contract would be worth millions less."

Notre Dame Stadium holds only 59,075 fans, so it is woefully inadequate to meet ticket demand. Expansion plans have been kicked around since 1991, but unless the stadium was doubled in size the public won't be satisfied. "It's amazing to see how important it is that people get tickets," said Bill Scholl, the school's director of ticketing and marketing.

Because of ticket demand, the school won't sell new season-ticket packages: those who have had season tickets get to renew them as long as they are still alive. "When they die, they will transfer back to the school," he said. "The only person you can transfer a ticket to is a surviving spouse."

Occasionally Scholl gets a letter informing him of the death of a ticket holder. Then he will get an address change notice allegedly from that same ticket holder. "We get letters from dead people all the time," he said.

Season tickets resumed go into a lottery pool for contributors to the school. On game days, thousands of non–ticket holders will gather outside the stadium, sniff for tickets, and then tailgate if they can't get them.

"At Gate 14, hundreds of people line up, almost to halftime, hoping that tickets get fumed in by the visiting team or whatever," Scholl said.

For the epic victory over Florida State, a mob of twenty thousand gathered outside the stadium. Fans went into the Athletic and Convocation Center to watch it on a big screen. Across the nation the game drew the highest rating since deregulation.

"Wherever we go in the country, we have supporters," former Irish linebacker Ned Bolcar once observed. "I think it's the people who are so special, who make up the Notre Dame family, who causes there to be a mystique. It's not the buildings, it's not the Golden Dome, or any of that stuff."

Constant Renewal

The Irish lose 14 starters off last season's team, yet a spring football writer's poll placed them second in the nation. Why? Because the top players keep rolling in.

A recruiting visit to Notre Dame can mesmerize most teenage athletes. Prep quarterback star Ryan Clement of Denver expressed his awe of the Irish tradition in a recruiting diary he penned for the *Rocky Mountain News*. He described game day: "The school lives and dies for the football team. Football is a religious experience there. Game day was incredible. It was hard to believe the people I saw—Spike Lee, Roger Clemens, John Kruk, and Paul Hornung were among them."

Alas, Clement chose not to sign with the Irish because phenom Ron Powlus was already there. Powlus lost his freshman season to a pair of broken shoulders. As a sophomore, great things will be expected of him.

He stands 6'4", he weighs a solid 210 pounds, and he led his high school team in Berwick, Pennsylvania, to a 15–0 record by throwing 35 touchdown passes. While participating in drills as a freshman, he impressed his new teammates with his maturity and ability to pick up the Irish offense.

Also, it appears he has Joe Montana skills. Had he not been injured last season, he may have started as a freshman.

"He's not fast or quick," Holtz said. "It's just that he does everything well."

The rich keep getting richer.

Player Development
No matter how many starters Notre Dame loses, the Irish always seem to have plenty of seasoned players. Under Holtz, the Irish develop depth while preparing their starting lineup for games. Their talent base never seems to get wobbly.

"During the course of the week, an average practice, coach Holtz strives for perfection in everything we do," said ex-Irish flanker Lake Dawson. "He always talks about what is important, doing all the little things the right way.

"College doesn't demand quite as much as the NFL does, but I'm sure that going to Notre Dame and being coached under Lou Holtz is going to help me and probably has helped a lot of other athletes that have gone through."

Holtz hopes that is the case. "Our athletes, besides having ability and intelligence, will really have a very good work ethic," he said.

Most Irish players develop plenty of patience as well. "At Notre Dame, there's quite a bit of talent, and you kind of have to wait in line," Dawson said. "I think Reggie Brooks is an example of that. You have a guy that's playing defensive back my freshman year and then all of a sudden going into his senior year, he rushes very well—he was ranked nationally—and now he did an excellent job his first year in the NFL."

Competition breeds excellence for the Irish. Holtz allocates his playing time with great care. "Todd Lyght, Tom Carter, Reggie Brooks, Jerome Bettis—I go against these people each and every day for months," Dawson said. "So as far as working against top-quality athletes, I've had that opportunity."

Corso lauded Holtz's ability to get the most out of his players. "You look at Notre Dame and study them and you see they sometimes don't get the greatest athletes in America, in terms of pure athleticism, speed, and agility," he said. But good results, under Holtz, have been consistent. "He does it the right way," Corso said. "Wherever he's been, he's had the ability to keep things in their proper perspective. If you're successful but you don't do it the right way, you only hurt your football program."

Cradle of Coaches

Because of all this success, fledgling programs routinely comb the Irish coaching staff to find new head coaches. Offensive coordinator Skip Holtz went to Connecticut over the winter, and defensive coordinator Rick Minter was lured by Cincinnati.

In earlier seasons, Barry Alvarez (Wisconsin), Ron Cooper (Eastern Michigan), Peter Vaas (Holy Cross), Pete Cordelli (Kent), Jim Strong (UNLV), and John Palermo (Austin Peay) have left the Irish for head jobs. Numerous others have gone to National Football League teams as assistant coaches.

"People say we can't keep coaches," Lou Holtz said. "That's not true. We have an obligation if a guy does a good job for us to help him advance. We lose them to the pros, where the salary scales are much higher. There are some schools that never lose assistant coaches because they never allow other schools to talk to them."

Why do athletic directors keep knocking at the Irish door?

"It's the pinnacle," Skip Holtz said. "It's Notre Dame. It's the top. Working at Notre Dame is different than working anywhere else. That's where people go to find coaches. They know what it takes to run a big-time football program. They know how to do things in a big-time way, and do them right."

Assistant coaches can wait decades to get their shot at a head coaching job. But that hasn't been the case with Irish assistants. "You kind of get spoiled," Skip Holtz said. "You think head coaching jobs are easy to get. Every year, it seems like guys are going. One or two guys a year are able to get a head job."

The challenge of head coaching is compelling, but it's tough to say good-bye to the Golden Dome. "The hardest thing I've ever done was leave Notre Dame," Skip Holtz said. "But head coaching jobs don't come around every year. You're not always going to have that opportunity. Connecticut is not Notre Dame, but at the same time we get a chance to build a program based on the same intrinsic values. Notre Dame is a special place. It's a different place. I don't honestly think there is another school in the country like it."

Because of that, Lou Holtz doesn't have trouble attracting quality replacements. And the turnover brings fresh ideas. "We like to think we improve our program with each new coach who comes in," he said. "The players coming in, they should expect the best coaching and the best teaching in the country."

Flip Side of Success

Naturally, a program as huge and prosperous as Notre Dame becomes an easy target for critics.

Dan Yaeger coauthored a highly negative book: *Under the Tarnished Dome: How Notre Dame Betrayed Ideals for Football Glory.* That book, plus subsequent newspaper stories, found a fair number of jaded ex-Irish players and recruits and told their stories. There were allegations that Holtz winked at illicit bodybuilding. "He made a clear priority on strength, letting players know it was OK if steroids were abused," Yaeger said.

Holtz was also accused of turning his back on injured players and trying to run them off. "He didn't give a whit about his players off the field," Yaeger said.

After Scott Bentley signed to play at Florida State instead of Notre Dame, he claimed Holtz berated him and chastised him for disappointing his father. "It made me cry, it made Scott cry," Bob Bentley said. "I'm not going to forgive him. Scott has to live with that the rest of his life. For him to say Scott let me down because of my closeness to Notre Dame is a despicable tactic."

Ex-Irishman Chet Lecheta claimed Holtz spit on him and blasted those who suggested critics were fabricating stories. "It's not like we've been calling each other," he said. "Think about it. It would take an unbelievable amount of planning to concoct something like this."

But Holtz defused the controversy within a few weeks by simply refusing to discuss the book or negative articles publicly. Earlier, he had made his feelings on criticism clear. "Notre Dame is judged by different standards than other school by the media and the public," Holtz said. "I didn't realize it, but I wouldn't want it any other way. There is a higher standard for Notre Dame, and we should take that as a compliment."

The Future

Holtz takes his Notre Dame tenure one year at a time. He chuckled when reminded how the interest an NFL expansion team showed in him over the winter caused quite a ruckus back in South Bend. "I try to look at the situation each and every year," he said. "If I ever left Notre Dame, I have several relatives who would disown me. You have to look at your health and if you have the enthusiasm to run it the right way, and I still do. I feel very comfortable at Notre Dame. I wouldn't stay here coaching if I didn't."

Though Holtz brought Notre Dame back to its accustomed glory, he always notes how the institution is far greater than its coach. "Every other program I've been in, the coach feels like it's his team," he said. "At Notre Dame, you don't feel that way. You're the custodian. You're just taking care of it."

BIBLIOGRAPHY